D1274602

Bitter Waters

Bitter Waters

Life and Work in Stalin's Russia

a memoir by
Gennady Andreev-Khomiakov

translated with an introduction by
Ann E. Healy

WestviewPress
A Division of HarperCollinsPublishers

Originally published as *Gor'kie vody: Ocherki na styke dvukh epokh, iz Vospominanii (Bitter Waters: Sketches at the Juncture of Two Epochs, from My Recollections)*, © 1954 Posev: Frankfurt

Copyright © 1997 by Westview Press, A Division of HarperCollins Publishers, Inc.

Published in 1997 in the United States of America by Westview Press, 5500 Central Avenue, Boulder, Colorado 80301-2877, and in the United Kingdom by Westview Press, 12 Hid's Copse Road, Cumnor Hill, Oxford OX2 9JJ

Library of Congress Cataloging-in-Publication Data
Andreev-Khomiakov, Gennady.
[Gor'kie vody. English]
Bitter waters: life and work in Stalin's Russia / by Gennady
    Andreev-Khomiakov; translated by Ann E. Healy.
        p.   cm.
    Includes bibliographical references.
    ISBN 0-8133-2390-8 (hardcover)
        1. Andreev-Khomiakov, Gennady.   2. Political prisoners—Soviet
Union—Biography.   3. Political persecution—Soviet Union.
4. Soviet Union—History—1935–1941.   I. Title.
DK268.A54A3   1997
947.084'2'092—dc21   96-53092
                                                                                CIP

The paper used in this publication meets the requirements of the American National Standard for Permanence of Paper for Printed Library Materials Z39.48-1984.

10   9   8   7   6   5   4   3   2

Contents

Acknowledgments

The self-educated Neposedov—a main protagonist in these memoirs—used a rich, colloquial Russian that was difficult to render in English. I owe many people my thanks for their contributions to this effort.

First, I would like to thank Rebecca Ritke of Westview Press for all her editorial help, but in particular for being as enthusiastic about Gennady Andreev-Khomiakov's memoir from the start as we both still are. Westview's anonymous readers greatly improved the contents of my introduction, as did my wise colleague and friend George Enteen of Pennsylvania State University. With his vast knowledge of the collection at the University of Wisconsin–Madison library, Slavic librarian Alex Rolich saved me endless hours of searching for photo-illustrated articles about Soviet logging during the 1930s.

Several native speakers of Russian also played a major role in the translation. Julius Nissen of Milwaukee translated and explained difficult technical terminology. Vladimir Gerzanich, then of Kiev and now a visiting researcher at the University of Pennsylvania medical school, spent hours helping me with perplexing colloquial expressions and idioms, as did Iuri Baibarak. An English teacher and translator in Kiev, Iuri also carefully checked the entire translation. Early help and encouragement for the project came from John Meredig, then a graduate student in Russian at the University of Illinois at Urbana–Champaign. Howard Goldfinger, scholar-editor of Milwaukee, and his Russian wife, Ira Ventsel, provided similar assistance during the final stages of the manuscript's preparation. Many important services were rendered me by the University of Illinois Summer Research Laboratory on Russia and Eastern Europe. The uniquely competent and helpful staff of the University of Illinois Slavic Library gave me invaluable assistance in tracking down information about Andreev-Khomiakov and his works.

Numerous improvements in my text are the result of the keen editorial skills of Martha Walusayi. As always, my husband and colleague in the history department at the University of Wisconsin–Milwaukee, David Healy, provided continuous support through every stage of the project. Ellen Healy, second-generation Healy historian, likewise gave the whole translation a careful reading, looking in particular for awkward turns of phrase and for terms in need of additional explanation.

Ann E. Healy

Introduction

The late 1920s witnessed the inauguration of one of the most colossal social engineering projects ever attempted. In a little more than a decade, Josef Stalin's "revolution from above" initiated the transformation of the Soviet Union's still largely rural and illiterate society into that of a relatively modern industrial state with a powerful arms industry. This was a full-scale socioeconomic revolution, accompanied by immense suffering on the part of a populace called upon to sacrifice elementary material needs, along with many of life's other satisfactions, in the name of a better, socialist future.

To a considerable extent, Stalin was building on historical traditions and institutions already in place under his predecessors. Tsarist Russia had experienced a marked increase in industrialization after the middle of the nineteenth century. Coal and iron production rose significantly, and the Russian empire led the world in oil production by the turn of the century. European Russia's railway network was almost complete, as was the Trans-Siberian Railroad, then and now the longest railroad line in the world. The empire's great cities were deservedly world famous for their architecture, museums, and cultural life. The country's well-educated and cultivated elite now included small but rapidly growing professional and business classes. The Soviet Union under Stalin also retained several other institutions from previous eras, including a one-party system, an arbitrary judicial system, and a secret police force. Thousands of citizens had already been arrested, accused of counterrevolutionary activities, and sentenced to forced labor.

Among the Bolshevik regime's many victims was Gennady Andreev-Khomiakov, the author of these memoirs. His experiences during the first two decades of Stalin's rule provided the material for this book as well as for several other autobiographical pieces. Andreev was living in West Germany when he wrote the earliest of these works, having remained there after his release from a German prisoner-of-war camp at the end of World War II. All of Andreev's works were published for the relatively small readership of the Russian émigré press, and this memoir is the first of them to appear in English translation. Haunted by the traumatic events of his early manhood, Andreev would spend the last four decades of his life in the West as an editor

and author, fighting the Soviet system with his pen and assisting fellow
Russian émigrés in their literary endeavors. Andreev had returned to his literary activities after an involuntary interruption of almost two decades.

After graduating from secondary school in Stalingrad in 1926, Andreev
had found a job with a provincial newspaper: "We had a literary circle at the
newspaper," Andreev recalled, a group "without remarkable talents," which,
however, included "several young people who were devoted to literature, in
love with it."[1] Andreev managed to publish several short stories before his
arrest for "counterrevolutionary activities" the following year. He did not
reveal the specific nature of the charges levied against him, charges that resulted in a sentence of ten years in a labor camp. There followed eight years
of "being dragged through all the circles of labor-camp hell," which included
two terms on the Solovetskii Islands, a small archipelago in the western part
of the White Sea. This former monastery and fortress was the most notorious of the Northern Camps of Special Designation (SLON). According to
Andreev, there were about 10,000 prisoners in the islands during his first
term (1927–1929).[2]

Andreev opens his memoirs with a graphic recollection of his sudden release from the camp in 1935, two years before he would have served out his
ten-year sentence. "During the years of my imprisonment all my ties with
freedom had been severed," Andreev wrote, claiming that "it made absolutely no difference where I went." His release on "general grounds"
meant that he could settle anywhere in the Soviet Union, with the exception
of forty-one cities and a two-hundred-kilometer-wide strip along Soviet
borders. He chose a small steppe town in southeastern Russia. Unable to get
his hands on anything but ragged camp garb, Andreev left with a travel warrant, twenty-five rubles, and a loaf of bread and five herring for "nourishment during relocation to the chosen place of settlement."

Andreev's release occurred during the respite of the mid-1930s—a respite
only in relative terms, but nonetheless a respite, compared to the previous
all-out push for industrialization. This temporary relaxation was signaled by
a decline in the population of the labor camps around 1936.[3] In addition,
Andreev mentions several other signs of the relative lull: Ration cards were
being abolished by stages, and the overall material situation in the Soviet
Union was more tolerable. All of the basic necessities were available in his
little steppe town, and even delicacies, such as jam produced by local cooperatives, were again appearing on the shelves. Collective farmers had recently gained the right to keep a cow and a few other domestic animals and
to cultivate a small plot for crops that could be sold on the open market.

Fruit, vegetables, and dairy products, although available only in small amounts and at high prices, assured that in his area at least, "people needed not go hungry." These products were easily accessible to Andreev after he found employment in the planning department of a small factory, because he earned a big salary by local standards and had only himself to provide for.

For the bulk of the population, however, goods remained expensive, although prices were somewhat lower than they had been a few years earlier. The free market prices charged by collective farmers had begun to fall from the astronomical heights of 1933, while some state-set commercial prices could at last be reduced. This upturn prompted Stalin's famous slogan, "Life has become better, comrades, life has become more joyous."[4] This slogan must have had a hollow ring to many of his fellow citizens as Andreev began his reentry into civilian life, a reentry into a social system and economy vastly transformed from the one he had left eight years earlier.

Andreev thanked fate for releasing him at a time "when the storms of the First Five-Year Plan and '100-percent collectivization,' which had so shaken our country, were dying down." Because he had been in camp during the crash collectivization drive and the famine of 1932–1933, Andreev encountered those horrors only afterward and mostly secondhand, in the accounts of people who had survived them. The First Five-Year Plan had both sparked and accompanied an all-out push for industrialization and collectivization of agriculture, marked by unrealistic predictions and incredible confusion. It was an era when extremes became the norm; a period of the heroic and the horrendous, of industrial achievements amid terrible waste, miscalculation, and error; of hatred of the regime and dedication to the cause of building a socialist society. The Bolshevik revolution had not spread to the developed capitalist world as Lenin expected it to do. Turning the Soviet Union into a powerful industrialized society, whatever the cost in human terms, had become the regime's top priority under Stalin.

Many Soviet citizens accepted Stalin's argument that the Soviet Union had to embark on this crash industrialization program if it was to survive in a hostile, capitalist world. In the late 1920s, Stalin and his backers got Communist Party approval of their plans, even overruling critics in top Party–government circles who had expressed opposition to rapid industrialization at the expense of the peasants. The blueprint for this industrialization drive became the first in a series of Five-Year Plans—cumbersome and confusing documents that set production and other targets for Soviet farms, mines, factories, retail outlets, offices, and other institutions. The Five-Year Plans also became propaganda instruments, spurring on the citizenry to strive to fulfill the regime's economic and other goals. Shortened, simplified versions of the plans, with appropriate sloganeering, circulated widely, often in the quasi-military terminology so characteristic of Soviet propaganda: "win the battle of steel"; "engage in a truly Bolshevik struggle for grain"; "deal a smashing blow to the kulaks" (a word allegedly referring to wealthier peasants, but in actuality to those who resisted joining collective farms). Nor was such language confined to the nation's economic and military sectors. In 1931, a general meeting of historians of the Institute of Red Professors lauded a recent directive of Stalin's as a "militant political weapon" that played an "exceptional role in mobilizing the historical front" to "confront tasks of party and socialist construction."[5]

However, drafting the First Five-Year Plan proved a more daunting task than its advocates had anticipated. Eventually, planners in the State Planning Commission (Gosplan) and the Supreme Council of the National Economy, the government agencies entrusted with the job, came up with two versions. Both were wildly optimistic, the first calling for an increase of 130 percent in industrial production, the second for an increase of 180 percent. The second version won the day as economists in these agencies found themselves under more and more pressure from committed planners: "We are bound by no laws. There are no fortresses the Bolsheviks cannot storm," insisted S. G. Strumilin, a major architect of the First Five-Year Plan.[6]

Unrealistic production goals in the optimal version of the first plan (already in full swing at the time of its approval by the Communist Party's Sixteenth Congress in April 1929) were soon discarded for even higher targets. Stalin himself discounted the views of comrades who were questioning the pace of the drive for industrialization: "The tempo must not be reduced! On the contrary, we must increase it," he declared in a famous speech in early February 1931, almost exactly a decade before Hitler's troops would cross Soviet borders. We are "fifty or a hundred years behind the advanced countries," Stalin warned; we must "make good this distance in ten years, . . . or we shall go under."[7]

These unrealistic goals forced people, including those directing the economy, to carry on in an economically irrational manner. Written from his vantage point in the planning-accounting departments of two provincial factories, Andreev's memoirs provide a uniquely detailed portrayal of just what it meant to do business under the Stalinist system. In an allegedly planned economy, the plans for their enterprises proved so inoperative that he and his boss regularly found ways, some of them quite ingenious, to get around the plan in order to stay in operation. They fiddled with the books, lobbied in Moscow, bartered construction materials produced in their plants for other essential (and sometimes not so essential) commodities. Andreev's account thus provides grass-roots confirmation of Hungarian economist Janos Kornai's analysis of the "socialist shortage economy" with its lack of normal budget constraints, inter-enterprise rivalry, gross inefficiency and corruption, and constant wheeling and dealing.[8]

Along with crash industrialization, a draconian campaign was waged for collectivization in rural areas. Millions of peasants died during the collectivization drive and the widespread famines that accompanied it in several regions. Although Andreev left camp after the worst of these terrible years, the resultant devastation and dislocation in rural areas is a recurrent theme in his memoirs. Andreev's responsibilities often included business trips through the countryside, where he was shocked and saddened by the neglected buildings, the crippling shortages of consumer goods, and the generally meager living standards of the downtrodden and demoralized inhabitants.

The leadership's constant proclamations that a marked increase in per capita consumption would follow all these sacrifices proved even more of a chimera than earlier, as the emphasis on the nation's military-industrial capacity prevailed over all facets of the economy. Heavy industry must not lag behind, so the disadvantaged consumer goods sector was even more neglected. New housing, needed desperately to shelter a rapidly expanding urban population, was not constructed. Trade distribution networks remained woefully inadequate, and shortages of basic items worsened, as living standards plummeted for urban workers and peasants alike. Yet, amid all this hardship, "a great industry" was built, to quote economic historian Alec Nove, although only as the result of sacrifices "on a scale unparalleled in history in times of peace. . . . The resultant bitterness, disloyalty, repression also involved a heavy cost."[9]

Stalin's revolution from above nonetheless had many supporters. Among the proponents of these vast changes were cynical careerists and dedicated Communist Party activists, non-Party opportunists, and ordinary people who sincerely believed that they were helping to build a more just, equalitarian world or that their country was endangered by "capitalist encirclement." Support came from some though by no means all of the millions of former imperial subjects who were experiencing upward social mobility. A host of new jobs were opening up for many in the rapidly industrializing and urbanizing society. Educational opportunities were also on the rise—never adequate to fill the growing demand for trained personnel, but nonetheless providing a gateway to a better job for thousands every year.

In addition, by the time Andreev left camp, in the middle of the Second Five-Year Plan (1933–1937), the situation in both urban and rural areas had settled down and improved somewhat. Agricultural output, decimated during the early thirties, had begun slowly to recover. The drive for industrial development was less frenetic. When finally adopted, the Second Five-Year Plan indicated more modest production targets than had its predecessor. Declines in monthly industrial output during the last months of 1932, involving "even such goods as steel and coal, so dear" to Stalin's heart, help to explain the partial retreat from the wildly optimistic production goals of the First Five-Year Plan (1928–1932).[10]

While many of the targets of the first two Five-Year Plans (1928–1937) were not met, the achievements in heavy industry were nonetheless impressive, even taking into account the chaos and enormous waste. The "planned, command economy" had demonstrated one thing: targeting key sectors and neglecting others could bring results. To paraphrase American historian Michael Kort, it was easier to build all those steel mills if planners need not worry about shoes and housing for the plant workers. Steel production rose from 4 to 17 million tons, coal from 35.4 to 128 million tons, and electricity from 5.5 to 36.2 billion kilowatt hours. Several new industrial complexes and whole new industries, such as aviation and automobile construction, came into existence. Railroad and canal networks were greatly extended, sometimes by prison labor. Moreover, because the central authorities planned and guided this industrialization drive, they deliberately located much of the new development in previously less developed regions to the south and east, areas safer from Western invaders.[11]

By the end of 1935 the Soviet Union was also the world's leading military power: It had 1,300,000 men in the armed forces, and 5,000 tanks, 112 submarines, and over 3,500 military aircraft. After 1936, military spending weighed ever more heavily on the economy, as the threat of a two-front war with more industrially advanced nations to the west and east loomed on the horizon. Soviet leaders were aware of a secret protocol of the Anti-Comintern Pact, signed by Germany and Japan in 1936, which explicitly mentioned the USSR: If either of those powers became involved in a war with the Soviet Union, they would confer with each other about measures safeguarding their mutual interests. Subsequent increases in military expenditures took scarce resources from an already overstretched Soviet economy. Overall, growth rates stagnated or declined from 1936 on, giving the lie to Stalin's promises, based on impressive 1934 and 1935 production figures, of future "miracles" and "great breakthroughs." On the contrary, from 1936 until Hitler's invasion in 1941, the general slowdown extended into ever more sectors of the economy.[12]

Andreev points up many of the consequences of this emphasis on defense. "The closer we came to war," the more strangers turned up at the sawmill, carrying briefcases bulging with rubles, at a time when such cash payments were strictly forbidden by law. Andreev and his boss sometimes found it difficult to weed out the swindlers from among the generally upstanding folk who were forced by circumstances to engage in illegal deals. Everyone needed lumber. And as military construction swallowed up more and more of the lumber, the state of civilian construction progressively worsened.

Thus, although the German invasion came to a nation much better prepared for war than it had been at the beginning of the decade, the industrial achievements of Stalin's command economy must be weighed against wasted resources and terrible human dislocation, suffering, and premature death in an often ill-directed and constantly overstrained Soviet economy and polity.

Among the brutal methods used to achieve these changes were extensive political purges. The onset of what Russians refer to as the Great Purges was marked by the June 1936 arrest of two formerly influential old Bolsheviks, Lev Kamenev and Grigory Zinoviev. By then, key areas of the economy were already suffering from major problems. The mass arrests of 1936–1938 were thus both a response to and a contributor toward the plummeting industrial growth rates, which had come as a shock to Soviet leaders who had been encouraged by the double-digit growth rates of the mid-1930s. Equally discouraging was the fact that after some progress toward mechanization of agriculture and a good harvest in 1935, in the midsummer of 1936 exceedingly unfavorable weather conditions were pointing toward a disastrous harvest that year. In addition, drought in many regions rendered rivers unnavigable, putting an additional strain on the already overburdened railroads and hindering deliveries of available raw materials.

Throughout the remainder of the summer a purge of many former Party oppositionists followed in the wake of the June arrest of the two famous old Bolsheviks. The terror of 1936–1937 would soon engulf many thousands accused of economic sabotage or "wrecking," as mounting shortages of vital materials, such as timber and coal, wrought havoc in widening sectors of the economy.[13] Gennady Andreev recalls that cries about the need for vigilance against spies, wreckers, and saboteurs began to dominate in the newspapers at this time.

To mastermind the campaign to "weed out the wreckers," Stalin appointed a man whose name was to become synonymous with the Great Purges (also known as the *Yezhovshchina*). Nikolai Yezhov, head of the Industrial Department of the Communist Party Central Committee at the time, took charge of the political police (NKVD) after an explosion in the Kemerovo Coal Mine in late September 1936. Under Yezhov, the accusations against most purge victims shifted from conspiracy against the Soviet regime to economic sabotage. Increasingly, industrial managers, engineers, factory and farm administrators, and Party and government personnel in charge of overseeing the economy became the NKVD's main targets. Evidence of failures and problems was widespread in this new, supposedly planned but in actuality very chaotic system. Many Soviet leaders as well as ordinary citizens tended to blame malevolent human design instead of more plausible causes such as sheer incompetence and human error; the economic impossibility of continuing to import large amounts of foreign technology indefinitely; irrational pressure to achieve the impossible; and forces beyond the planners' control, such as world economic conditions and the weather.[14]

As Andreev remembered it, the Great Purge trials and the *Yezhovshchina* had "almost no echo in our plant." Andreev himself remained untouched, and not one of the factory's employees was arrested, although district Communist Party propagandists held meetings at the sawmill to explain the search for enemies of the people. Aware only of the arrests of two high-level regional officials whom they did not know personally, "we tried not to pay too much attention to what was going on in higher circles." Andreev's recollection that "the violence was occurring far away somewhere, at some inaccessible height" supports the arguments of Roberta Manning, Robert Thurston, J. Arch Getty, and other scholars that the vicious cycle of denunciations, arrests, and trials, however horrendous, was confined to certain elements of the population and less widespread than is often alleged.

The international climate of the mid- to late thirties increased the insecurity of the regime and heightened the terror. The Soviet press emphasized the tense situation on the country's long border with Japan after the latter's recent conquest of Manchuria, as well as aggressive actions and expansionist saber rattling by fascist Germany and Italy. Soviet citizens in responsible positions began to be "unmasked" as agents of the Japanese and German intelligence services. The terror exacerbated the country's economic difficulties, as arrested technicians and managers had to be replaced by less trained and more inexperienced people. Efforts to cope with declining production by raising work norms led to more problems due to frustrated managers and technical personnel, who were forced to impose higher production targets on their already overextended workers, and to the resentful workers, who were incapable of meeting the new, unreasonable goals.[15]

All these cataclysmic developments of the 1930s take on concrete reality in Andreev's memoirs. Their author gives readers an overall view of the era by telling his own individual, yet not atypical, story. And he tells it well. His poetic descriptions of northern forest landscapes and southern steppe lands reflect the deep love of so many Russians for their vast land. Gennady Andreev had a keen eye and was an effective raconteur with a fine sense of the ludicrous, the ironic, and the amusing. The memoirs open with the author's discharge from concentration camp in 1935 and conclude with a marvelously vivid portrayal of a bewildered and terrified people during the first weeks after the German invasion of 1941: refugees fleeing eastward; empty store shelves; jammed train stations; and *apparatchiki* and their families fleeing Moscow in overloaded automobiles. Andreev is at his best when writing about the human side of historic events, and he lived through a host of them.

The author breathes life into textbook accounts of the Soviet "planned, command economy" through well-chosen incidents and deftly drawn characters: A concentration camp inmate driving down a desolate road sells him fifty liters of gasoline, then shrugs off Andreev's concern. Who's to discover the shortage upon his return to the camp? A chap in charge of "out-of-plan" procurements arrives at the sawmill, authorized to pay in cash from a bulging valise "without a bill of sale, at any price you choose." (Mission not accomplished.) Andreev brings the reader into his planning department, right onto the mill floor, out into logging regions. At one timber operation their factory had to get by with twenty horses instead of seventy, and less than a fifth of the necessary workers.

As a result of the labor shortage, Andreev wrote, the lumber industry began to use women both for hauling and for felling timber, a practice that had not existed in the Russian empire. Reflecting women's diverse roles in the rapidly changing Soviet economy, a variety of women—from a young female truck driver "of Herculean strength" to Aunt Pasha the cleaning woman—frequent the pages of this memoir. They work on kolkhozes (collective farms), in day-care centers, at various factory and office jobs; however, undoubtedly reflecting reality in traditionally male-dominated industries, there is no mention of a woman working in management in any of the plants where Andreev was employed. Some of Andreev's stories convey traditional male attitudes toward women in the workforce. His boss once tossed out a public reprimand, in jest, to a "pug nose" in the front row for laughing during his presentation at a plant meeting, and then followed this up with the suggestion that the male workers "see to" those chatterbox girls. On another occasion, the wives of the director and head mechanic were waiting impatiently for a male-only discussion of upcoming affairs in the sawmill to end. Finally, losing her patience, the director's wife threw a bundle of office papers onto a desk to get the men's attention. Unfortunately, one cannot tell whether the wives of the management team were a part of the workforce because Andreev made little or no mention of their careers or contributions.

Incidents from Andreev's own experiences, along with well-chosen anecdotes about the people he encountered, reveal much about Soviet society. He selected each character and incident carefully, to make a point, and his account never rambles. Unlike most Soviet memoirs, these are the recollections of an ordinary citizen who, aside from a year in an unspecified regional capital and a period working in Moscow just before the German invasion, spent his time outside the Soviet Union's large urban centers. *Bitter Waters: Life and Work in Stalin's Russia* thus sheds considerable light on provincial life in the 1930s.

Focused largely but not exclusively on his experiences in the timber industry, Andreev's account corroborates 1936 Soviet press stories bemoaning the fact that the output of lumber, a key construction material as well as a fuel, was lagging behind plan targets and failing to attain the growth rates achieved in certain other sectors of the economy. Moreover, demand was on the upswing, and persistent lumber shortages were causing disruptions and hardships in many a factory and collective farm. To cite a couple of rural examples: Herds of animals had to spend harsh winters in the open or in half-built barns. Sick and healthy animals were often housed together, sometimes bringing charges of "wrecking" because government quarantine regulations were not being enforced. ("Enforce the unenforceable" suggests itself as an appropriate slogan.) Timber shortages were exacerbated by the mounting labor crunch in an industry with an excessively high rate of worker turnover, due largely to the unusually poor working and living conditions in remote lumbering regions.[16]

Andreev's experiences in the timber industry provide specific examples of these general trends as well as an insider's view of Soviet planning. As the head of planning departments in two different plants, Andreev was one of about a half-dozen people on their management teams. Andreev was on excellent personal terms with the director, who kept him well informed about the whole operation and relied on him heavily. In the second plant, a sawmill, it was Andreev's job to keep track of daily production figures, draw up the annual plan, and then defend his figures in bargaining with Moscow. The people's commissariat in turn defended their interests—higher growth indices—while Andreev attempted to provide for reserves to give the plant more slack and maneuvering room during the coming year. In the event, like everyone else in a position similar to theirs, the mill management team then expended much energy getting around the plan in order to locate needed resources and supplies in a desperately straitened economy. Their access to lumber, which as a *defitsitnyi* item could command high prices or be used in barter exchanges, was a great boon. In theory, supplies could be obtained and paid for only in the quantities and at the rates designated by the Plan. In reality, plant managers regularly turned to agents who specialized in obtaining scarce commodities for a fee. Andreev's portrayal of a couple of these talented procurement agents are among the most colorful sketches in his memoirs.

However, Andreev's memoirs are much more than an account of daily operations at the factory. A restless and adventuresome sort, our author was very creative at thinking up reasons for leaving planning department routines behind and going on business trips that took him into remote corners of the Russian countryside. An astounding zest for these adventures in the boondocks of the Soviet Union sparkles throughout what might otherwise be depressing accounts. Some of the author's recollections are hilarious.

Gennady Andreev was a great storyteller who would have spent has entire life as a writer, had not circumstances intervened. The thirties in the Soviet Union was hardly the time for a former internee accused of counterrevolutionary activities to resume a writing career. With survival the issue, Andreev sought work using skills he had reluctantly acquired in the camps: "By a quirk of fate and against my will, I had come to master the art of bookkeeping," although before his imprisonment, the "prospect of an accounting office evoked waves of revulsion in me." Stable employment as a planner came only after a discouraging series of rejections, short-term jobs, and an arbitrary firing. Andreev spent four months in an unnamed regional capital, making the rounds of hundreds of institutions and enterprises. Often they had a great need for workers in his specialty; however, once potential employers saw his camp release paper, their friendly manner would turn cool. As in the nearby steppe town where he lived before moving to the regional center, "no one refused me outright, but no one hired me, either." Discouraged, Andreev nonetheless empathized with those who refused work to a stranger with his past: "Who would be inclined to risk his position, maybe even his neck, by hiring a suspicious and unfamiliar person like me?" One temporary job came to an abrupt end when his employer, who had scarcely looked at Andreev's documents when hiring him, considered shifting him to more permanent status. As soon as Andreev filled out a personnel card, he was fired for "concealing" his past: "My coworkers stared at me in terrified disbelief. At that time, few people were acquainted with the camps."

By lucky coincidence a telegram with a job offer, signed "Neposedov" (a coined name, meaning one who cannot sit still), arrived shortly after that dismissal. Andreev had worked for Neposedov for a year and a half in the steppe town, his first locale upon release from the camp. Boss, friend, and fellow adventurer, Grigory Petrovich Neposedov is a main character in these memoirs. It was Andreev's wonderful portrayal of this vital little man that first inspired me to translate these memoirs. An amazing fellow who would have been outstanding in any society, Neposedov was also a typical product of his era. He was a prime example of what social historian Moshe Lewin called *praktiki,* Soviet citizens with no formal preparation for employment, who were forced to learn on the job because the schools could not yet satisfy the voracious demand for trained cadres (the Soviet term for skilled workers). Such persons were promoted en masse during this period to fill ever more complex jobs in the industrial sector.[17]

A self-educated orphan who grew up in children's homes, Neposedov was the manager of a factory by age twenty-five. He had joined the Komsomol, the Communist Party's youth organization, at the electric motor factory where he began working as a teenager, and somehow caught the eye of an official who occasionally visited the factory. Under his patronage, Neposedov rose rapidly from his position as the director of small workshops to the position of plant manager. Membership in the Communist Party, as well as the increasing need for people in a widening range of jobs, opened doors for Neposedov and many of his fellow citizens of humble origins. Not surprisingly, many of these new cadres, whose formal training was often nonexistent, were ill fitted for their positions as technical personnel, administrators, political leaders, indoctrinators, and educators.

In that respect, however, the rash, dynamic, and resourceful Neposedov was atypical. Highly energetic, in love with technology, Neposedov also had a valuable talent for small-scale wheeling and dealing within the constraints of a supposedly centralized, planned economy. He and Andreev regularly bartered valuable lumber to procure commodities for the mill and its employees. On a small scale this bartering paralleled transactions still taking place in the higher echelons of the Soviet economy fifty years later. As Boris Yeltsin recalled, he and Mikhail Gorbachev got acquainted when they were Party bosses of their respective regions in the Urals and the Kuban: "Our first conversation was on the telephone. Quite often we needed to extend each other a helping hand." Gorbachev would often supply his future rival with food products from Stavropol in return for Sverdlovsk metals or timber. While Yeltsin claimed that "anything over and above the limits imposed by Gosplan" seldom arrived, he also admitted that Gorbachev's shipments nonetheless "did help us build up our stocks of poultry and meat."[18]

Neposedov originally hired Andreev because he needed a literate employee. He was ashamed because he himself was practically illiterate and wrote in an unimpressive, childish script, making awful mistakes. But Neposedov made up for his inadequate formal education with his native ability and great practical know-how, which enabled him quickly to absorb new information and practical skills. Neposedov was constantly designing and working out the technical aspects of various new projects. However, not one of these projects could be set in motion without various reports, explanations, and estimates being approved by the appropriate bureaucracies in Moscow. This is where Andreev came into the picture. Andreev had luckily found a bold and courageous boss who appreciated his abilities and was willing to overlook his camp background. The two became fast friends, working as a team until shortly after the beginning of World War II, when their paths separated forever.

A.E.H

Bitter Waters

1 ↩

A Second Birth

There is nothing new in these memoirs. But time takes its toll, and our view of past experiences tends to become not only fixed but distorted; therefore it does not hurt on occasion to recall the recent past, which in many ways remains our present, alive and in motion. To that purpose I have dedicated these sketches—which perhaps might better be called "notes," as they were written in both the memoirist and journalistic genres, with no attempt being made to fit them into a literary mold.

Leaving the Netherworld

I have long been haunted by a memory from my early childhood: Along the dusty streets of the city where I was born and grew up there wandered a moss-grown old man with a twangy hand organ. This simple, one-legged box dolefully revealed a pearl of wisdom to us children, till then innocent of fate's existence:

> *Fate toys with a man,*
> *She is fickle always.*

This hand organ's truth could never be erased. The revolution blazed up; there came years of unrest, famine, firing squads, gallows. Life, rearing up on its haunches under the powerful whip of some unknown driver, jerked free and bolted ahead like a whirlwind, pummeling its passengers mercilessly along countless bumpy roads—and the ride has not yet ended. One had no choice but to submit to this wild galloping, surrendering to the will of an incomprehensible, inscrutable fate.

Caught up in the insane whirlwind, in the second half of the 1920s I found myself in a penal labor camp. The hand organ's motif also followed me there. "Fate toys with a man," sang thieves who'd been thoroughly trounced at cards or locked in a punishment cell for stealing. Fate was written, too, on the faces of innocent people dying in the camps by the hundreds, marked for sacrifice—to whom, for what? In most cases, they died submissively, without a murmur. They no longer had the strength to murmur, and doing so was useless. For these people there was no other consolation but simply to say, it's all up to fate!

Recalling the hand organ's motif, one moment bobbing to the surface, the next down in the most abject depths, the netherworld of camp existence, I constantly defied fate, walking the tightrope between life and death. More than once I miraculously evaded the grim reaper. But in the end, I, too, resigned myself to it: well, that's fate! How many incomprehensible tricks I've endured at the hands of that villainess![1]

Everything comes to an end, and fate's wrath sometimes turns to kindness. After I was twice threatened with execution and had spent eight years being dragged through all the circles of the labor-camp hell, in 1935 fate suddenly summoned me to the office that issued release papers, in the registration-distribution department of one of the large camps.

In anticipation of this day, I had long pondered what I would do next. During the years of my imprisonment all my ties with freedom had been severed, and it made absolutely no difference where I went. I might just as well pick up a map, close my eyes, and randomly point—wherever my finger landed was where I would go.

The worker at the release office, also a prisoner whom I knew well, greeted me lightly: "Enough idling your life away, I am releasing you to the four winds! Tell me, where will you go?"

"To Moscow," I said, jesting halfheartedly.

"Fat chance. Talk sense!"

"All right then, *you* tell *me* on what grounds they're releasing me," I retorted angrily.

"General grounds."

I understood: I was free to settle anywhere in the Soviet Union, with the exception of forty-one cities—Moscow, Leningrad, the capitals of the Union republics, and other large manufacturing centers—and a two-hundred-kilometer–wide strip along Soviet borders. I chose a small town in a rural district of southeastern Russia.

Two days later I received my documents and left the camp. I wore a plain black work jacket, trousers that were none too skillfully patched in the rear, and a pair of serviceable shoes. I did not want to return to freedom in ragged camp garb but I had been unable to get my hands on anything else. In my pocket lay my release paper, a travel warrant, and twenty-five rubles. Under my arm was a packet with a loaf of bread and five herring issued "for nourishment during relocation to the chosen place of settlement." With these provisions I was to begin my new life.

During my last years of imprisonment I had thought agitatedly about the new life in store for me. Although reason told me otherwise, I couldn't imagine it being anything but wonderful. It seemed that there could not be a more joyous day than the one when I would leave the camp. I imagined that I would be dancing instead of walking, that when I finally got my freedom I'd be drunk with it. But when I actually was released, I felt none of this.

I walked through the gates and past the last guard, experiencing no happiness or sense of uplift. With a heavy feeling, I left the camp, repeatedly looking back at the long barbed wire fence with towers at the corners, at the rows of unseeing barracks, pressed low to the earth as if by a heavy fate. I was leaving a large part of myself there. Eight years earlier I had entered one such compound as a youth, still understanding nothing of life. In the camp I learned about life. Now freed, I was still a very young man, but could I really experience again the strength, health, and confidence in self that make youth what it is, that lend it wings? I certainly could not leave the ever-present barbed wire behind, nor the heavy burden of what I had endured, seen, and experienced. What was there to be happy about if I, only one of millions, could finally go beyond the fence, when my friends and acquaintances, millions exactly like me, remained behind it? No, there was no reason to be joyous.

Feeling tense, I boarded the train. Among other passengers in the car was an artel[2] of seasonal laborers carrying saws and axes. I felt I was seeing them through a transparent shroud, which imperceptibly separated me from everyone else. Beyond the window, forests, lakes, and granite cliffs floated past—that gloomy, wild, northern landscape, so familiar in its smallest detail. To me it seemed a lifeless image painted on canvas. In the stations people were coming and going. I looked at them as though they were wax figures in a museum. Were they really—actual people? There along the sun-drenched platform ran two young girls in light dresses, merrily laughing about something. I looked at them in astonishment. How could they laugh? How could all these people walk around conversing and laughing as if nothing unusual was happening in the world, as if nothing nightmarish and unforgettable stood in their midst? Did they really know nothing, truly not sense the barbed wire and the man with a rifle at their backs? I was numb, almost as though I were paralyzed, unable to feel what those around me were feeling.

I had to spend the night in Leningrad, waiting for a connecting train. I walked the streets of the Northern Palmyra till morning, bathed in the irresistible soft charm of a white Petersburg night. I sauntered down Nevsky Prospect toward the Neva. The city was slumbering. From time to time I met a solitary pedestrian or heard the rustle of a passing motorcar. I stood on the embankment and stared a long time at the movement of the wide river's silvery waters, as illusory as the city itself, magnificent and regally cool. The Admiralty's spire, familiar from postcards, pierced the sky; the bulky Peter and Paul Fortress loomed ahead blackly. A drawbridge along the dark roadway led across to the other bank. Frozen in silent dreaming stood the city of Peter, itself a wondrous and mysterious dream, a symbol of the empire. The city slept—or could it be that it did not exist, that it was only a specter, a moonlight mirage evoked by the witchcraft of the darkly and inconceivably beautiful white night? Perhaps I, too, was a ghost, having fallen under the spell of this beauty so soon after leaving the netherworld. Could it be that I was only dreaming and that the very next moment, the harsh, shrill cry, "Fall out!" would resound, breaking the magic spell and melting away the mirage, and I would awaken again in a plank bed and run like a crazy man, in formation, toward the man with the rifle?

Early the next morning I boarded the train and traveled farther. Toward evening of the third day, I arrived at my destination.

First Steps

My first task was to seek out the only hotel in town, as night was falling. The young woman on duty at the desk surveyed my release paper and explained that she could not check me in: They only rented rooms to people on business trips. The prospect of spending the night on the street, however, was not a pleasant one. No, I had to make a better arrangement. I would find out exactly what my new life held in store for me: Having thought it over, I went to the police.

The sleepy duty officer perked up a bit after he'd read my document. He turned it this way and that, and then inspected the newcomer curiously. His curiosity was transformed into astonishment when I told him I had nowhere to spend the night.

"So what do you want from me?" the policeman inquired.

"Surely you will help me find a place to stay for the first few days, until I get settled," I replied, a little surprised by my own audacity. Like it or not, to some extent I was still a prisoner. So to clarify matters, I added, "I did not exactly come to you of my own free will."

The officer scratched the back of his head and said indecisively, "I don't know how I can help you."

"Telephone the hotel and have them give me a room."

"Oh, you can stay in a hotel?" exclaimed the policeman, obviously delighted at the prospect of disposing of his strange visitor.

"I should think so, but they won't let me in because the hotel is only for those on business trips."

"They won't let you in?" frowned the officer. "I'll just see about that!" And he snatched up the telephone receiver with a resolute gesture.

About ten minutes later I settled myself onto a cot in the hotel dormitory. After three days and nights on the train, that night I slept like the dead and did not even dream about the camp.

In the morning I thought things over. On the way there I had gone on a bit of a binge—I bought white buns and spent a tenner on beer and sausage, the taste of which I had long since forgotten in the camp. In all, I had only about ten rubles left. The cot cost three rubles a day, and I had to eat. I was going to have to look for work. We had no unemployment in Soviet Russia, there was work enough for all; but for me, newly released from the camp, and given "the organized recruitment of the work force," it would hardly be easy to get a job.

First, though, according to the instructions on my release paper, I had to present myself to the local authorities. I again went to the police station, where they pointed me toward the district representative of the NKVD. A young man in a crisply pressed military uniform greeted me pleasantly, invited me to take a seat, and in a friendly tone asked about my offenses against Soviet power. "What do you intend to do?" asked the official at the end of this conversation, smiling sympathetically.

"Live, work," I answered vaguely.

"You won't return to your old ways?" he inquired, smiling even more broadly.

"No, thanks to you, I've had it up to here." Smiling back at him, I pointed to my release paper.

"I can readily believe that. So I wish you success in your new work life." The official got up from his chair. "Did they warn you that it would be better not to spread the word about what life was like there?"

"Oh, I took that for granted!" I also stood up. "Can I ask you one question?"

"Of course, ask away!"

"I fear that I may have difficulty getting hired. If they will not take me because of my past, can I turn to you?"

"Yes, yes, of course!" the official exclaimed warmly.

Well, my backside was covered. It was not so bad to have a firsthand knowledge of the NKVD—we understood each other perfectly. You could get right to the point with them. "Even a mangy sheep yields a little wool," thought I, leaving the attractive NKVD building in its verdant setting. "And now we plunge into battle."

And I took off. The little town, its only charm being its location on the banks of a large river, had about 20,000 inhabitants and some thirty different enterprises and institutions. The latter included everything you'd expect to find in a southern steppe town: a creamery, a steam-powered mill, a winery, various workshops and artels of craftsmen and handicapped workers, district commerce and consumer goods bureaus, a branch of the state bank, financial and statistical bureaus, and other district institutions. Mountains of paper were generated by all of these institutions. It would not be difficult for me to get a job in one of them, I thought. In the camp, through a quirk of fate and against my will, I had come to master the art of bookkeeping, although before my imprisonment the prospect of an accounting office evoked waves of revulsion in me. At a time like this, there was no question of changing my specialty; I had to get established very quickly. Furthermore, as was customary almost from the beginning of the revolution, the jobs of bookkeeper, planner, accountant, and store-room attendant provided a piece of bread for "suspicious elements." Former White officers,[3] merchants, peasants who were evading *dekulakizatsiia*,[4] priests, and members of the intelligentsia who were considered undesirable frequently sought refuge in these occupations. Far be it from me to change established tradition and avoid the common lot!

Within three days I had made the rounds of almost all the city enterprises—and found a job in none. No one showed any confidence in my release paper. Two or three suggested that I stop back in a week, but in such a tone that only a child could fail to understand that returning was fruitless. I did not have even a kopeck left. Yet I had no grounds for going to the NKVD official for assistance. No one had turned me away because of my past; they rejected me without offering a reason. I was sinking into deep depression, when on the fourth day, fate unexpectedly smiled on me.

The chief bookkeeper at a sawmill inspected my release paper thoroughly, but without subjecting me to the usual song and dance. He seemed to be eyeing me sympathetically. Looking thoughtful, he went in to see the director. I waited, a bit agitated: The director was a Party member, and this was no cause for optimism.

About five minutes later I was summoned to the director's office. He turned out to be a very young fellow, about my age, small in stature and skinny, wearing an embroidered shirt with an open collar. His keen eyes were alert and full of life.

Sunken into an easy chair behind a desk, under a portrait of Stalin, the director was holding my release paper. Inviting me to sit down, he said: "This little paper of yours is pretty frightening. How did you manage all that?"

The director's eyes were laughing, so I smiled back at him. "It's a long story. If you find it frightening, then we have nothing to talk about."

"Perhaps I am not among the fainthearted," laughed the director. "I need workers, but only good ones. If you have such a paper, that means you have a head on your shoulders," he blurted out, apparently unaware of the double meaning that could be inferred in his words. I could only smile in response.

"What can you do?"

I told him about my work experience.

"What about planning? We need a planner."

"I have never worked in planning," I admitted.

"Eh, it's nonsense, foolishness," he replied scornfully, waving his hand and nodding at the head bookkeeper. "You will quickly become familiar with it; Ivan Ivanovich here will explain."

"Nothing we do is very complicated. For the time being you will just be doing some statistics, and you'll soon catch on. Agreed? What kind of salary would you expect?"

To refuse when a job for pay was in front of me would be frivolous. I said that I would agree to take a job there, not as a planner but in some other, minor position and at the lowest salary level. Even a hundred rubles a month, just enough to live on, would satisfy me. Later, say in a month, once they saw whether I was capable, we could talk about the future.

The director laughed. "Okay, we will see, as they say. It's settled. Come to work tomorrow."

The next morning I learned that the director had not agreed to my proposal. Instead, he had allotted me 250 rubles a month. This was as high a starting salary as I could have anticipated.

"It doesn't take a genius to make a pot," as they say. Planning, especially for an experienced bookkeeper, proved uncomplicated. After a couple of months I completely mastered it, and two months later I was already the director of the planning department and earning 500 rubles a month. I could only thank fate, which continued to protect me.

Freedom

The beneficence of fate was reflected also in the fact that it released me from the camps at a time when the storms of the First Five-Year Plan and "100-percent collectivization," which had so shaken our country, were dying down. Ration cards had already been abolished and the material situation in the country was tolerable. I had been in the camps during the terrible famine of 1932–1933 and could judge it only from the terse accounts of townspeople, who unwillingly recalled the overwhelming hunger and instances of cannibalism. Thank God, I was seeing the town in different times. One could buy all the basic necessities in the local stores. Local artels even began to sell delicacies like jam, halvah, and other confectionery. Not long before my release, Stalin had decided to permit *kolkhozniki*—that is, workers on collective farms—to own one cow and a few small livestock and chickens per family, and freely to dispose of what they grew in their tiny private garden plots. Neighboring *kolkhozniki* brought butter, milk, eggs, meat, and vegetables to the market. And although all this was available in meager amounts and at high prices, nonetheless people in our town need not go hungry. I had even less reason to be hungry than most: I was single, and by local standards I received a big salary, which even permitted me gradually to acquire a wardrobe of sorts and a respectable appearance.

These circumstances facilitated my mental recovery after the camp. I settled into a little room in the small home of a worker's widow. The house had a typical provincial yard, spacious and thickly covered with a shaggy grass—called "broomstraw" by the locals—lilac bushes, and dozens of fruit trees. In the back yard the widow kept a goat and five or six chickens. The animals, the fruit trees, her handknitting, and my rent were her livelihood. Constantly busy with her domestic chores, the fussy old woman inaudibly and unhurriedly moved about the house, accompanied by a lazy old cat whom fate also smiled upon.

Evenings I went out into the yard, lay down in the grass, and for hours idly gazed upward at the magnificent sky, the brilliant, starry abyss. I left the camp behind. Alone with the rustling grass, the lilac bushes, and the dark foliage of the trees in the quiet reverie of the southern night, I slowly shed my disfigured camp hide, becoming accustomed once again to the eternal and simple elements of life.

The process of internal liberation took quite awhile. For a long time I still looked incomprehendingly at people and things, watching them from the sidelines. Words and actions all seemed unimportant and inessential because inside me remained the unanswered question: What is it all for? Why bother, if somewhere back there what I cannot, must not forget still exists? I was unable to share the interests of people around me, and my life became sharply divided into two parts. At work I tried to act like everyone else; but only at home, in the company of the quiet old woman and the silent grass, lilacs, and stars did I feel truly at ease.

My remoteness was noted in the factory, and at first I was considered an unsociable crank. But my past, which soon became known to everyone there, evoked their sympathy. After a short time I began to detect this in the glances of the workers and from the fact that in our factory neighborhood, women that I had never met, workers' wives, gave me a friendly nod in passing. No one asked me about anything, no one directly expressed their sympathy, but it hung in the air, it was evident from their glances and the tone of their voices. And this sympathy from simple, good-hearted people really bolstered my spirits.

The town had a movie theater, a park, and a workers' club that was uncomfortable and always empty. The young people preferred the dance floor in the park or the furnished foyer of the movie theater, where they also could dance. There was a small but decent library with a reading room. Of an evening one could sit on the lush cliffs above the river, forgetting about everything, calmly yet excitedly watching as the dark tent of the velvet night covered the river and the expanses beyond. Life flowed on peacefully. People worked at their jobs during the day, and in the evenings they visited each other, gossiped good-naturedly, sat over tea, bared their souls in long conversations, and like their bureaucrat predecessors, spent hours playing preference or mouse for small stakes.[5] Events far away in the regional capital, in Moscow, and in other big cities seemed to bypass our backwoods corner, hardly touching us—or perhaps bouncing off the solidly entrenched daily routine that in many respects echoed the previous good life of the provinces.

I can never thank fate enough for freeing me at that period, in those brief two or three years when the country was slowly recovering from the upheavals of the first onslaught of "building socialism" and people could catch their breath for a minute—before they were again besieged by the authorities, and before that other terrible event, that destructive maelstrom we call war, which erupted four or five years later. I was very happy to spend a year and a half in a quiet steppe town. Simple people, human relationships, and the uncomplicated, eternal beauty of the grass, sun, and stars, along with the tender care of my elderly landlady and her purring cat, helped me slough off my labor-camp hide, gradually convincing me that reality was not whence I had returned, but here.

I worked conscientiously, and after the numbness subsided, I even began to enjoy my work—thanks in large part to the director of the factory, Grigory Petrovich Neposedov.

Restless Neposedov

Neposedov[6] was an extraordinary fellow. He never knew his parents: His father was killed during World War I, and his mother died at the beginning of the revolution. Neposedov grew up in children's homes, although he ran away from them more than once. In spite of all this, at twenty-five he was already the director of a factory. It was not because he was "devoted to the Party and the government," but because he was an energetic and able man; and besides that, he "got lucky."

As a teenager, Neposedov went to work in an electric motor factory. He soon became a fitter, joined the Komsomol,[7] and somehow caught the eye of a people's commissar who occasionally visited the factory. For some reason, he made a great impression on the people's commissar, who took the young fitter under his wing. After two or three years, Neposedov became a director of small workshops, then of a small plant, after which he was appointed to run the factory where I met him. Neposedov raced ahead without stopping to catch his breath, constantly fired up and always in motion—and that's just how he was all the while I worked for him.

He was unable to move quietly. Skinny and short, he moved around the plant so quickly that he seemed to be running, not walking. Keeping pace with the director, the fat chief mechanic would be steeped in perspiration. The shift foremen used to laugh at Neposedov, saying that he was "propeller driven." He rarely sat in his office, and if he needed to sign some paper or other, you had to look for him in the mechanic's office, in the shops, or in the basement under the shops, where the transmission belts and motors that powered the work stations were located. There you could often find him covered with grease, wrench in hand, cursing out the machinists and metal workers, furiously letting them know that they did not understand a damn thing and that it was essential to do what he said. He remained unflustered if the machinists managed to demonstrate that *they* were right. Without admitting his error, Neposedov would rapidly make the adjustment suggested by his opponents. Only one thing could get to him. Dragging him away from a dispute with the "smudged faces," as we called our brigade of metal workers, I would bring the director into the daylight and point to his recently snow-white trousers: "Your wife will bawl you out today!"

"She'll make me take a bath, all right," Neposedov would shake his head, examining the black spots on his pants and trying to remove them with a shirt sleeve, which also became black in the process. "So whoever thought up wives, anyway?" Nonetheless, Neposedov loved his wife and two children and was a good family man. After signing the paper, he would forget both his trousers and his wife and take off again for the depths of the basement.

This enthusiasm of his, this ability to lose himself completely in a genuinely creative exertion, to give his all selflessly, was contagious. It was impossible to be around Neposedov without being infected by his energy; he roused everyone, set them on fire. And if he did not succeed in shaking someone up, it could unmistakenly be said that such a person was either dead or a complete blob.

Neposedov made up for his inadequate education with native ability and great practical know-how, which enabled him to absorb knowledge in a flash. But he also delved into every detail. He wanted to get to the bottom of everything on his own, and if he encountered something he did not understand, his fidgeting quickly disappeared. He would sit down with books and charts or spend the whole night in conference with the chief mechanic, forcing him to explain matters until everything was clear. After this he would walk around beaming, with even more faith in his own powers and in the power of technology, striving rapidly to put what he had learned into practice, to apply it to life.

Technology, the factory, the shop—there Neposedov was in his element. Given these all-consuming passions, one might have thought he would scorn bureaucratic red tape. However, this was not at all the case. I was struck by the fact that his love for petty detail almost equaled his passion for technology. He liked the florid, elevated style of official documents. He had an even greater regard for imperceptible "underwater reefs" placed in agreements with our suppliers and purchasers. Whenever we succeeded, thanks to some trick of pettifoggery, in winding a client around our little finger, Neposedov would be delighted, and his face would take on the look of a sharp lawyer. Moved by his propensity for hairsplitting, Neposedov pressed the head accountant to teach him bookkeeping. Afterward, to his great satisfaction, he could use his knowledge to impress the other bookkeepers, most of whom thought directors did not have even the slightest understanding of accounting.

Neposedov wrote in an unimpressive, childish scrawl, making dreadful mistakes. He was ashamed because he was almost illiterate. Nor did he possess verbal eloquence, although he loved to attend meetings. In general he liked to swagger a little, to project a "this is how we folks are!" image. But all this came out ingenuously, without the slightest sense of superiority or the least desire to put down or humiliate his fellows.

So Neposedov needed a literate assistant. He was constantly full of new projects and ideas, since he could not be satisfied with what already existed. He conjectured and experimented; he designed and worked out the technical aspects of his projects with the mechanic; but he still needed help in preparing the financial and other paperwork—the reports, explanations, and estimates for Moscow, without which none of his projects could be set in motion. In addition, Neposedov had no special liking for either the head bookkeeper or the technical director, who were elderly and sluggish fellows. He needed people who quickly responded to his feelings and ideas. Even a negative reaction stimulated Neposedov. Fate designated me for this role, as Neposedov quickly sensed that I found his enthusiasm catching. Over the course of time, we also became friends.

Neposedov's enthusiasm and restlessness were harmless and only evidenced his strength and health. Although he generally liked to use cunning and play a trick when the opportunity arose, he was a wholehearted and guileless man with an open and sympathetic nature. As I got to know Neposedov better, I realized that his attitude toward the Party was similarly original. He submitted to the orders of the district Party committee and fulfilled his Party obligations, but when alone with me he would growl that the district committee was pestering him with "all kinds of nonsense" and hampering his work. He had no liking for politics; and although he had been promoted by the Party and it would appear that he should be thankful for this, he felt no gratitude toward the Party. Neposedov seemed subconsciously certain that he had achieved his position on his own strength and that it suited him and his abilities perfectly. He took the system that afforded him this station completely for granted, as though it were borne of life itself. He never stopped to ponder the matter.

I must admit that we botched things up a lot during the first year and a half that Neposedov and I worked together. We were still inexperienced with lumbering. Moreover, the factory was old, with equipment that was worn out and functioning only so-so. Nonetheless, Neposedov was able to modernize the equipment so that we almost doubled production and fulfilled our annual plan in less than eight months. Everyone was satisfied: the People's

Commissariat of Forestry;[8] the district and regional organizations, because an enterprise under their supervision was producing at a remarkable tempo; the workers, with their raises; and we, with our success and bonuses. Neposedov felt like the birthday boy, walked around for awhile with a grin on his face, and tried to raise production even higher. We were still pouring on the steam when we noticed that our raw materials were almost gone, and it looked as if no one was going to give us more. And that's exactly what happened: The people's commissariat, viewing our factory as relatively unimportant, decided not to send us raw materials, which were in short supply, and ordered the factory to "conserve." We settled accounts with the workers, paying them the prescribed severance allotment, and drew up a liquidation order two months later. Then we withdrew our own severance pay and said farewell to each other and the factory. We felt awful. We had not anticipated such an outcome. The factory could have operated at least another half-year, and during that time we might have succeeded in obtaining raw materials. Now all we could do was blame ourselves and vow never to overdo things in the future.

They summoned Neposedov to Moscow as one of the reserve workers in the people's commissariat, and I decided to move to the regional capital.

More Tricks of Fate

By this time, I had all of the documents that a normal citizen needed in order to survive—passport, workbook,[9] and military and trade union cards. Once again I appeared to possess all the legal rights of citizenship. Thinking that I could count on finding work without too much difficulty, I moved to a city with a large university. I intended to enroll in evening courses in order to continue my education, which had been interrupted earlier by my arrest. I would work days and go to school nights—in my mind, everything fell into place perfectly.

I rented a room from another working-class family. The husband and wife had a separate room, a bit larger than mine, and their teenage son slept in my room. He was a quiet fellow and did not disturb me.

Filled with the best of intentions, I began to look for a job. Now fate again turned villainess. For four months I walked around in search of work and could not find it.

I made the rounds of hundreds of institutions and enterprises. Everywhere it was the same story. First, I would ask whether they needed workers of my specialty in their enterprise. Usually it turned out that they had a great need, since enterprises were always short of workers. Next, I would offer my services, which were readily accepted; but then came the process of surveying my documents and the inevitable question. Where was I employed before being let go from the factory? Once more, I had to show my release paper from the camp. They would read it as if they were holding a bomb that was about to explode. Their friendly manner would suddenly turn dry and official, and I would hear that they could still manage without new workers, or that they would need time to consider whether to hire me or someone else. As in the steppe town, no one refused me outright, but no one hired me, either.

I could worry about it all I liked, try every possible approach—nothing helped. I understood those who turned me down. The newspapers had begun to be filled with cries for vigilance and warnings about spies, saboteurs, and wreckers. Once they knew I had been in a labor camp for counterrevolutionary activities, everyone was afraid to hire me. Who would be inclined to risk his position, maybe even his neck, by hiring a suspicious and unfamiliar person like me? As for acquaintances in that city, I had none. Only such personal networks might have helped me at that time. I recalled a saying that was common in the camps: "*Blat* (pull) is higher than the Council of People's Commissars."[10]

I made no progress at the university, either. It was impossible to study without being employed, anyway, so I gave up on enrolling in classes there. However, I did manage to register as a correspondence student at an economic-planning institute that had opened recently in the city.

Fortunately, my previous modest lifestyle had enabled me to accumulate savings. These small reserves, along with my severance pay, enabled me to survive for four months without work. But no matter how much I economized, I finally used up all my resources. It might have been possible to locate some kind of menial job, but with my past even that was not easy. There was no way to conceal my past. Even if there had been, there were no opportunities that held any promise of building for the future; and I was still entirely too young not to count on the future.

The endless search for work wore me down. Having no prospects, I finally decided to return to the steppe town, where they already knew me. But fate once again struck with a bolt from the blue.

While walking down the street one day, I saw a notice on a door: "Urgent need for accountants." I looked up and read a sign over the entry: "Regional Branch of the All-Union Fish Trust." I mechanically opened the door, located the head bookkeeper, and offered my services. And then a miracle happened. Barely glancing at my workbook, the head bookkeeper said that he had an immediate need for temporary workers at a rate of 300 rubles a month, and that if I agreed I could come to work the very next morning. This all happened in no more than five minutes, and I was a little stunned. I left, still not fully realizing what had happened, forgetting to rejoice at finally locating work.

The miracle was clarified the next day. It was a simple matter: The regional branch of the all-Union fish trust had totally muddled its accounts with its contractors and received a stiff reprimand from Moscow with orders to straighten out the mess quickly. The administration had no time to be interested in the pasts of those who were offering their services, especially since the job was temporary, to last only three or four months; so the first four persons who turned up were taken on. This was a lucky break for me.

The work was excruciatingly dull. For two years, the would-be record-keepers before us had misrecorded shipments. Goods that had been directed to Moscow, for example, were entered under Yaroslavl or Rostov, and those sent to Rostov were entered under Tambov or Penza. Goods received were recorded in exactly the same fashion. The region contained more than thirty districts, and the records of shipments to and from the thirty receiving and distribution centers were so completely muddled that one might well be driven to despair. This could hardly have been a surprise to anyone: The young girls who had kept these accounts, barely out of high school, undoubtedly had had no knowledge of or interest in their work. We had to go through a mountain of documents, check each entry, and verify the new data with the contractors, all of which took a tremendous amount of time. The contractors' situations frequently proved no better than ours, as they had the same kind of young girls working for them.

As for balancing the accounts between the various offices, while still in the camp I had developed a kind of special flair for catching mistakes, so I got right down to business. Like people everywhere who are inclined to introduce order, I systematized the checking process. I also suggested speeding it up by going directly to the contractors. The administration approved my work, gave me a little raise, and designated me "head of the brigade of controllers." Their approval of my travel proposal pleased me. It would be far more pleasant to visit the various towns and villages than to sit in the office of the fish trust. I felt almost as free as a bird.

For three months, I traveled around by automobile, train, and ship, visiting several large towns and many rural district villages. Sometimes I got so far into the "boonies" that there was no passenger service. Then I had to hitch a ride on the cart of a passing *kolkhoznik* or go to the nearest highway and patiently await the occasional motorized vehicle. When one approached, I would flag down the driver, who would stop to pick me up, and we would take off, sending up clouds of dust.

These drivers were like the coachmen of yore—they generally drove like the whirlwind. I remember one time when I thought I wasn't going to make it. The young woman at the wheel, of Herculean strength and deeply tanned, had been busy at some urgent task and had not slept for two nights. She kept dozing off, drooping over the steering wheel, but the vehicle would race along as if we were riding on a smoothly paved runway rather than a bumpy steppe road. Twice we drove into the shallow ditch along the road, and several times we scraped the truck's sides against telegraph poles. Whether saved by a miracle or the strength of the handmade sides of that three-ton truck, we escaped accident. The driver would shake her head to clear it, rub her half-closed eyes, curse out whoever in the world had moved that pole out of place, and drive on, her head again slumped over the wheel.

People who have ridden only in city traffic cannot comprehend what our drivers are like; this can be experienced only on the steppe expanses. Only there can one fully appreciate what old foxes these people are. They keenly sense who can afford to pay what, and if they could wrest a ruble from a *kolkhoznik* for a ride, then they knew they could pry ten out of me. But I wasn't too upset by it: The bureau paid for my transportation at the going rate, and this stipend, combined with my living allotment, provided ample funds. The drivers had to make a buck, too.

As a teenager I had been a great wanderer and loved to spend the whole day out in the steppes. Traveling around the district, my former passion was rekindled. Sometimes I would walk ten or fifteen kilometers just to feel again the thrilling closeness to nature that I have fully experienced only in the steppes: the road, weaving in and out among the hills and foothills; the endless hum of wires buzzing overhead; a dung beetle suddenly appearing out of nowhere, droning resonantly; the song of an invisible bird filling the endless sky. Vast expanses, and in my chest the exact same expansiveness, happiness, and light, peaceful calmness. No one is visible for tens of kilometers around. I walked alone, with nothing but the eternal quiet and calm of the steppe surrounding me—no fish trust, no past, no future. Walks like these are like a bath. You are absorbed in them, cleansed; and afterward, you breathe more easily.

Instead of three or four months, the verification process took more than five. I finished up alone, as the other three bookkeepers had already been let go. My position in the branch office had become more secure and I was now a member of their regular staff. I was slated soon to take up the post of senior bookkeeper in one of the departments. But for some reason, I had a dark premonition that I would not be entering the inner circle of the fish trust.

The premonition proved accurate. One day, the office secretary approached me, put a form in front of me, and said, "For some reason we don't have a personnel record for you; please fill this out."

I filled out about sixty sections on the form, tracing my genealogy and my every step, thinking that this was surely my last task at the fish trust. After I handed the form back in to the secretary I soon noticed that the head bookkeeper was staring at me, panic-stricken. Before, no one had taken much interest in me. Now, the assistant to the director went wandering by, then the secretary, just to have a look—or so it seemed. They peered at me as if they had never seen me before, as if I had become someone else. I concluded that the form had made a strong impression.

Our head bookkeeper was a heavy-set, mellow, and reasonably good-hearted man, but in the director's presence he became timid and totally subordinate. He detained me after work, and after everyone had left, inquired, his eyes popping out: "How can this be, old fellow? Why didn't you say so earlier?"

"And what should I have said?"

"What do you mean, what? That you were in a labor camp!"

"But no one asked me about that," I objected. "If they had asked, I would have said something, but why should I broadcast it of my own accord?"

"Well—but why didn't you even breathe a word to me?" the bookkeeper offered reproachfully. "Do you know what went on in there?" He nodded in the direction of the director's office. "Such a storm God has never seen. Everyone got it, especially me. 'Why did you hire him without a background check?' Why me? Checking up on employees is their job, not mine. He's going to fire you for sure."

I shrugged my shoulders. Fate would decide.

Before that, I'd had no occasion for close contact with the director. From the accounts of my coworkers I knew that he had served as a sailor in the Baltic fleet, that he had been a member of the Party since 1918, and that he was an obtuse and hidebound fellow. Stubborn and narrow-minded, he was wholly devoted to fulfilling the orders of the Party and the higher authorities and would permit no deviation from them. With subordinates he was cold, often rough, and he had no contact with them outside of work. As an old Bolshevik, he had close connections to the regional Party committee.

There was no reason to hope for humane treatment at his hands. I knew that my employment at the fish trust was over.

The next morning, they sent me official notification that I was fired "for concealing my past." My coworkers stared at me in terrified disbelief. At that time, few people were acquainted with the camps.

A Fateful Summons

My discharge was illegal. Shortly before, in one of his speeches, Stalin had announced that the "son did not answer for the father" and that it was forbidden to judge a man by his past. My discharge also ran contrary to the spirit of the "Stalin constitution," which had just been published. In addition, a decree had been issued by the Soviet Control Commission to the effect that a previous conviction could not be an obstacle to employment, whatever the job. The director must have known that his order was against the law. But he was just as surely aware of the worth of Soviet legality—and so was I, he must have thought—so he must have expected me to submit quietly to his will.

But I decided not to do that. There were reasons for my decision. One was frivolous. I was simply fed up and thus opted to measure swords of unequal strength with one of the new petty tyrants. The second reason was more serious. If the director himself entered a discharge order in my workbook, it would be impossible for me to find other employment. I would be turned into a suspicious character once and for all; such an order would add an even more frightening aspect to the blot on my record, and the document would get me blacklisted for sure. I had to try at least to get the wording of the order changed.

I saw a way to do that. Because I was a "counterrevolutionary," it would be too risky for me to bring a lawsuit against the director—I might again be summoned to the NKVD. However, knowing the mechanics of the Soviet bureaucratic machine, I hoped to avoid that outcome. I would make cautious use of all the circumstances in my favor, proceed quietly, and try to get the matter resolved locally and by lower-level bureaucrats, on a strictly documented, legal basis: The red tape and the fine print in the laws could actually work to my benefit with such people. It was crucial that I preserve the strictly labor-oriented nature of the conflict in order to avoid arousing the interest of the NKVD. In this effort I knew I would be aided by the increasing alarm among Party members due to the *Yezhovshchina*.[11] If the director decided to denounce me to the NKVD and have me arrested, he could not guarantee that I would not in turn maliciously slander him and his office to the NKVD; and while they were sorting it all out, he might well be sitting in prison. So the director would hardly be likely to turn to the NKVD for a minor affair like mine.

Having weighed all the pros and cons, I lodged a complaint about my discharge with the Rates and Disputes Commission (RKK) of the director's office. Our RKK consisted of the assistant to the director, also a Party member, as a "representative of the administration"; the secretary of the local trade union committee (he was also the office secretary), as a "representative of the trade union"; and a female accountant, as a "representative of the workers." I knew that the last two would not dare go against the director's wishes, and that as a result, the RKK would deny my request. Nevertheless, I had to go through all the proper channels, beginning with those at the lowest level.

That very day, the RKK issued a confirmation of the director's order. The next day, I lodged a protest against their decision with the regional committee of our trade union, which was presided over by a woman who was also an old Bolshevik and a personal friend of the director's. I had no doubt that she, too, would deny my request; but this was a necessary step. About five days later, I received a notice from the regional committee of the trade union to the effect that it found the RKK's decision correct.

I had one last resort—the central committee of the trade union. What were the relations of our regional committee with the central committee? This I did not know. But I was aware of the central authorities' general tendency to treat their subordinates in a condescending manner so that they would not get too cocky. I also knew that one could hope for an objective hearing of this sort of case in Moscow. The higher authorities sometimes liked to demonstrate their "fairness," which they hoped would make people recognize they were not guilty of being arbitrary. Arbitrariness went on without their knowledge, at a lower level. Did the president of the regional committee have "a lot of pull" in Moscow? How would they receive me there? I had to see my case through to the end. Of course, I could simply have written a letter to the trade union's central committee; but then I most likely would have had to wait months for a response, or my appeal might easily have sunk without a trace into the sea of paper. Having thought it over, I boarded a train for Moscow.

During all this time I had strange, contradictory feelings. I felt like a dwarf going into battle against a giant. To the huge government machine, I was a nonentity. The machine could wipe me out at any minute and leave no trace, as though I had never existed. So I acted cautiously; but of what use was caution, when I would be confronting a soulless, irrational machine, the conduct of which I could not predict? The movement of its levers was imperceptible, and I could neither modify it nor defend myself from it. The machine would swallow me up. I was nothing to it, a nonentity. At times, I even felt like a "nothing," and this really seemed strange: There I was, sitting on the train, but at the same time it was as if I did not exist. I felt as if I were slipping now to one side, now to the other side of the borderline between the real and the unreal, existence and nonexistence. One might well be surprised that this "nothing" was still trying to oppose reality; but I was merely acting on the stubbornness that I felt inside, which was irrational. I decided to pursue the matter to the end, regardless of the consequences.

In Moscow, I went straight from the train station to Solyanka Street, to a huge House of Edification, the "Palace of Labor." Wandering along endless, dark corridors, I located the offices of our trade union's central committee and, a bit diffidently, eased open the heavy door.

The chief counsel for labor conflicts, a fat man with a flabby, markedly indifferent face, received me. Immobile, deeply ensconced in his armchair, almost merging with the dusty furniture, he appeared to have been sitting there for many a year. He had grown gray anchored in his post, and he certainly knew it no worse than I knew inter-office accounts. My impression proved accurate. The trade union bonze barely glanced at my papers, and without raising his head or looking at me, he intoned in a deep basso: "These decisions run counter to the labor laws. The matter will be reviewed tomorrow in the meeting of the presidium of the central committee. Stop back in two days."

I left with a feeling that a mountain had slid from my shoulders: I had made my case.

For two days I lightheartedly wandered around Moscow, going through all the rituals appropriate for a provincial visiting the heart of his homeland. I went to the Tretyakov Gallery and the Historical Museum, saw the Kremlin, took a jaunt through the Vorobev Hills, strolled the streets in the evening. Moscow was changing. Older buildings were being demolished and moved and new ones constructed; but it was still the same old mishmash, bustling, yet also homey and intimate. I did not get to the Khudozhestvennyi or the Bolshoi theaters; the tickets were all sold out, and I could not afford the scalpers' prices. Instead, I went to the people's commissariat that oversaw Neposedov and me and learned that he had recently been appointed the director of another sawmill, not far from Moscow.

Two days later, the same trade union bonze, again without looking up from his desk—as if I really were a nonentity to him—silently handed me a copy of a resolution of the union's central committee. Thanking him, I went out into the corridor and read it: "On the basis of such-and-such regulations, the decisions of the RKK and regional committee of the trade union concerning the complaint of Citizen Andreev are rescinded and he is granted the right to appeal to a people's court with a complaint against the unjust action of the administration."

I returned from Moscow in buoyant spirits. I had won my head-to-head battle on all counts. On my copy of the resolution was a stamp with the words "central committee" and "Moscow." It stated that the action of the administration was illegal. What judge in the provinces could refuse me and go against those magic words? If the director did not pull something unexpected, my success was guaranteed.

Immediately after arriving home, I filed suit. The case came to court two weeks later. Legal counsel for the defense was an elderly lawyer from the fish trust, a kind and goodhearted fellow. While awaiting the court's settlement of the case, we sat together in the corridor and talked about my trip, about Moscow, about my reception by the central committee's legal counsel. The advocate sighed. "I have never seen such a blockhead," he said of the director. "Stand firm, like a stump; you should win your case. How could I win, going up against a decision made in Moscow?"

The hearing lasted all of five minutes. The document from Moscow was incontrovertible. The decision of the court read: "The discharge was improper. Citizen Andreev shall be reinstated in his job, and the administration shall be obligated to pay his salary from the day of discharge because his absence was the fault of the administration."

With the lawsuit resolved in my favor, the next day I went to the fish trust and delivered two papers to the head bookkeeper: the court's decision and a request that I be released from employment. There was no sense in testing fate further. After this, it would have been risky for me to continue working for the fish trust.

The head bookkeeper disappeared into the director's office for a long time. Then they summoned their legal counsel. Finally, the chief bookkeeper returned and whispered to me: "Another storm. He shouted, insisted on filing a complaint. Surely this undermined his authority, undermined discipline. You see what's at stake here! We finally convinced him that we would just lose anyway and only waste more money."

A half-hour later I received my back wages and signed the newly phrased order. Paragraph 1 read: "Bookkeeper Andreev reinstated in his job. Basis: Court decision." And Paragraph 2: "Bookkeeper Andreev discharged from work at his initiative. Basis: His resignation request." The secretary wrote what I demanded in my workbook: "Discharged at his own request." I exchanged good-byes with my coworkers and left the fish trust forever.

At home I found a telegram awaiting me. Several days before my case came up, I had sent Neposedov a letter saying that life in this city was not to my liking and asking whether he had a job for me. Tearing open the telegram, I read: "Come at once. I will pay your way. Neposedov." I smiled, thinking that under the Soviet system I could apparently work only for Neposedov. I went to the station to buy a ticket.

Neposedov's Misadventures

Neposedov and I greeted one another like old friends. He brought me to his apartment to rest up from the trip. He was still as explosive and restless as ever, but I noticed a change in his appearance. If he'd been thin before, now he was emaciated. Hollow cheeks, wrinkled brow—he looked five years older, as though he'd had a serious illness. I asked about the reason for this alteration. Pacing around the room, Neposedov related what he had been doing during the interim.

"At first, they designated me an employee for special assignments. I did not like trouble-shooting: today here, tomorrow there, like an errand boy. All the while I kept insisting that they give me my own responsibility, put me into production. And I got what I wanted, to my great misfortune—they gave me a task fit for a Goliath.

"They sent me to Noginsk to manage a brick works. I arrived and looked it over: the factory was fine, fully mechanized—a plum. So why was it fulfilling only 30–40 percent of its plan, and why was it as silent in there as the graveyard? What's the matter, I inquired. No workers. Technical personnel were available, skilled workers as well, but there was no permanent force of unskilled workers to haul clay. Why not? Because, they said, the factory does not have money to pay wages. Utter nonsense, bricks are worth their weight in gold, and you do not have money? The reason, they answered, is very simple: We supply a carload of bricks according to the fixed price of 200 rubles; according to our plan it costs us 250, but in reality the cost is 500–600. Well, clearly the factory has nothing but debts. In debt to the bank, in debt to the central board, in debt to tens of other enterprises; and we ourselves have gone two to three months without wages. And you understand, they say this in such a hopeless tone, like a bunch of dead flies, that I explode. You aren't worth a damn, yourselves! You've got to get to work instead of chasing butterflies; then there will be money. 'You try,' they say; 'maybe you will succeed.'

"So I set myself to task. First, I had to get workers. I went to the regional soviet executive committee [Oblispolkom] and put on the pressure. They gave me two districts for recruiting. I mobilized my staff and threw them into recruiting, but the districts wouldn't give us any workers. So I went to them myself, applied some pressure through the district Party committees, got the backing of the district soviet executive committees, and they referred me to some village soviets—but then the kolkhozes wouldn't give us anyone either. Nothing could be done about it, they had no labor to spare. For a month I made the rounds of the kolkhozes, talked, grew hoarse, cussed, plied the chairmen with vodka, and extracted three or four workers from each. By hook or by crook I collected about a hundred workers. I bought their tickets myself and put them on the train. To prevent their running off along the route, I sent one of my own people along with each group. We did everything but wipe their noses for them!

"Well, now I'd brought people to the factory. But they had to be fed, and they hadn't a kopeck on them. What was I going to feed them? Our dining room was closed, there wasn't a coin in the cashbox, and we were overdrawn at the bank. What was I to do? I felt sorry for these people. They were half starved—what kind of workers would they be?

"I galloped off to Moscow, to the central board, to the people's commissariat: save us; extend a hand! I got nowhere with them. 'Our funds,' they said, 'are exhausted; we can give you no more credit. Try to find the resources locally, show initiative'—the usual runaround. I argued that this was impossible, that with such a gap between selling price and cost, the factory could not survive. 'Fine,' they said, 'we will take this into account when composing next year's plan and we'll bring up the question in the people's commissariat of raising the price of bricks and increasing your loans.' They, as you know, look at things on an all-union scale; you can't get through to them. And what would I do until next year?

"I could think of nothing else to do. The factory is a good one, but what headway can it make without funds? We ship out bricks, but the bank won't leave us a kopeck for them; everything goes to pay off our loans. The sons of bitches won't even allow us a wage exemption; they dispense as little as possible. And our debts are so huge that we would have to work about two years just to pay them off. What could we do? There was only one recourse: We'd have to sell bricks for cash on the side, skirting the bank.

"So we got by for three months. Bricks are a *defitsitnyi*[12] item, so people grabbed them up. You sell a carload or two to some craftsmen's artel, not at the fixed price, but for what they are worth; and then you pay off the workers with a tenner each, and they are satisfied. And then, another two or three carloads sold on the side—and you survive another week.

"So we carried on. Carried on, and got burned. A son of a bitch of a bank inspector got wind of it, checked our shipments through railroad documents at the station, compared them with our records of shipments at the bank, and reported that we had disposed of about a hundred carloads on the side. What an uproar! It was against the law, a scandalous violation of financial discipline. We were in a real pickle! They handed the matter over to the public procurator. The director of the bank hauled me before the district Party committee for punishment. The committee chewed me out for illegal activities. My feathers were flying! Well, they were not attacking a docile fellow. I also raised such a stink that you could not tell who was the guilty party. How often, I asked, did I turn to you? And did you help me? I struggled so desperately, I did everything I possibly could to increase production. Would you lift a finger to help me? It didn't matter how much I suffered, so long as your red tape wasn't disturbed! And who do you think I did it for, anyway—do you really think I was trying to line my own pockets? In short, I got off with a tongue-lashing, on the condition that I sell no more bricks on the side.

"The affair was hushed up, but there was still no money at all. And although the workers in the barracks were under guard, they still ran away. And why wouldn't they run off, with nothing to eat?

"So we rolled along for another three months, I'm not sure how, myself. You beg at the central board for a thousand or two; you bring it to the plant. It all disappears like water. I go to the bank, grapple with the director to the death—scratch out another thousand. They were stealing the bricks themselves: Someone would arrive from Moscow at night with a couple vehicles, quietly load them up, and take off, unseen by a single eye.

"I got completely worn out by such dealings, started having bouts of insomnia. I couldn't sleep nights, thinking about the factory. As soon as I dozed off, some kind of demons would appear. I lost my appetite and walked around as if in a fog. Once I was going to Moscow in a taxi and suddenly I felt sick—nauseated, dizzy, weak all over. Well, I thought, I am sick, and I have to go to bed. As if that weren't enough, there was a terrible gnawing feeling in my stomach, so awful that I could hardly stand it. What was this knot in my stomach, and what was causing it? I recalled that I hadn't used the toilet in three days. Well, that was it—I was sick! I must go to the doctor. I told the driver, 'Pal, take me to an internist, I'm not well.'

"We went to the doctor. I explained to him that my stomach hurt. I undressed, and he examined me, poked around, listened, and asked, 'Have you eaten today?' No, I replied—not enough time. Besides, I have no appetite, I don't feel like eating. 'And you ate yesterday?' I thought about it for a minute—no, I hadn't eaten then, either. 'And the day before?' I got furious. Why are you asking me about what I ate days ago, when I have a stomachache *now*? If you can cure it, then do so. If not, I will go to another doctor. And he laughed heartily. 'You,' he said, 'are as healthy as a bull; however, for the last few days you have apparently only been drinking a little tea. This is what's causing your pain. You have an empty stomach—that's all there is to it. Go and eat a hearty meal, and you will feel better right away. Maybe you don't have enough money for dinner, and I'll have to loan you some?' he added, jokingly.

"From the doctor's office I went directly to the people's commissariat. Either get me out of this situation, I said, or in a month you will have to put me in a mental institution. They laughed too, the devils. 'Ah,' they said, 'so the brick factory is too much even for you! Not one of our directors can last there for more than half a year.' They let me go, I took a month's vacation, and then they sent me here."

We both laughed over the tale of Neposedov's ailment.

"The hell with it, that brick factory," Neposedev concluded his story. "That was in the past. Now *this* factory is a different matter. A picture! Here is the kind of operation that can really be developed. You are nodding off!" Neposedov had again come to life, and his eyes sparkled. "First-rate mechanization, modern, rapid frames. Here we'll show them what a hundred blades can do! There is one catch, but we can manage. I just arrived two weeks ago. Tomorrow I will show you the factory and you can roll up your sleeves! Here, dear friend, you will never be bored. This is not your little burg in the steppe."

"And what about raw materials?" I inquired, recalling the embarrassing debacle in which our previous efforts had ended. Neposedov disdainfully waved his hand: "Here we are rolling in raw materials. We are in a forested area, in the very heart of timbering operations. Don't worry your head about raw materials."

Forgetting that he had brought me there to rest, Neposedov got out a map of the region and set about showing me which districts were in our territory and would supply us with raw materials. We sat up until midnight, making plans for our future work.

2 ~ঽ

Squeezing Credits
from Trees

The Socialist Intrusion

Before the revolution, our forest industry did not cope badly with its tasks. The explosive growth of industry in the final decades of the nineteenth century and in the beginning of the twentieth dramatically increased the demand for building materials. The forest industry completely satisfied this demand. Whether for manufacturing, housing construction, or other general needs, Russia never experienced shortages in lumber, fuel, or other raw materials. In addition, Russia was one of the major timber exporters on the world market.

These achievements were won without any kind of extraordinary measures, without "all-hands efforts," "all-out offensives," "mobilizations," "mechanization," and of course without sacrificing millions of people—in other words, without any of the characteristic methods of the Bolshevik era, not to mention plunder, mismanagement, and squandering of the country's timber reserves. Forest valuation surveys—inventories of those reserves—were conducted in the last decades before the revolution. Proper forest use was enforced, and logging, as a rule, was carried out with care so as not to disturb the ongoing renewal of timber reserves.

There were undoubtedly inadequacies and scandalous practices in lumbering.[1] Where and when have there not been? There also was "exploitation of the workers by the capitalists." But this did not at all compare with what happened in the forests after the Bolsheviks' incursions. About twenty years after the seizure of power "by the most just people's government," I happened to be in some of the main logging regions of the country, both in the northern region and around the upper Volga and its tributaries, the Vyatka, Kerzhenets, Unzha, Sheksna, and Mologa. From the loggers' homes and the traces they contained of bygone days, even more than from the tales they told, I saw that it would take many, many years for the loggers to live as they had previously. Before the revolution, despite their supposed lack of civil rights, the loggers actually had been masters of their own affairs and therefore also masters of the land. Under the "people's government" they were transformed into menial laborers of the socialist state.

Bolshevism caused incalculable harm to our forest economy, introducing a chaos into lumbering that has not been overcome to this day. From the time of the changeover to a "planned economy," there has not been a single year when the lumber industry fulfilled its plan or satisfied the insatiable demand for timber materials.

In the early years of the revolution lumbering almost stopped entirely. The forest industry began to be restored only after the proclamation of the New Economic Policy (NEP)[2] in 1922–1923. It was renewed quickly, not so much by government efforts as through cooperative initiatives. An All-Russian Cooperative Timber Union sprang up, uniting the majority of the timber artels and small firms, and leasing a fair number of sawmills. Workers' artels of former employees were formed. They, too, leased state factories, repaired them, and put them into operation through their own efforts. For two or three years, these artels prospered: The demand for timber was high, and the artels were run by experienced people. The state lumber trusts operated alongside them. Until roughly 1928 lumbering was conducted normally, with attention to correct forest usage and the traditions of the lumber industry. But by 1928 timber production was still far from attaining its prerevolutionary level.

The year 1927 saw acceptance of the First Five-Year Plan and the rush to "build socialism." Exiling Trotsky from the country, Stalin took for his own Trotsky's idea of rapid industrialization. This led to a sharply increased need for construction materials as well as for massive amounts of capital in order to purchase foreign equipment. There was no hard currency, so Stalin also adopted Trotsky's idea of "squeezing credits from the forests." The Bolsheviks hoped to earn essential hard currency by a dramatic expansion in logging and the export of timber.

The concomitant reestablishment of state socialism brought with it the liquidation of cooperative artels. A number of small lumber firms also ceased being cooperatives at this time, having been placed under the complete control of the government. The All-Russian Cooperative Timber Union was liquidated and its reserves were turned over to the state lumber industry, which now would have to fulfill its Five-Year Plan alone, single-handedly squeezing "credits from the forests."

From the very beginning, the Bolsheviks encountered difficulties that could not be surmounted by normal methods. The liquidation of the artels, the introduction of collectivization, and the subjection of forest villagers, along with the rest of the village population, to *dekulakizatsiia* sent a tide of workers out of the forests. An acute labor shortage was the result, and no one could produce credits from the forests.

The worker shortage was covered in part by the labor of prisoners. As early as 1929, about 500,000 prisoners were at work felling trees and readying timber for export in Karelia, the northern territories, Perm, and other regions.

The "specially resettled"—peasants who had been forcibly exiled from various parts of the country during *dekulakizatsiia*—were also widely used for logging. North of a line extending roughly from Leningrad through Vologda to Vyatka and Perm, about a million "specially resettled" peasants, whose labor was even less productive than that of prisoners, were occupied in logging. Thrown into the forests with their families, the peasants had no tools and few if any other provisions. Some managed to survive in huts and dugouts, but thousands of others died under the exceedingly harsh conditions.

Thus, at the cost of compulsory labor, a workforce was procured for logging operations; but catastrophically, there were not enough horses to haul the timber once it was felled. This difficulty in many places was overcome by felling trees along the banks of flotable rivers, or as close as possible to railroads, or locations where logs could be floated, with no regard for the rules of timber cutting.

During the years of the First Five-Year Plan, the rules of forest usage were generally forgotten, and the Forest Protection Department was deprived of its rights. Trees were felled any old way, leaving tall stumps; and afterward, areas were not cleared out properly. This led to a cluttering up of the forests and a multiplication of pests. But even worse, within two or three years this excessive logging had cleared out huge expanses along the banks of the rivers, and the rivers had become clogged with silt and reduced to shallow meanders. Snow on these open expanses melted quickly, partly evaporating, partly being absorbed into the ground—moisture that later dried up over the summer. But much of it poured too rapidly into the rivers as spring runoff, causing massive groundwater loss in the forests and flooding downstream. The forests were now nearly barren of the lakes, swamps, and streams that had formerly been replenished gradually by melting snow and then in turn had fed the rivers over the course of the summer. This resulted in shallower rivers for floating timber, while along many tributaries navigation stopped altogether. Formerly tugboats on the Volga pulled barges fully loaded with oil from Astrakhan almost to Nizhnii Novgorod. In the mid-1930s, they could not even be loaded half full of oil. The Volga was covered with new sandbars, and in its lower reaches shoals appeared, making that stretch navigable only with shallow draft vessels.

This development evoked considerable alarm, and at the end of the First Five-Year Plan the Forest Protection Department managed to obtain government resolutions that established water preservation zones. Felling timber within twenty kilometers of any river now was forbidden. The rules of forest usage again began to be observed. However, the harm was already done. By this time, huge expanses near the upper Volga and the Kama and in the basins of the Northern Dvina and Onega had been stripped bare, and many other forested areas had been left a shambles. In many places loggers did not even leave a scattering of standing trees to reseed stripped areas. Forests no doubt will rustle in these expanses again, someday—maybe in a century or a century and a half.

Chaotic and haphazard logging during the First Five-Year Plan caused another misfortune. Having obliterated the forest reserves that were located near water or road transport, in subsequent years loggers had to penetrate farther and farther into the depths of the forests, which doubled or tripled the demand for timber removal and raised the cost of timber.

Such was the devastation wrought in Russia's forest industry by Stalin's interpretation of Trotsky's proposal to "squeeze credits from the forests."

The Rationalization of Lumbering

Before the revolution, lumber was produced by old-fashioned methods. The basic tools of logging were the saw and ax, and for hauling, the horse and sleigh. Had lumbering not been disrupted by the revolution, surely the necessary mechanization would have gradually penetrated the forests. Russians generally have been quick to adopt technical innovations profitable to our economy. Take for example the Volga river fleet, already one of the best river fleets in the world at the beginning of this century. A parallel, in lumbering, was the rapid changeover of sawmills to Swedish equipment, which began shortly before the revolution.

The revolution delayed the introduction of new methods into lumbering. By shifting to rapid industrialization, mainly because of shortages of workers and carting facilities—the Bolsheviks hoped to make up lost ground with a dramatic surge forward. Huge efforts and resources were expended on the effort. However, to this day, the felling of trees by hand has been only partially replaced by mechanization. Many domestic and imported portable saws of varied design, powered by gasoline, kerosene, or electricity, have been tried time and again. These saws were capricious, broke frequently, and required regular maintenance; but there were no workshops, spare parts, or mechanics in the forests. The basic means of lumbering have remained the saw, ax, horse, and sleigh.

The inadequate carting facilities led to a search for a method of rationalizing and mechanizing timber delivery. Transport was rationalized by the introduction of a new type of sleigh and the improvement of forest roads so that the load per horse could be increased. But improved roads required constant snow removal, upkeep, and repairs, which in turn necessitated a larger workforce. Even without these added tasks, there were not enough workers to go around.

A great deal of effort was spent on introducing tractor transport. But tractors and automobiles demand even better logging roads, which, given our winters, also need constant maintenance. Moreover, that kind of transport is feasible only in big timber regions, where the laying of roads can be justified economically; but since the First Five-Year Plan, as a rule, lumbering has been conducted in regions with small forest reserves. A single, integrated, logging-lumbering unit conducts logging in dozens of areas—and it does not have the wherewithal to lay roads adequate for motor vehicles in each area.

A large number of technical personnel and adequate technical supplies are also needed to maintain motor-tractor stations but neither was available. During the attempt to shift over to tractor transport, graveyards sprang up throughout the forests—the final resting places of broken, discarded machines, dilapidated shops, garages, and fuel bases for gas generators, and all sorts of tractors, automobiles, and tractor-drawn sleighs.

More than twenty years of efforts to introduce mechanization into the forests did eventually result in more or less effective power-driven saws as well as transport by tractors and motor vehicles and, in some places, by narrow-gauge railroads. A technical base and service personnel were also established to maintain these machines. However, as a rule, such technology is only applied to part of the timber industry; little more than 25–30 percent of all timber in Soviet Russia is logged with its help. The rest is being logged by the same antiquated methods used before the revolution.

Efforts to change over to year-round work in the forests were no more successful. Given our weather conditions, summer work in the forests is unsuitable because of the impossibility of transporting timber from remote, often swampy places. It can only be done by certain operators in locales where the necessary infrastructures are present. Basically, logging remains a seasonal, winter business: Today, at least 75 percent of our forests are logged only in winter.

A huge effort was made in the early 1930s to rationalize the flotation process on the Vychegda and Northern Dvina rivers. Seeking a way around the usual slow and costly rafting process, which required a large workforce, and to demonstrate that it was feasible to float logs down the large rivers without joining them in these costly rafts, it was decided that a "loose flotation" should be attempted.[3] Shipping was temporarily curtailed on the two rivers. Then the rivers were dammed just above their mouths with holding booms, and tens of millions of logs were tossed into their upper reaches. But the Bolsheviks were unable to storm the watery fortress: The booms broke, and more than two million cubic meters of timber escaped into the White Sea and the Arctic Ocean. That year, factories in Arkhangelsk were left without raw materials and the Timber Export Board failed to fulfill its plan.

Thereafter, timber industry leaders refrained from rationalization by "loose flotation" and continued to operate as they had for centuries. Improvements were introduced into the raft flotation process, and some rafts were towed by steamships—a very costly way of speeding the delivery of timber to factories and construction sites.

During the 1930s, large-scale logging began in Siberia and the Far East, but it was intended only to supply the Siberian market. At the time, transporting a train car of timber, from Omsk to Kharkov, for instance, could cost as much as two and a half thousand rubles. So in Kharkov a cubic meter of Siberian timber sold for 150–160 rubles instead of the official rate of 20–25 rubles fixed by the People's Commissariat of Forestry. Because of the shortage of construction materials, Siberian timber was often shipped west, even as far as the Caucasus, despite these high prices.

The timber processing industry also was operating at a fevered pace. The locational distribution of sawmills, which had taken shape in response to market demands and had more or less satisfied that market, was greatly altered. New construction demanded an increase in the manufacture of wood products. Obviously, existing factories would have to be refitted at the same time as new ones were built. But the opposite was done: Seventy-five percent of the old factories were abandoned and many new ones were built, helter-skelter, without taking into account either the demand for lumber or the availability of raw materials in a particular location. During the middle and late 1930s a number of new factories stood idle, while others worked at only 40–50 percent of their capacity, due to a shortage of raw materials.

And these new factories had enormous capacity. Some were absolute titans: for instance, the twenty-frame factory in Arkhangelsk, surely unique in the world, and the nine-frame factory in Kem. Huge plants also were built in Kandalaksha, in Soroka, in Onega—all to process lumber for export. Due to raw material shortages, not one of these factories ever operated to full capacity.

Furthermore, since the People's Commissariat of Forestry was unable to supply enough lumber for the construction of the new factories, almost all of them, even the smallest, were forced to build their own temporary sawmills. This led to an unbelievable dissipation of resources and greatly increased operating costs. Such is the immutable law: The forceful subordination of life's variety into a single mold will be avenged by that variety's becoming nothing but chaos and disorder.

An Unsystematic System

The free and "unplanned" and therefore ostensibly chaotic character of lumber production before the revolution in reality possessed a definite order. As the season approached, hundreds of thousands of forest workers gathered in small artels of loggers, rafters, and floaters, hired themselves out to entrepreneurs through their foremen, and got all the work done. The Bolsheviks, concerned with "putting order" into life and organizing it according to their single scheme, destroyed that order and introduced their own—and arrived at complete chaos in lumbering.

Large lumbering operations are conducted by the NKVD-MVD. This institution works according to its own laws and generally falls outside of any kind of system. The MVD produces lumber for export, for its own construction, and for the internal market. It conducts these operations with the most primitive means, by forced labor—even using prisoners quite often as horses, to haul the timber.

Overseeing the timber industry is the People's Commissariat of Forestry (now the Ministry of Lumber Production). Its subordinate trusts carry out timber production, designated mainly by territory (Kalinin, Yaroslavl, and so on). Each trust administers dozens of "integrated logging-lumbering units," which directly engage in lumbering operations. These units are full-time institutions with a permanent staff of technical and office personnel as well as a number of skilled workers. Since lumbering remains a seasonal business, the existence of permanent logging-lumbering units presents a huge problem. In summer neither the service personnel nor the workers have anything to do, but they must be paid. During the summer these units keep their employees busy mainly with subsidiary tasks unrelated to production, trying to hold onto them by all possible means because they are an operation's only hope for fulfilling its plan. When the lumbering season begins, these workers form brigades of fellers and haulers, and some become foremen and brigade leaders. They are the last logging specialists remaining of a former army of forest workers whose villages once peppered the countryside. As the lumbermen's villages have dwindled and been incorporated into collective farms, and as collective farmers are far from timber specialists, the lumbering-logging units prize their own skilled workers.

To fulfill its plan, a logging-lumbering unit needs hundreds and thousands of workers during the timber season. Regional and district soviet executive committees assign each unit a particular territory "for recruitment of a workforce." Each village soviet and each kolkhoz within that territory is given orders to supply the unit with a certain amount of workers and carting facilities, or alternatively to fell and deliver to the unit a designated quantity of lumber.

Wages for lumbering are extremely low. Through various measures a logging-lumbering unit tries to keep the pay of its year-round workforce at the general level in the country, but it pays seasonal kolkhoz workers according to a fixed scale for forest work. During the 1930s in the central zone the wage for seasonal fellers was 5–6 rubles a day, for haulers 4–5. At that time workers in other branches of industry received from 6–7 to 10–12 rubles a day. Furthermore, the *kolkhoznik* received only half of his nominal wage; the operator paid the other half to the kolkhoz.

Such miserable pay was no enticement, so the *kolkhozniki* went to great lengths to avoid work in the forest. A logging unit had to keep up continuous recruitment, making the rounds of the kolkhozes and demanding workers for dispatch to the forest. This did not help much, so they assigned legal responsibility to the chairmen of the kolkhozes and to the *kolkhozniki* themselves for failure to show up for work in the forests. That didn't help much either: After collectivization, the villages were depopulated and the kolkhozes did not have enough people for their own work. As a result of the worker shortage, they resorted to using women both for hauling and for felling timber, a practice that had never existed before in Russia.

The use of what was essentially the compulsory labor of the *kolkhozniki* explains both the low output and the unsatisfactory products of the lumber industry. Forced laborers will work any old way, just trying to get through the day; therefore, you cannot expect satisfactory work from them.

The acute shortage of workers and carting facilities in the forests was one of the main reasons for the People's Commissariat of Forestry's regular nonfulfillment of its plan and the poor supply of forest products to the country. This forced the government to allow many people's commissariats, builders, and enterprises to conduct lumbering with their own means, outside of the People's Commissariat of Forestry. After this the People's Commissariat of Forestry was referred to as the "primary provider" and other organizations as "self-providers."

Virtually all branches of industry that are engaged in production and do their own construction have to conduct lumbering operations. Even military bases and factories frequently resort to their own lumbering because the People's Commissariat of Forestry cannot fully supply even them with lumber. The food and other light industries also engage in lumbering. It frequently turns out that the "shoemaker bakes the pies,"[4] which magnifies the chaos in the forests.

Usually the worst timber reserves, situated far from flotable rivers or roads, are earmarked for the self-providers. Details of workers are also assigned to them, but only after the demands of the People's Commissariat of Forestry are satisfied; the latter, as the primary provider, takes priority over the self-providers. Thus, the self-providers often have to bring in workers from as far away as two or three hundred kilometers from the logging areas, since all the neighboring kolkhozes have already been hit up for workers by the People's Commissariat of Forestry.

Self-providers are supposed to operate according to the rules, norms, and rates of the primary provider, but they pay little attention to these rules. They have but one goal in mind: to obtain lumber by any means. Frequently having more means available than the People's Commissariat of Forestry and, given the pressing demand for lumber, disinclined to spare those means, the self-providers pay their workforce at a much higher rate than does the people's commissariat. The self-providers entice workers away from the people's commissariat by paying them wages that are two, three, or even five times higher. The People's Commissariat of Forestry calls the self-provider to account legally for violating the required pay rates, but while the case is being investigated and prosecuted, winter passes and the commissariat's plans remain unfulfilled.

In the early 1930s, in order to attract workers into the forests and improve their standard of living a little, the people's commissariat succeeded in distributing foodstuffs and manufactured goods to the workers. The food went to the workers' cafeterias, while manufactured items including footwear were distributed as part of their wages. From 20 to 25 percent of the average worker's pay was in the form of such goods. This kind of remuneration did encourage the fulfillment of plan norms; but the People's Commissariat of Forestry distributed manufactured goods only to its year-round workers, leaving the kolkhozes, agricultural cooperatives, and state stores to look out for the seasonal laborers from the collective farms.

Self-providers such as the People's Commissariats of Food Production and Light Industry compensate their workers—including their seasonal workers from the kolkhozes—with a greater number and variety of goods. Thanks to this, both seasonal and year-round workers try to transfer from the People's Commissariat of Forestry to the self-providers, since there is a constant and acute hunger for manufactured goods in the villages.

Consequently an endless struggle goes on in the forests between the integrated logging-lumbering units of the People's Commissariat of Forestry and the army of self-providers. This struggle occupies much of their and others' time and energy and is not easy for the integrated units. Like any established and continuously operating enterprise, the logging-lumbering unit is more inert, slow, and sluggish—the self-provider is nimble, assertive, and energetic. If he is fined and his workers are put in prison, new ones come to take their place and continue the work of their predecessors. For the self-provider one task prevails—to obtain lumber for himself by any means. The integrated logging-lumbering unit of the Commissariat of Forestry is not producing the timber for its own needs but merely to fulfill the plan. In the Soviet milieu, the basic task of the self-provider turned him into a *partizan* (a risk-taker who operated illegally, outside the centrally planned economy), a bird of prey: His job was to swoop down into the forest, snatch a shred for himself, and hastily devour it. This brought the self-provider into frequent skirmishes with the Forest Protection Department.

The forests are managed by the General Directorate of Forest Protection and Replanting, which also maintains tree farms and forest reserves, with a staff of foresters, wardens, and other employees. Its relations with the lumber operators of the Commissariat of Forestry are normal and usually flow on without major conflicts, but it sees the self-providers as its mortal enemies. The self-provider frequently operates arbitrarily, tries to evade cleaning up an area after felling, cuts down trees where logging is forbidden, and generally ruins the timberlands. The Forest Protection Department mercilessly prosecutes self-providers who commit these acts and battles them unceasingly.

The *partizanshchina* of the self-providers—that is, their economic activities unaccounted for by the plan—can be expensive. If the price of a cubic meter of logs, fixed by the People's Commissariat of Forestry, is 15–16 rubles in Moscow, it can be raised to as much as 60–80 or even 100–120 by the independent operator. And there is no way out: Industry and construction need lumber products, and the Commissariat of Forestry is unable to supply them. The only way to get the job done is to pay as much as 100 rubles a cubic meter. In the final analysis, these costs hit the pockets and stomachs of the basic consumers, the workers and peasants of the country.

That was how the lumber industry functioned in the era of "building socialism." Having first liquidated private enterprise in the forests and then the cooperatives, which were working productively, and finding themselves incapable of supplying the country with lumber by "socialist methods," the Bolsheviks introduced private enterprise of a distorted, surrogate form into lumbering, leading to enormous expenditures and inflicting great harm on the forests.

Timber Graveyards

It frequently turns out that the self-provider, in pursuit of good timber and neglecting to take his resources into account, manages the easiest work, the felling, but is in no position to transport the timber. The felled logs remain in the forest and rot. Many such timber graveyards are scattered throughout northern Russia and Siberia.

I happened to visit one of them at the end of 1941, when it became apparent that we urgently needed to build new factories to replace those occupied by the Germans. I was sent on special assignment to Siberia to organize the transportation of about twenty thousand cubic meters of logs to a railroad line.

This timber had been sold by some self-provider to our People's Commissariat of Forestry as far back as 1938. Arriving at the locale, I sought out the timber. Excellent material for any construction project, it was partially gathered in piles, although the greater share lay scattered about, exactly where it had been felled three or four years earlier. These scattered logs were no longer suitable for construction. Damaged by rot and eaten away by pests, they could be used only for firewood. The timber lay about twenty-five kilometers from the railway, at the end of an impassable, overgrown road. One could not imagine how the self-provider had planned to remove it from such a desolate, almost uninhabited place. The employee of our commissariat who bought this hopeless timber for some reason was also a dunce.

After checking in the neighboring villages, I became convinced that it was impossible to transport the timber using local labor. The population was sparse, and besides, the men had been drafted into the army. The horses also had been requisitioned. I sent out feelers about recruiting a workforce to the regional soviet executive committee. The committee threatened instant arrest if I took even one worker from their region, in spite of the fact that the lumber was needed to construct factories that would supply the army. Our commissariat also lacked the means of conveyance. I had to leave, as nothing could be done. The logs most likely perished there in the forest.

Pondering such graveyards, I could only conclude that the very same people who had formerly coped perfectly well with the tasks of lumbering could not work productively under Soviet conditions. Even with the best of intentions, people's efforts ultimately led to absurdity, getting them nowhere.

One time I stopped at the Yaroslavl Lumber Trust on a business matter in connection with rafting. They directed me to the inspector of rafting, who to my surprise turned out to be an attractive young woman. I could not believe that I had come to the right address. With her delicate oval face, magnificent hair, and striking figure, the rafting inspector radiated so much femininity that it was quite impossible to envision her being connected with rafting. To think of rafting—which required brute, masculine strength, a command of "technical terminology" (vulgar language)—and then all at once to be confronted by this embodiment of femininity!

The inspector of rafting proved to be a very nice person, the tender, loving mother of a delightful daughter. Introducing myself, I asked her to disclose the secret of how she had become a "raftsman."

"Some raftsman!" the woman replied with a bitter, ironic smile and told me her story. She was the daughter of a forester, and the forest was her natural element. She grew up there, and it was her cherished home. So as not to be parted from the forest, she enrolled in an "Institute of Afforestation and Forest Improvement," upon graduation from which all students were to work in the forest industry. She studied for two years; suddenly an order came from Moscow to change the institute into an "Institute of Timber Rafting." It was suggested that the students continue their studies in order to become "engineers of timber rafting."

"That's how I became an inspector of rafting. What rafting? I sit in an office, composing briefs and drafting reports. And that's about as useful to me as last year's snow."

Looking at her, I involuntarily thought how useful her deft hands would have been in our forests! What great benefit her love for the forests would have brought, had she been given work that she could put her heart into, work that she so desperately wanted to do. Instead, they'd played a bad joke on her. Could anyone imagine a greater mockery?

Such was the general situation in the forest industry, into which, under the direction of Neposedov, I was fated to plunge headlong.

3

Wrenches
in the Works

The plant, which Neposedov showed me the day after my arrival, was truly fine. A small, single-frame factory that once had belonged to a merchant stood near the site. It was abandoned during the years of the First Five-Year Plan and a large, triple-frame factory was built alongside it. Of the old factory, only crumbling walls and rusty equipment remained. Still salvageable, the equipment could have been functional with minor repairs, but by then no one was interested in it.

The new plant was constructed according to the latest technology, with a good log conveyor of Swedish design and a pool for washing the logs. From the pool, the logs were moved by conveyor belt to the shop. The excellent, high-speed frames from the Moscow factory "Ilyich" (patterned after a Swedish model, with slight modifications), together with the automated removal of finished products and the mechanized sorting, waste collection, and delivery of sawdust into the stoker, all lightened the workers' load and ensured high productivity. A separate building held a planing shop with imported machinery. In addition, there was a box shop that turned out small boards from scrap lumber, for making crates. The factory had everything it needed in order to function optimally.

A 200-horsepower steam engine put the sawmill's frames into motion and turned an electrical generator that powered the other machinery and mechanized equipment. There was also a separate engine for the generator. The factory was fully outfitted with all the machinery and equipment needed to process roughly 120,000–130,000 cubic meters of logs annually and to turn out high-quality products; but the yearly plan for the factory was fixed at only 75,000 cubic meters, and of this amount only about 70–80 percent, at most, was achieved.

The reason for the factory's reduced plan was a shortage of raw materials. The People's Commissariat of Forestry could not supply it with more resources. The nonfulfillment of even this lowered plan was in turn due to certain other "shackles," to which Neposedov had alluded when we talked the day before.

The matter could be explained simply. The builders had rashly overspent their budget on the shop and were forced to economize on the boiler. So instead of first-class steam power to back up the state-of-the-art equipment, the builders settled for an old-fashioned steam boiler of the sort used on ships, made of numerous pipes enclosed in a casing. That type of boiler worked right only under certain conditions. Before six months had gone by, its pipes overheated, an accident occurred, and work ground to a halt. The ancient steam boiler from the old, abandoned factory was quickly dragged over and put into place, and somehow they managed to hobble along.

The boiler produced roughly half the steam needed, so neither the engines nor the frames could operate at full capacity. From the day the plant went into production, it never fulfilled even its understated plan. At first it was the "start-up period," then it was the lack of steam. The first-class equipment on which several million rubles had been expended was good for naught.

It was evident from the documentation that the plant director had petitioned tirelessly for a new boiler, but boilers were in such short supply that it was almost impossible to get one. The factory could not even obtain new pipes for the old steam boiler; they, too, were worth their weight in gold. Though the pipes would have cost about two thousand rubles at most, the factory spent over five thousand rubles on business trips and solicitations for them—and still received no pipes.

In such circumstances even the energy of a Neposedov was of little help. Neposedov was unable to compensate for the steam shortage. He sat in the factory around the clock, consulted with the mechanic and the technical director, but this did not raise production.

I so wanted to help Neposedov: Working in a plant that is not fulfilling its plan is no good at all. You can never be rid of the feeling that something is not going as it ought and that you are somehow to blame. Daily reports from the shops with figures of 70 to 80 percent of plan targets act as a depressant; you wish that 100 percent would somehow appear in their place. You see embarrassed or guilty expressions on the faces of the mechanic, technical director, skilled workers, the president of the factory Party committee, the head bookkeeper, the Party organizer. Everyone in the plant is glowering, unhappy, irritable. The atmosphere of despondency and hopelessness results in a general melancholy.

There is another reason for the melancholy mood: A factory that does not fulfill its plan is always at a disadvantage because it will have a chronic shortage of funds. It is all right if the bank dispenses enough money for wages, but then the head bookkeeper still has endless worries about whether money can be obtained for operating expenses. Since shift norms are not met, hourly workers receive minimal wages and salaried employees can forget about bonuses and occasional extra pay. The management is generous only when the work is going well and bringing in profits.

Depression reigned in the factory, and there was no help for it: Without a new boiler or those ill-starred pipes, we could neither increase production nor improve the lot of our employees in the least.

Not Far from Moscow

While still en route to the new plant, I had decided that my rebirth was completed. By this time my camp impressions had receded to some part of my subconscious. I had already had a taste of my new life and was familiar enough with it. In the new locale, under Neposedov's guidance, I could feel more or less secure. Here no one but Neposedov knew about my past; here there was no employee information form to fill out, because I had been brought in by the director and was one of the "production captains" in the plant. No one showed much curiosity about my background. It was enough for them that the director himself knew me. Consequently, with nothing holding me back, I had only to familiarize myself with my new post and get down to business.

My new locale differed sharply from the steppe town where I had worked with Neposedov earlier. That was a remote corner with an established way of life that moved along slowly, impervious for the most part to any innovation. Here, one sensed the proximity to the center, to Moscow: life was more anxious, more hectic, more exposed.

In the steppe town, we could at times forget about the Party, and the Party only occasionally remembered itself. Here, meetings were often held, where propagandists from the regional or district Party committees would speak. The young people were forced to attend reading circles that studied the history of the Party and Marxism-Leninism, whereas in the steppe town they could ignore such things and go dancing. In the steppe, we could let calls for socialist competition and intensely heightened efforts go in one ear and out the other. Here, even if we put no more stock in them, we had to appear to take them seriously. Placards clamoring about *udarnichestvo*[1] and Stakhanovism[2] hung in the offices and the shops. This clamor somehow seemed to remove the warmth from life, the caressing simplicity that imperceptibly had enveloped our uncomplicated steppe existence.

One also noticed a difference in the times as 1938 approached. Trouble hung in the air, borne in from the west. It was reflected in increased military construction, with more and more military factories going up, right in our neighborhood. Delegations from these construction projects kept converging on us, while our superiors in Moscow kept pressing us to hurry up our timber shipments. All this heightened the anxious atmosphere that was so unlike the quiet life of the steppe town.

The events of the *Yezhovshchina* and the Moscow trials found almost no echo in our plant. We attended meetings where propagandists from the district Party committee spoke about the "search for enemies of the people." According to the prescribed order, we dutifully voted for the death sentence, but we almost never discussed such things among ourselves. The violence was occurring far away somewhere, at some inaccessible height, and people sensed that it was better not to talk about such things. It was a spontaneous conspiracy of silence. We would hear of the arrest of the secretary of the regional Party committee, and then of the president of the regional soviet executive committee—but we did not know them and had not elected them. No one in our factory was arrested, and we tried not to pay too much attention to what was going on in higher circles. It was better to tend to our own affairs—and that's just what we did.

I likewise remained untouched during the *Yezhovshchina*. Whether because I had changed my residence three times after my release from the camp and had therefore disappeared from the NKVD's field of vision or for some other reason, the NKVD left me alone. Considering what was happening, I was naturally uneasy, but I continued to believe that fate would have the last word.

About four hundred workers and over a hundred white-collar employees, guards, firemen, and other "nonproductive elements" worked in our plant. Some lived in the nearby countryside, some in town, and some at the factory. The factory had dozens of small homes and a long, two-story building with eighty rooms that was nicknamed "the ship." It was constructed at a time when such standardized buildings were all the rage, during the First Five-Year Plan. Assembled from planks, the ship had already rotted and was listing to one side as if it were ready to sink. A town commission termed it unsafe for habitation, but since there was no substitute housing, the residents had no choice but to continue to find shelter in the ship, risking life and limb.

Until there was a room available in the residence for engineering–technical personnel, I settled in a village near the factory, in the home of one of our workers. Observing the way he and his family and their neighbors lived, I was struck by their poverty.

In that regard, it was worse here than in the steppe town. In the favored south, living is always cheaper and more abundant, with many fresh fruits and vegetables. Here, there were significantly fewer vegetables and no fruit at all, and wages were too low to support a family.

Our skilled workers received about 200 rubles a month, unskilled workers about 150–180, while cleaning women, watchmen, and firemen earned only about 110. With the cost of bread at 1 ruble a kilogram, meat at 10–12, butter at 16–18, and cereals at 3–4, a family of four or five persons that also had to pay for living quarters, clothing, and shoes could not live on one salary.

White-collar workers did not get much more, except for those in managerial positions: The director earned 900 rubles, the technical director 700, the mechanic, head bookkeeper, and I, as director of the planning department, about 600. The departmental bookkeepers and the Party organizer (in our factory they were included in the personnel department) received about 300–400 rubles a month, while other white-collar employees were paid from 150 to 200. Shift foremen got about 250. Thus, out of five hundred people, only five received wages that were more or less adequate to live on, and the rest had a hard time of it.

These people managed to cope with their low wages in various ways. Most of them resorted to subsidiary economic activities, such as family gardening. In the spring all employees were allotted a plot of land for cultivating a garden. It yielded vegetables—and even more important, a supply of potatoes for the winter. Some kept cows, selling part of the milk at market and using the rest to feed their families. Almost everyone kept chickens, a pig or two, or a goat, which also helped to supplement their diets and their incomes. In large families, all adults had to work, including older children and aged parents; frequently, both husband and wife were employed. In such cases, they took their children to a day-care center. After work some people engaged in crafts at home: They made shoes, did carpentry, even wove baskets to sell. Firewood was never purchased; instead, scraps were taken quietly from the factory. Everyone knew this and looked the other way. A few families did quite nicely, thanks to their enterprising women. These pushy wives went to Moscow, bought clothes and shoes there, and sold them in our town at speculators' prices. The countryside was again suffering from a shortage of goods, and speculation brought these clever people big profits.

Thus, reconciling themselves to the fact that mother, wife, and children must work, and by combining labor in the factory with work at home and in the subsidiary economy, our workers somehow managed to make ends meet. But they still lived poorly. Their homes were unattractive inside, and halfway decent clothes could only be seen on young people of an evening or a Sunday. More often than not, the adults went about in the same clothes they wore to work.

Reason told one it was impossible to help these people without reconstructing the entire Soviet economic system, which functioned not to satisfy the needs of the population but to develop and strengthen communism. This economy seemed unable to cope with people's basic needs. However, the heart refused to listen to reason's assertion that in such a situation any measures could only be palliatives. It wanted to help somehow, even if only temporarily. There was just one way to do this: We would have to increase the productivity of the factory and thereby the wages of the employees.

The Captains Confer

Neposedov's ardor could not increase the steam from the ancient boiler, but his nose for detail led to the unearthing of quite a number of mistakes that also were lowering productivity. People in the factory had become accustomed to an attitude of hopelessness and blamed everything on the ill-fated boiler, which served as a scapegoat for all mistakes. But Neposedov refused to accept this. Within a month he had composed a detailed chart of factory operations and outlined a strategy for "liquidating hitches." Neposedov called a meeting of the "captains of production" to discuss this strategy. The technical director, head mechanic, shift foremen, chief accountant, Party organizer, president of the factory's trade union committee, and I met in his office.

Senior engineer Kolyshev, our direct supervisor for production technology, came to this meeting from Moscow. He arrived just as the meeting was beginning and barely had time to exchange greetings with us before Neposedov laid out his plan. Neposedov gave major attention to little inadequacies, which he discussed in great detail, suggesting ways to eliminate them. He outlined measures for more efficient coordination between the various teams involved in production and proposed decreasing the number of workers in several departments in order to lower costs a little. He concluded with general remarks about the need for shock tactics and competition, thus taking cognizance of the tone of the times.

Silence reigned in the office after he finished speaking. You could feel the awkwardness. We smoked, avoided looking at the director and each other, not because the report was poor or absurd—Neposedov had laid out his plan thoroughly, with a good grasp of the operation. But the part devoted to technical defects was clear and familiar to everyone and could not evoke any discussion; and on the whole, the director's plan offered no hope of radically improving the situation. People sensed this but could not bring themselves to say so, and therefore we kept silent.

The silence dragged on. This wounded Neposedov: "Well, comrades, are we going to have a discussion or sit in silence?" he asked aggrievedly. "We are at a production meeting, not at a cell meeting of the International Organization for the Promotion of the Revolution." Turning to the shift foremen: "You, shift foremen, why are you so quiet? You see everything firsthand."

Foreman Komlev, a broad-shouldered, red-headed fellow with a full, fiery beard, who had worked in the factory a very long time, droned: "Ah, what can I say, comrade director? The malfunctions are known and must be overcome, and so—we are in agreement with everything."

"In agreement," growled Neposedov. "That's what you always say. You agree to everything, but when it comes to implementation, you hide in the bushes or walk around in a dream world instead of using your heads. 'We're agreed!' Your agreement is good for nothing. You have to mean it, to ask yourself, Will the work go forward or not?"

"And why wouldn't it?" asked Komlev, so dumbfounded at the sharp tone of the director that his eyes bugged out in a comical manner.

Neposedov started to laugh. "Okay, bearded one, I'll talk with you later. . . . Comrade Utkin, your opinion?"

Elderly, with a bony face and an ungainly build, technical director Utkin, a modest fellow and diligent worker but not a very deep or original thinker, coughed a little in embarrassment and remarked that he welcomed Neposedov's suggestions of a technical nature, but that one should consider carefully the matter of reducing the workforce. Would doing so be beneficial?

The mention of workforce reduction aroused the chairman of the factory's trade union committee, Dolgov. A worker and Party member, he had long ago metamorphosed into a *zavkomshchik* [professional trade unionist]. Dolgov had been reelected to his post many times. A representative of the workers' interests, Dolgov restricted his activity to club work and mutual benefits funds, to collecting union membership dues and making annotations on sick leave certificates. But he sometimes permitted himself to come out "in defense of the workers." He announced that he saw no need for cutting the workforce, that this would be contradictory to the collective agreement, which, Dolgov added clumsily, "in any case has to be upheld."

The meeting limped on. The Party organizer, likewise a former factory worker, said indecisively that a Stakhanovite unit should be organized, but he was not clear on how this was to be done. And again there was silence.

"Yes," proffered Neposedov, "we have as much enthusiasm as we have steam in our boiler. Perhaps Comrade Kolyshev will share his ideas?"

"You're right, you have no enthusiasm—because you haven't enough steam in your boiler." Kolyshev smiled. "Let me tell you what I think." And he thoroughly analyzed the director's plan as if he had composed it himself and knew the situation in the factory as well as we. In general Kolyshev approved of Neposedov's plan, but he said what no one else could bring himself to say: that this plan alone could not save us.

Kolyshev's arguments were reasonable, substantive, and persuasive. One sensed that he knew the situation well. And with his wide, calm face and compact figure, Kolyshev himself had real impact, gave an impression of solidity and thoughtfulness. Listening to him I thought: "Neposedov is impetuousness itself, and God knows where he might lead us. But this fellow can be relied on."

Kolyshev disapproved only of the proposal to cut the workforce. "You won't gain much, and it could worsen your position in the future. If you attain high productivity, then you will not have enough workers. And you will hardly be permitted to restore the former number. So, generally speaking, any gains made by such means would ultimately be lost. No, I do not advocate anything that would harm the working class," Kolyshev jested in his low-key way. "I propose something else. Work out some type of graduated bonus pay system; that will surely help."

I liked Kolyshev very much. And his joke about the "working class," in which one sensed both irony about the typical terminology and sympathy for the "working class," gave me great satisfaction. Everyone was listening attentively.

"I saved the main item for last," continued Kolyshev. "I will tell you now, but with the proviso that you first put all your plans into practice and only then resort to this main item: I've brought you an order for pipes. You can send people to pick them up."

"What? Can it be? Pipes?" Exclamations poured out. The somnolence vanished as if by magic. Everyone jumped from their places and stared excitedly at Kolyshev. Springing up from behind the table, Neposedov rushed over to him. It was amazing what a magical effect one word had produced: pipes!

Smiling, Kolyshev removed the requisition from his briefcase. Neposedov snatched it, ran his eyes over it quickly and flourished it in the air: "Pipes, my friends, pipes!" Everyone crowded around the director, trying to get a peek at the order.

"It's high time," hissed Komlev, standing next to me. "The rest is just hot air, but this will be of real use."

The meeting could be adjourned. The pipes had solved everything.

Launching the Offensive

Kolyshev's suggestion about graduated bonus payments pleased me to the core, so I got right down to business. I went to the People's Commissariat of Forestry and picked up the standard regulations for such payments in the timber industry. I didn't think much of them because they were designed to compel a laborer to work harder for not much more pay. If a worker over-fulfilled his norm to 105 percent, his pay was increased by only 6 or 7 percent. This obviously did not adequately compensate the worker for the extra effort that enabled him to exceed the target. In addition, the regulations provided for the introduction of progressive bonus payments only to workers of leading sectors, while other workers would receive the usual piece rates. This was clearly unfair: In a case of overfulfillment of production targets by a leading sector, the rest of the enterprise's workforce also had to work harder and participate equally in the overfulfillment of the norms by that sector.

I decided to work out another, more just wage system, taking advantage of the fact that the regulations were not legally binding on us because we were not subordinate to the People's Commissariat of Forestry. I knew Neposedov would approve, and I was reassured by Kolyshev's visible sympathy for the "working class." All of the employees in the shops, including metal workers (*slesari*), machine operators, and even those who swept up shavings, would be included in my plan. And my plan would offer real wage increases, so that a worker might double his pay for overfulfilling the norms by 25 percent—or even triple it with a higher percentage. Now that's what I would call a progressive bonus! It might seem overly generous, but careful calculations showed that in the case of overfulfillment of the plan, even with this payment system the plant would earn high profits due to reductions in production costs and overhead.

Neposedov endorsed my plan without probing into the details; he knew we were governed by the same instincts. So I took the plan to Moscow. Kolyshev looked at it, carefully checked the figures, and smiled: "They're pretty high, but so what; we mustn't wrong the working class. Your situation is lousy and it won't be tragic if you pay a little more and perhaps improve it. I will try to get your plan approved by the people's commissariat as is."

I liked Kolyshev even more. Anyone else in his place, fearing "what might come of this," would carp about why it was not being done according to the usual regulations. I would have had to wrangle with him over every percentage point of pay increase, then arrive at some compromise and find that almost nothing was left of the original project. Not only did Kolyshev not wrangle, he was not afraid to accept responsibility himself for our plan after he had carefully checked it out. And it was better, in this case, to have a careful review. I felt more confident myself, knowing that no mistakes had crept in. Yes, one could do business with a fellow like Kolyshev.

Meanwhile, Neposedov was tormenting a brigade of metal workers, machinists, and a mechanic, sometimes even keeping them at the plant for two shifts in a row. He couldn't bear to lose a minute in his battle to eliminate minor deficiencies. The pipes arrived, and some of the smudged faces undertook the repair of the boiler. One sensed excitement in the factory, as if we were gearing up for an offensive.

After about two weeks our proposal for progressive bonuses was approved by Moscow. We decided to acquaint the workers with the new payment system. During a break between shifts, about four hundred people assembled in the shabby factory club. Neposedov, presiding, announced that from the first of the month—which was just four days away—the factory would change to a new wage system. I explained the system in detail, then Neposedov asked whether there were any questions.

The hall was silent. But it was not the profound, heavy silence that usually accompanied political lectures at factory assemblies. People were whispering, coughing, and talking to each other. One sensed that this information was not going in one ear and out the other, but being slowly digested. Interest was written on many faces and bewilderment on others. It was as though people were trying to decide what kind of wind was blowing. Was this talk in earnest, or was it only the usual hot air? Was there some ulterior motive? How should they respond? Currents of curiosity and disbelief rippled through the hall.

"Well, what's the matter?" Neposedov pressed. "Don't you get it? Come on, brothers, use your heads. Why do you think we called this meeting? I am telling you myself that you are being given a chance to better your situation. I'm not just dishing out propaganda. What use has propaganda to me?" Neposedov added, dismissing it. "Just look at the situation. In the first place it is a shame and a disgrace for us that we cannot fulfill the plan. How does that look? It's laughable. We are as capable as anybody else, but we work like complete misfits. Not a single enterprise in the district functions as badly as we do. What good is that to anyone? How long will you go on working for the same daily rate, making a hundred and fifty rubles a month? What's with you, don't you need money? Clearly we're in a worse mess than I thought. What about you, pug nose, laughing when the director is speaking?" He turned unexpectedly to a young female employee who was laughing at something in the first row. "You, smudged faces, why don't you tend to those girls? Chatterboxes, I'll fix you," jested Neposedov. People began to laugh in the hall, and the girl also burst out laughing, covering her face with her kerchief. Her neighbor shouted daringly: "What about us in shipping, will there be a bonus for us?"

The laughter and the female worker's question broke the ice, and the questions poured forth. Workers who delivered raw materials to the shops, sawyers, metal workers, sorters—everyone wanted to know if they were included and what the new pay scale would be. I explained, but I had to repeat myself again and again so that everyone could understand. The hall buzzed; you had to shout to be heard. The time came to start the next shift, but passions had begun to flare and arguments had broken out in various corners of the hall.

"Enough!" shouted Neposedov, quieting the noise. "You have the general idea. More talk won't help, and the details will get clearer as we go along. This meeting is closed. Second shift, you've just about got time for a shave, and then it's off to work."

Some of the workers who were crowded around the doors started to leave; but workers from the first shift stayed to discuss the news, gathering in groups in the club and outside. Going from group to group, I answered more questions and listened in on their conversations.

"The main thing is that there be no slowdown in supply!" fretted a frame operator in one group. "Give me a steady supply and there won't be any lagging on my part."

"And will you take the place of the engine that turns the frame?" objected another worker. "If the engine doesn't work, that'll be the end of the story. It's a lot of bunk."

"To you everything is bunk!" a feisty female employee attacked him. "We know, you've got it made. Your wife ran off to Moscow, you've got a little money in your pocket, and life is a bed of roses. But I'm counting every kopeck."

"Everyone knows that you don't find money just lying around on the ground—enough said," a third worker added, in her support.

Foreman Komlev stood a little way off, in another group, staring sternly at the workers crowding around him and counting on the fingers of his left hand. "Supplies—that's the first thing! And keeping a sawyer in his place. As it is, you can't even track one down with bloodhounds. That's number two. And enough of frame operators sitting in the smoking lounge; they have been sitting there long enough. That's number three!"

"Don't forget the metal workers, those devils—you can call for one until you are blue in the face," someone interjected. Komlev lost his train of thought and involuntarily glanced at the person who had interrupted him.

"The main thing is, everything's got to go like clockwork. The engine will do its part, once the boiler is fixed!"

Gripping me by the arm, Neposedov led me to the plant office. He, too, was happy and excited. "We really lit a fire under those workers. Did you see how it got to them? This is what we call the ruble test!"

The Secret of Our Success

On the first of the month, when the day shift had ended, foreman Komlev brought us the shift reports himself. He did not hand them to my coworker Valya as usual, but instead laid them on the desk in front of me, saying, "Well, add it up."

While I was figuring, he sat opposite me and followed my pencil with concentration. I calculated the percentage of target fulfillment—96 percent. I had not expected this: The day before, Komlev had projected only 85 percent. I held out my hand to the foreman: "Congratulations, dear comrade Komlev! This is not like yesterday."

Komlev did not take my hand. Looking at the figures, he smiled into his beard. "Hold your congratulations—we have a ways yet to go. Maybe tomorrow we'll have something to celebrate."

The next morning, the night foreman, Kudryavtsev, came in—lean, gypsylike in appearance, with coal-black eyes under black shaggy brows. Likewise an experienced worker and a skilled foreman, Kudryavtsev was a silent and serious fellow. His reports showed 95 percent. In disbelief, Kudryavtsev carefully looked at the figures, growled something, and left.

At the end of the day Komlev again appeared, this time with an accounting clerk and two frame operators. Gathering around my desk, they tensely followed the calculations. The figures showed 102 percent.

"Heh-heh-heh!" Komlev chuckled contentedly. "See that, you big louse? Looks like we're still good for something. Now you can congratulate us!"

The frame operators and the accountant were smiling, their faces glowing with utter contentment. I too was happy.

"Now figure out how much the boys earned on the shift," begged Komlev.

I began to calculate the bonuses, and although it was a lengthy procedure, my visitors waited patiently. It turned out that the frame operator, who formerly did not even receive 8 rubles a day, had earned 11. The shipping clerk earned 8 instead of 5 or 6. This added fuel to the fire, and the contented faces became gleeful.

"Oh, sweet mama!" rejoiced Komlev. "And if we make 105 percent? Three-ruble increases—do you know what this means?" He nudged one of the frame operators in the side. "A quarter-liter of vodka at one go!"[3]

I went to tell Neposedov that we had finally broken 100 percent, and we had barely begun to implement the measures he'd proposed. Neposedov rejoiced: "I always said the boiler wasn't the only problem! Who was right? We've got two more weeks to go till the boiler is ready, and 100 percent is already in the bag. They won't let up, now, and when the boiler is put into operation—*mama rodnaia!*—there will be no holding us back!"

"Maybe it's due more to the progressive pay scale?" I egged him on. Neposedov began to smile.

"A little of this and a little of that; whatever it is, we're holding the trump card!"

Let's hope their trump card doesn't trump ours, I thought, but squelched this pointless worry.

Kudryavtsev's shift made 101 percent. Having already learned about Komlev's shift's 102 percent, Kudryavtsev growled: "They work in the daytime, and the day shift always produces more. Next week, we will reach that level too!"

The next days yielded insignificant increases of 0.5 to 0.75 percent. Production was greater than 104 percent on the day shift, but less than 103 percent at night. This meant that the workforce was really trying, squeezing all it could out of the equipment in its present condition. They'd reached the limit; but we would have to raise production to at least 110 percent in order to make up for the losses during previous months of the year and assuage the plant's financial difficulties.

About ten more days elapsed before the repaired boiler went into action. It was tested on a Sunday. On Monday, Kudryavtsev was the first to arrive with news. He came with an accounting clerk and stood outside in the corridor by the office, while nearly his entire shift—dozens of workers—waited in the yard to find out how they'd done. Neposedov, Utkin, the Party organizer, Dolgov, and the head bookkeeper could not wait, and they besieged my desk from all sides.

Finishing the calculations, I could not believe them myself: 118 percent. Checking a second time, I got the same results. The uproarious crowd that had gathered tore out of the room to spread the happy news, with Neposedov running proudly ahead, beaming like a general who had just won a battle.

Komlev's shift yielded 115 percent. In the days that followed, I never knew whom to congratulate: The numbers increased like rabbits—120, 122, 125, 130 percent. I began to worry. After a week, the numbers rose beyond 140 percent, passed 150 percent, and approached 160 percent. The daily earnings of the frame operators galloped to 20 rubles, passed 25, and were approaching 30. I clutched the back of my head—look out! Soon the frame operators would receive more than the director! What would be left, then, of our plant's profit from overfulfilling the plan? What if I had made a mistake somewhere in my calculations?

Such a mistake could have deplorable consequences—I might wind up in the "enemy" category. I carefully verified my figures for the new wages. They were accurate. Even when paying the employees triple wages based on overfulfillment of the plan, the factory nonetheless made a large profit. I was relieved: My figures and the new pay scale that had been approved by the People's Commissariat of Forestry were accurate.

In the first month under the new payment scheme, the workers' earnings more than doubled. Now the chief bookkeeper, too, was clutching his head: There was no money coming in yet, and he could barely scrape together enough to pay the wages. After tax deductions and credit repayments, the frame operators cleared almost 500 rubles. Workers of other ranks were making between 350 and 400 rubles, and even the cleaning staff, who formerly earned about 110 rubles, now got about 220 to 230 rubles. For the first time in many years—and for the younger workers, the first time in their lives—the employees were happy when they left the cashier's office, feeling that they had been adequately paid for their work. Earlier the bookkeepers had been besieged on paydays by glowering and irritated workers demanding verification that the office had not erred in their calculations and underpaid them, but on this payday there were no malcontents. The payment process went surprisingly smoothly, without the usual arguments and verbal abuse.

One could only rejoice, seeing people's satisfaction. We were happy, too, with the results of our work. The factory not only fulfilled a monthly plan for the first time, it even exceeded it by 50 percent—a huge success.

Celebration in the Factory

The factory was transformed. Animation, contentment, near bliss was written on the faces of the employees. Even the sullen guards at the entry gates looked friendlier, although it would seem that there was nothing for them to be happy about; the upsurge in the shops could not have affected their situation. But the elevated mood of the shop workers infected everyone. They were all somehow related to one another, and if the son, daughter, son-in-law, or daughter-in-law of an elderly guard worked in the shop, then the improvement in their lives made the guard happy, too.

Work was in full swing. Before, when you would drop into a shop, you'd find five or six fellows, without fail, sitting near the water cask in the smoking lounge, chatting peacefully, and puffing on cheap tobacco. A frame or two would be at a standstill, while for the sake of his conscience the foreman would be wrangling idly with the metal worker who had caused the stoppage. Now everything had changed. The smoking lounge was empty. The sawyers, who used to think they were doing the foreman a favor by readying the saws at his request, now began to show up a half-hour early on their own initiative in order to adjust and align the saws and not let a minute be wasted on their account. A progressive piece-rate system of payment was in effect, and bonuses for those guilty of wasting time were lowered or not given at all. The metal workers were arriving half an hour early to check out their machines before work started, and the entire shift was applying itself zealously to the task. Before, no one had been in a hurry and everyone blamed the other guy. Everyone was paid the same paltry amount. Now, the whole shift was working at the same quick tempo.

I asked my coworker Valya, the daughter of one of our workers, to draw graphs on large sheets of paper, showing the shift output and workers' earnings by category, and to post them daily in the shop. Valya carried out my instructions with pleasure; she also wanted her father to see the result of his efforts. Before starting work each day, the employees looked at the figures, comparing their own shift's earnings and output with the other's. The numbers not only made them happy but also provided inspiration for the day ahead.

About three days later, as production rose higher, the Party organizer and the president of the factory's trade union committee began to fuss: "We should draw up agreements for socialist competition between shifts! Each worker must fulfill his socialist obligation! Organize individual competition between the workers!"

With a look of incomprehension, I asked the Party organizer: "Why draw up individual agreements, if the whole shift is working to fulfill a single, common norm? Is there any sense in that?"

The Party organizer did not understand: "What do you mean, sense? Let them work more zealously at their own jobs, not hold back the others."

"They already have no interest in holding back the others. Everyone knows that would only mean depriving themselves of earnings."

"That's beside the point!" exclaimed the Party organizer in vexation. "They now hurry subconsciously, but give them a socialist obligation and they will know exactly what's what. We have the complete picture."

I smiled to myself, thinking, It isn't the picture you're after. What drives you is the need, according to the prescribed Party order, to beat down the impulses of people, to saddle them and make them your dependents by creating the impression that their success is due to "socialist methods of labor." But the people themselves, without any compulsion, have grasped the why and wherefore perfectly. There was already competition in our factory—not socialist, but simply human competition.

Komlev arrived, having learned from the figures that he was behind Kudryavtsev by two or three percent. Komlev grunted, pulling at his beard. "Outgalloped by that skinny devil. We slipped up. Well, you just wait. We'll wipe their noses. They'll find out what kind of a fellow Komlev is!"

This was said without any trace of ill will toward Kudryavtsev, and there was nothing offensive about Komlev's boasting. It was merely an unceremonious expression of healthy fervor from a man who had realized that he, too, could play this game.

Formerly, when we were hopelessly behind, none of the local authorities ever appeared in our factory. Now the district Party secretary paid us a call. He accompanied Neposedov around the shops, talked with the workers, and congratulated them on their success. A representative of the regional newspaper showed up: "Will you reveal how you have achieved your success? Share your experience with other enterprises."

Again, I chuckled. I could tell him that the secret was very simple: We repaired the boiler, put the equipment in order, gave the workers a chance to earn a bit more. Those were the reasons for our success, but I knew they would not satisfy the reporter. It would have better suited his purposes to have Neposedov or the Party organizer talk about their "socialist methods" or "shock work tactics and competition" and other propagandistic nonsense.

After the reporter left, Neposedov summoned me. He was alone in his office. "Who can you come up with as our Stakhanovites?" he asked, grinning.

I shrugged my shoulders: "Just who are our Stakhanovites, Grigory Petrovich? Each shift fulfills its own general norm; everyone is working equally hard."

"That's so," proffered Neposedov, "but the district Party committee demands it, so we have no choice. How can there be an enterprise that overfulfills its targets by almost 200 percent without Stakhanovites? It just won't do. Don't our figures show which workers are the most productive?"

"Absolutely not. The figures are broken down only by shifts."

"Well, all right. I will settle this somehow with the Party organizer and Dolgov. We'll find some Stakhanovites."

Several days later, four photographs of our workers, two from each shift, appeared in the district newspaper. There was a banner headline spanning the page, under which ran the captions: "Stakhanovites of a lumber factory, front-runners of socialist labor," and "Shock workers in a socialist enterprise of the district." The article said that these workers had exceeded their quotas by 150–160 percent.

The articles and photographs distressed me. Other workers had similarly overfulfilled their norms. Why single out a few and thus offend the others? They all worked equally well, so why honor these four with special praise? And why all this praise, if we were doing nothing more than attaining a more or less normal work pace? Why raise such a fuss about that? Because a "socialist economy" cannot function without constant, noisy propaganda to intensify the mood and without, however unjustifiably, singling out one person at the expense of the others, on the principle of "divide and conquer." All this had nothing to do with production but was really about politics, a domain in which I had no desire to get involved.

The sharp upward trend left me with just one misgiving: Would they raise our future targets, so that instead of being in the vanguard we might be bringing up the rear? When it was opportune, I shared my concerns with Kolyshev. He tried to reassure me. "Why would they? Your norms are the usual, the same as others' throughout the Soviet Union. So why would they be raised? If they raised them in all sawmills, that would be a different matter—but for you alone? I can't imagine that happening. Your plant is small, not in the forefront. Who is going to pay any attention?"

After a month and a half the rumpus over the Stakhanovites and the competition died down and our achievements began to seem routine. Neposedov ordered a more careful watch on the quality of production, and fearing that the boiler pipes might again burn out, he established a special regimen. Both of these measures lowered production somewhat and held it more or less stationary. Targets now were overfulfilled by 130–135 percent. This guaranteed double payments to the workers. Because the production norms were above the plan targets, the factory overfulfilled its goals by 150–160 percent. Those were outstanding figures, and we could be content merely to maintain them.

4 ↙∂

Private Initiative, Socialist Reward

Neposedov's Toy

As a reward for our factory's achievements, the People's Commissariat of Forestry sent us a motorcar, an M-1, for the director's transportation. Neposedov's happiness was indescribable. He had long dreamed of having an automobile—and now his dream had come true. At first Neposedov neglected all his factory duties and occupied himself solely with the car. Walking around his own "Little M" ten times a day, he gazed at it with tender fondness, stroking its shiny fenders caressingly as one might a racehorse. He took driving lessons for a week and obtained an amateur chauffeur's license. Henceforth he went everywhere in his "personal" automobile.

It seemed that most of all he liked to honk. Leaving a parking spot, he would compulsively toot the horn, like an engineer starting up a train. Spotting a person or a chicken two or three hundred meters ahead, he would blast away frenziedly. Neposedov had a garage put up in the courtyard of the engineering-technical workers' building, which cost the factory about five thousand rubles, although the object of his passionate love was rarely out of his sight.

In his free time Neposedov occasionally gave his wife and children a ride in the car; and he never passed up the chance to transport the cashier or chief accountant to the bank in town, willingly exchanging his director's hat for that of a chauffeur.

It's hard to say whether this fascination of Neposedov's was more touching or comical. Unable to conceal his feelings, Neposedov openly rejoiced in the car, like a child who has received a long-wished-for, absorbing toy. People at the plant laughed at Neposedov, and sometimes they became indignant because his car so absorbed him that he was referring visitors with all manner of business to the technical director. They especially laughed at his passion for honking. Detecting their amusement, Neposedov got flustered, but he could not overcome his love for the auto and totally succumbed to it. After his initial passion cooled, he did return to his duties as director. However, he continued to drive the car himself, resolutely rejecting suggestions that he hire a chauffeur.

The car was truly comfortable and fine. Almost new, with no more than five or six thousand kilometers on it, the car still glistened, gladdening many hearts besides the director's. But it had one defect—someone in Moscow had switched its new tires for a set that were completely worn. Neposedov immediately put in a request for new tires, but since rubber was in short supply and could be squeezed out only with strenuous efforts, one could easily wait a year for a satisfactory reply to such a request. It was easier to buy tires from Moscow taxi drivers; they could *kombinirovat'* [pull strings],[1] and they always had tires to sell *nalevo* [literally, on the left, that is, on the unofficial or "black" market]. But a set of "left" tires cost 600–800 rubles, as opposed to 150–200 at the official rate of the Machine-Tractor Trust. The factory could not pay the black-market price for tires. The need to acquire new tires was a topic of agonizing concern to Neposedov.

Once I was getting ready to go to Moscow on business. Neposedov, who had no travel plans, suddenly announced that he was going, too. He proposed traveling by car via Rybinsk and Yaroslavl. I was surprised: "For pity's sake, Grigory Petrovich, that's more than six hundred kilometers away! What do you think we are, champion auto racers? Six hundred kilometers on our roads! We would devour so much gas that it would cost us a fortune. And your tires couldn't take it."

"That is exactly why I am going—because they cannot take any more," winked Neposedov. "We can swing by Volga Construction in Rybinsk and buy tires from the chauffeurs there at a good price. Get my drift? The gas is a trifle, and the road from Rybinsk isn't bad; we can somehow manage up to Rybinsk as well. How about it? I don't want to go alone."

It would be easier, of course, to go by train and be in Moscow in three hours. Neposedov's route would take a minimum of twenty-four. But the weather was marvelous and the thought of more travel to new places was tempting. I agreed.

Not Everything in Technology Has Its Place

It was mid-morning, about ten o'clock, when we left. We drove hastily through town, scattering chickens in the dusty streets on the outskirts, then set off down a soft country road. A cool breeze wafted through the open windows. The road wound along a meadow with yellowing birches, set like a picture in the quiet drowsiness of Indian summer.

We drove on for a couple of kilometers and entered a forest. Suddenly the motor coughed once or twice and froze. I glanced inquiringly at Neposedov. Confused, he was pumping the gas and pulling on the choke. We weren't moving.

"What nonsense is this, this has never happened before." Neposedov muttered, hurling himself out of the car. "The carburetor must be clogged."

We checked the carburetor, and it seemed in order. We got back in the car and tried again—no reaction at all. We began searching for the cause of the problem. We were in a good mood. It was just some little thing, and we'd find the hitch in no time. I had no doubts about Neposedov's technical competence. He would find the problem, fix it, and we would continue on our way without a care. We unscrewed one part or another, blew on it, wiped it off, and put it back in place. Neposedov tried to start the motor—with exactly the same result. What the devil! A half hour passed, then an hour. I began to get worried. Did Neposedov also appear to be getting nervous?

Then he located the defect! The gas pump wasn't working. "Here it is, the scoundrel," Neposedov said affectionately, gazing fondly at the detached pump. "Now, my dear friend, we will fix the blessed thing. The main thing is that we've found the problem, and now, in a flash . . . "

He took the pump apart, cleaned it, then carefully reassembled it and put it back in place. For the tenth time we pumped the gas pedal, for the fifteenth time Neposedov sat down behind the wheel. "Get in," he invited me. "Now we're off!" But I couldn't quite believe it—and for good reason. The engine coughed a minute and died again.

"Ah, the son of a bitch," scolded Neposedov, though still affectionately. "Why is it kicking up such a fuss? We will see, we will see," he repeated, again unscrewing the stubborn pump. It appeared that he even enjoyed fooling around with it—the better to know it.

Again we disassembled and reassembled the pump, put it back in place, gave it gas. The car stood as if rooted to the ground. "Well, blast it!" exclaimed Neposedov, beginning to curse in earnest. "Now what's the matter? Everything seems to be in order, but it won't work. Look here." And for the tenth time he explained the construction of the pump. I listened in boredom to his chatter about the little lever, membrane, valves.

"And what the devil is this little ball for?" Neposedov showed me a little ball made of cork. "I just don't get it. It acts as a valve, but what the devil for, if there's another valve? However, if they put it in, that means it must be nec-

essary. Machines don't have any superfluous parts," Neposedov philoso-
phized. "Well, we'll check it in water, see if it works, the devil," he proposed,
walking toward a brook along the road.

Perhaps the pump preferred the crystal water of that little forest stream,
the only water it would pump correctly.

"Just look at that!" Neposedov marveled. "Look, it works! So let's give it
one more try." We put the pump back in place, but the car stood stock-still.

"I'd like to tear you apart!" Neposedov cursed heartily, again grabbing a
monkey wrench. He furiously removed the pump and morosely twirled it in
his hands.

I felt a gnawing sensation in my stomach, so I looked at my watch. It was
three o'clock. In five hours we had traveled only two kilometers from town. A
strange fear crept over me. Clearly we would not be moving from this ac-
cursed place. Neposedov had also noticeably cooled down and was examining
the pump with a frown, not knowing what else to do with it. I got my briefcase out of the car, sat on the grass, and took out some sandwiches that I had
had the foresight to bring along. If you plan on a day, bring food for three.

"Have some lunch, Grigory Petrovich," I suggested. Neposedov, who was
absentmindedly wiping his hands on his trousers, abruptly came to, plucked
some grass, carefully wiped his hands, then cleaned his trousers with his
handkerchief. "You can't go to Moscow looking like a chimney sweep," observed the director, knitting his brows. Devouring a sandwich, he grinned
sarcastically. "Anya slipped some sandwiches into my briefcase and I threw
them out. I even swore at her: Why are you fussing? In two hours we will be
in Rybinsk. Are we going on horses? These are not the olden days! Such id-
iocy, it's enough to make you sick!" sputtered Neposedov.

Finishing our sandwiches, we sat and had a smoke, in no hurry to get up.
There wasn't much we could do.

"Just think," Neposedov remarked irritably. "The top of the line, and they
couldn't even design a little thing like the pump properly. What good are
they? They're idiots, not designers!"

"Perhaps we might go back to town for help while it is still light," I proposed, "and spend the night there."

Neposedov gave me an indignant glance and jumped to his feet. "And be
the laughingstock! Are we little kids? A spectacle in front of the whole
town!" And he again threw himself into battle with the pump. Five or six
more times we disassembled and reassembled it—but the pump refused to
work. Long shadows extended from the trees; the coolness of the evening
had arrived. Without even glancing at me, frowning, menacing, Neposedov

did battle with the pump. I had already lost interest in it and was no longer watching what he was doing.

He put the pump in place once more, poured in gas, and sat down silently behind the wheel, looking stormily ahead. And suddenly the engine came to life! The car shivered and crept forward. Neposedov drove it a short distance and stopped. Hurriedly gathering up the tools, we got in. The automobile, as if rested, joyously raced through the already darkened woods.

"The bastard works!" shouted Neposedov. The scowl had disappeared from his face, and once more he looked happy and confident.

"What did you do with it?" I asked, still not believing that we were actually moving.

"I threw out that little ball!" exclaimed Neposedov. "Threw it out, and off she went! Did you see what happened? This means that not everything in technology has its use. She'll run fine now, I can sense it! When we get back to the factory I will install a little gas tank, three or four liters, here in front. I've already figured it out. I will insulate it with asbestos. Gravity will bring gas from the tank right into the carburetor through a tube, like trucks have. In any case, that pump will never again let me down. Fiddlesticks, you can't fool me!" laughed Neposedov, cheerily.

Twilight was rapidly approaching. The farther we went, the worse the road got. The car tossed about mercilessly on bulges in the pavement, pushed up by tree roots. "Let's hope we don't wreck the shocks," worried Neposedov, letting up on the gas.

"Shouldn't we stop for the night in the next village?" I suggested. "The road is lousy, and our tires are no better; if we rip them up, we'll be stuck."

"I'd rather not," Neposedov said, twisting around in displeasure, "but since there's no hurry, I suppose we can stay over one night."

A Night's Lodging

The forest released us, and it grew lighter. We came out into a huge field, in the center of which stood a tiny village, its single street running parallel to the road. There were seven or eight peasant homes, at most, on one side of the street, and an equal number on the other. Not a soul was in sight, although it was already evening and one would imagine that this would be the time for the old folk to sit on the *zavalinki* [mounds of earth along the outer walls of a village house], discussing their affairs. What was even more surprising, not a single dog yelped at us or ran to intercept our car, barking ferociously. The village appeared deserted. This impression was strengthened by the fact that almost half of the high, generously proportioned log homes were boarded up; crisscrossed planks covered the windows, as if the houses had closed their eyes.

"The Land of Nod," muttered Neposedov. "Well, we'll arouse them." He stopped the car and gave a despairing blast on the horn.

A disgruntled, unshaven face appeared in the window of the nearest home; then a hatless, disheveled man in a patched coat came out. Looking unfriendly, he was in no hurry to reach us.

"Where does the executive of the village soviet live?" inquired Neposedov.

"I am the executive," the peasant replied, looking at us gloomily.

"We need to spend the night. Where could we sleep?"

The executive did not hurry with his reply, continuing to stare at us sullenly. He seemed to be sizing us up. We came in a car—so it followed that we were officials, but what kind? Did we have business with him, or were we just passing through?

"And who might you be?" he asked, without a shadow of obsequiousness or any desire to render service.

"I am the director of a lumber factory. We are on a business trip. Can you direct us to one of the cleaner and roomier cottages?" asked Neposedov impatiently.

With no change in expression, the village executive reluctantly responded, pointing with his hand: "Third cottage on the right side, Sidor Silantev's."

"These devils are not of our God," laughed Neposedov, starting the car. "He certainly did not wish to chat. And with such we are building socialism."

Silantev's high cottage with four windows also looked uninviting. The walls had been darkened by time, and paint was peeling from the intricately carved window frames, which were rotting in places. The sharp peak of the roof leaned forward, as if the house were frowning morosely. Yet the thick log walls revealed that in its day the house had been built wonderfully well, to last many years.

We rapped on a small, sturdy gate, which also had weathered many a year, but received no answer. We went into the yard—not a soul in sight. There were no carts, sleighs, or harrows leaning against the barn, either. The doors of the wide barn had been thrown open, and one surmised that it was also empty in the darkness behind them. Beyond the barn, a few sheds and coops huddled together. Farther on, behind a picket fence, there appeared to be a kitchen garden. The yard, too, had been converted into a garden. The only footpaths were right next to the house and farther back, near the coops. Cultivated beds, either bare or with the withered remnants of potato plants, occupied the remaining space. There was no movement or sign of life anywhere. A broom leaned against the door on the high porch—evidence that the master of the house was away.

Both of us were accustomed to the bustle of factory and town and had begun to feel uneasy in this quiet desolation. "Is there a living soul here?" shouted Neposedov. No one responded.

We sat on the little porch for half an hour, awaiting the owner. It was already dark when a tall, spare, sinewy old man of about sixty appeared from the back yard. He greeted us without apparent surprise. We informed him why we were sitting in his yard.

"You can spend the night, we'll make room for you," the owner responded unenthusiastically, stepping up onto the porch. "Come on in."

In the house he lit a little kerosene lamp and we looked around. The room was orderly and clean: a table; a wide bench along the outside wall; several Viennese chairs; a little fireplace; darkening lithographs on the walls. The place looked shabby, but it was evident that at one time its inhabitants had lived well. Neposedov inquired whether we could get some milk, eggs, something to eat.

"Of course you can, but do you know what they're charging for milk and eggs these days?" asked the owner in a dry, unfriendly tone. "They really sting you."

When Neposedov responded that we would pay city prices, the owner softened a little. "My wife will be home soon and give us a bite to eat. Till then, why don't you have a seat?"

We sat down. Our host puttered around the house morosely. Conversing with him was going to be a hopeless task. His wife turned out to be the exact opposite. About ten years younger than her husband, friendly in appearance and efficient in movement, she greeted us cheerfully: "Welcome! Be our guests."

She brought us an earthenware jug of fragrant milk, some bread, and a bit of butter. Supper for herself and her husband was bread, milk, and boiled potatoes. "Take some potatoes, too; so tasty with milk! And even more so with butter; they will jump right into your mouth!" the loquacious woman rattled on in a pleasant Yaroslavl accent. Neposedov, who always felt very much at home with simple people, began to joke. By the end of supper the host had also thawed, and he did his part to keep up the conversation.

After supper we sat and rested, offered cigarettes to our host, and chatted about life. The old man had come out of his shell completely and now talked readily. Before the revolution they had lived well but were hard put for land. After the revolution they had more land, and with the help of his two teenage sons, the man built up his farm during the NEP period. He had owned four Yaroslavl cows, a mare and foal, sheep, pigs, and chickens. The old man said he had felt as if he had attained everything he had ever dreamed of. But when collectivization came, his dreams turned to ashes.

"You ask why there is no one in the street," said our host. "And who would be in it? We had twenty households in the village. Four were dispossessed as kulaks and deported—so there you have four boarded-up houses. Five families moved to the city—another five homes boarded up. Eleven are left out of twenty. And half of the members of these families are not here. My two sons went to a factory in town. My daughter is studying at a technical school. Who would you meet on the streets? Not even dogs; there aren't any leftovers for them to eat—we have nothing to spare. The only people still here are either those who have no choice or those, like my wife and I, who have no time."

"We haven't even a free minute to relax on the bench in our yard," he continued. "Days at the kolkhoz, evenings digging in our own garden. If you don't dig, you will swell up from hunger. This past year my wife and I received three pood [a pood is 36 pounds] of grain from the kolkhoz for the whole year. Although it is not enough, you have to be content with this. What can you do with three poods? Every day our cow gives about six liters of milk, while in the kolkhoz the cows only give about three or four. We have six chickens. My wife takes a dozen eggs and a kilo of butter to the market—there you have twenty rubles. With them we buy twenty kilos of wheat in town. In the kolkhoz we have to work three months for that. We have potatoes in our garden for the entire winter—and so we live. But what we live for, I do not know," the owner concluded unhappily.

What could we say to these people? We could not bring ourselves to utter false words of consolation, so we were silent, perhaps revealing our sympathy only by our expressions. They gave Neposedov the master bedroom, put me on a wide bench, and settled themselves in an alcove near the entry, where they always slept in the summer.

The next morning, I had a chance to see just how eagerly *kolkhoznik* Silantev rushed to work at his favorite kolkhoz. About six o'clock someone in the street knocked on the window frame with a stick and yelled: "Uncle Sidor, get up for work."

From the alcove came the disgruntled voice of the master of the house: "I hear you. Go call the others."

Our host dressed, washed up, and then sat down to breakfast. He did all this at such a leisurely pace that a good half-hour passed. Again someone knocked at the window: "Come on out, Uncle Sidor!"

Our host got up from the table and leaned out the window: "So, is every-one ready?"

"Almost everyone. We're waiting for you," they answered from the street.

"I'll be right out." Noting that I was awake, he turned to me. "You see how we get ourselves going? We'll be in the field about eight o'clock. But if I worked for myself, I would be up with the sun and in the fields without a clock. . . . You can stay in bed awhile yet. Soon my wife will come and get your breakfast. She's already milked our cow, so she went to the kolkhoz to milk theirs. She'll be back to feed you." Saying good-bye, he sauntered out.

I understood the man's attitude so well. It was plain what was eating him. While I was in the camps, I heard about what a disaster collectivization was for the peasants. I heard it from those just like Silantev, people who had been sent to the camps for opposing collectivization. Neposedov understood him, too. Three or four times a year, he, Dolgov, the Party organizer, and several of the most active members of the Komsomol, along with other Party people from the town, disappeared from our sight for a week or two. The district Party committee had sent them off on the latest "campaign," into the villages to sow, harvest, or procure grain for the state. In order to compel peasants to work more intensively during the busy season and to give up their grain, the Party had to send Party controller–urgers—into whose ranks Neposedov fell—to the kolkhozes.

Neposedov would be morose and angry when he returned from these trips. Sometimes he would let slip a terse sentence or two about what he had ob-served in the villages and what he personally had to do there; but even with-out his accounts, I could well imagine what kind of "work" this was and how it went against his nature. He could not have refused to do it, though, or he would have been expelled from the Party and quite possibly sent to the camps for refusing to fulfill "tasks of the Party and government." Then he would have to say good-bye to his position and his beloved routine. After each dis-appearance into the countryside, Neposedov would resume his factory work with even greater frenzy, as if to forget the unpleasantness more quickly.

Where There Is a Will, There Is a Way

It had rained a little in the night, and the sun gleamed brightly in the puddles as we drove on. The dust had been dampened down by the rain, the air was intoxicatingly clear, and we cheerfully rolled along the soft country road.

Neposedov was concerned; we did not have much fuel left. But fate res-cued us. We had driven no more than half an hour when a gasoline truck appeared, rumbling slowly toward us. Neposedov stopped the car and waved his hand. The fuel truck also stopped. A lone driver sat in its wide cab. I knew from his dirty uniform shirt that he was a camp inmate employed by the NKVD's Volga Construction, which was building electrical power stations and dams nearby on the Volga, near Uglich and Rybinsk.

"Hey, pal, could we get a little of your gas?" shouted Neposedov. Looking at us, the driver thought it over a minute, then got out of the cab and jumped to the ground. "You need much?" he inquired.

"Could you give us about fifty liters? If not, then maybe just fill our tank. Do you have a lot?"

"Flowing over," the driver waved. "A whole cistern. Take it quickly, while no one is around."

In a flash, we got the spare gas cans from the trunk. Volga Construction fuel flowed into them in generous spurts. While the car's gas tank and the spare cans were being filled, I asked the driver: "What did they get you on?"

"The law of August 7, 1932."[2]

"How many years?"

"Ten."

"And how many are left?"

"Five."

"Won't you get caught for not having enough gas?" broke in Neposedov.

"Who's going to check?" the driver brushed it aside.

"They let you drive without an escort?"

"They know me; I have been working there a long time."

"You don't happen to have any tires?" queried Neposedov.

"No tires."

"Do you know whether I might buy some from your chauffeurs?"

The driver shook his head. "It would have been possible earlier, but now we don't have any. Half of our own vehicles don't even have tires."

The gas tank was full, so Neposedov asked how much we owed him.

"The official price," grinned the driver. "Ninety kopecks a liter."

Neposedov gave him fifty rubles, and we said good-bye and left.

"I gave him a little bit extra," remarked Neposedov. "He's a prisoner, so he has no way to make money. Let him benefit from our generosity. And we can relax, now that we have a full supply of gas! It will get us all the way to Moscow with no problem."

There wasn't even a whisper of trouble in the air, and we were in a great mood. The weather was perfect, the car was running well, the road was smooth, we had lots of gas—what more could we want? Forgetting that good fortune always goes hand in hand with bad, we would pay dearly for our complacency.

We had gone about ten kilometers when the car began to weave strangely, as if it were lame on one foot. Neposedov's face fell. He stopped the car and threw himself out of it as though it were on fire. Following after, I found him already squatting next to the right, rear wheel, somberly examining the tire casing.

"Well, here we are," growled Neposedov in response to my inquiring look.

The casing had come apart—lengthwise, no less. Not only the rubber, but the inner cloth layer had been abraded, leaving only a swatch about a foot long, riddled with holes, through which the reddish rubber of the tender inner tube shone pitifully. Give it a little more pressure and it would completely disintegrate. We could go no farther; we were finished.

"Well, here we are," Neposedov repeated thoughtfully. "What should we do?"

What *could* we do in such a situation, stuck without a spare tire in a dense forest about fifty kilometers from Rybinsk, on a country road traveled only by a Volga Construction gasoline or other truck once or twice in twenty-four hours? There was no way out of this situation.

"If only we had something to hold the casing together," remarked Neposedov. "Perhaps we could somehow hold out until Rybinsk. But what could we tie it with? We have nothing."

We dug around in the trunk, in the tool box—sure enough, nothing there. We looked around: a wide clearing, with forests on both sides. No sign of anything we could use to secure the casing.

Suddenly I detected an amused glimmer in Neposedov's eyes. Smiling, he flung open his coat and took off his belt.

"Uncinch yourself!" proposed Neposedov, laughing. "Your trousers won't fall down, and if they do, you can hold them up with your teeth! We won't be sitting in the middle of the road, but getting out little by little."

With absolutely no other way out, I also removed my belt. Fortunately, my trousers stayed up without it. We bound the casing tightly with the two belts and proceeded cautiously. But no matter how soft the road, the belts did not hold very long; they were worn out after a few kilometers. However, we had gotten closer to civilization. A field appeared on the right, surrounded by wire fencing. In it we found good pieces of telephone wire for binding up the casing.

"Just hope it doesn't cut the inner tube," worried Neposedov. So we crept along at the speed of a horse, checking the casing frequently.

A farm village came into sight. There Neposedov bought dozens of rawhide thongs—long, thin belts. We substituted the thongs for the wire and crawled along farther at the same pace.

The stops, the unwinding and rewinding of the casing took up a lot of time. The hands of the clock passed twelve. It was more than a little wearing on the nerves. At first it was funny; then dealing with the casing became tedious; finally, we were fed up. Sitting next to Neposedov, I recalled that I had seen mountains of new casings not long ago in Yaroslavl, on the banks of the Volga, near the Rubber Combine. Where did they all disappear to? Neposedov sighed heavily: "What can you do with such an economy? Those casings are not for us. Seventy-five percent of the production of the Rubber Combine goes to the army and into reserves in case of war. And as for us, well, we have to drive on our belts."

After a couple more hours we came to a large village. In its center stood a rural cooperative retail store. We went in and greedily eyed the shelves. Wouldn't something be suitable for our casing? Learning what we sought, the saleswoman led us to the harness department. It was a treasure trove of hame straps, saddle straps, and small belts of all kinds. We were dazzled. We picked over strap after strap, testing its durability and elasticity, and stumbled on some thick, soft rawhide strips, as wide as the palm of one's hand, which could not have been more appropriate for our purpose.

"What are these things for?" queried Neposedov.

"I do not know, myself," responded the saleswoman phlegmatically. "On the invoice they appear as lassoes, but nobody knows what they are for. They are not in demand in our locale, so they have been lying here since they arrived. No one has bought any. Almost all the goods here are defective: either too short, too narrow, or too wide," the saleswoman explained with the same indifference.

"Well, we will relieve you of some of your defective items," remarked Neposedov. "Give us five of those lassoes."

Not to be embarrassed in front of anyone, we drove out of the village and stopped in a field for capital repairs. We wrapped the torn casing so well and firmly with a lasso that all of the holes were covered. We also wrapped another casing that looked to be in danger.

Finishing our work, we stepped back, entranced: The vivid, bright yellow belts looked splendid against the black background of the automobile. "They turned out fine," Neposedov shook his head. "We'll be just like a circus, entertaining the public. Since everyone who sets eyes on us will be amused, we can collect money for providing a diversion."

At first we drove slowly, frequently checking the patches. The straps held. We quickened the pace—the straps held. Our spirits rose. Perhaps we would get to Rybinsk? We arrived in Rybinsk—the straps were holding and nothing had happened to them.

We could find no tires either in Rybinsk or in Yaroslavl, so we traveled on the lassoes all the way to Moscow, which we reached only toward evening of the third day. Neposedov had driven the car from Yaroslavl to Moscow at a good clip, because by then we had a strong faith in the durability of the lassoes.

In Moscow I informed Neposedov that I did not wish to be put to shame, riding around the capital in a car with bright yellow patches, and I parted from him. Simply put, I was fed up with the excessively prolonged trip. Finishing my business on that same day, I went back to the factory by train.

After a couple of days, Neposedov returned. Looking at the car, I gasped; it was radiant with new tires. "Where did you get them?"

Neposedov grinned boastfully, like a thief. "I got them at the people's commissariat." Then he took me aside and said quietly. "Don't tell a soul, especially my wife; she'll chew me out! Warn the head bookkeeper not to let the cat out of the bag when the notification arrives. I received a bonus of a thousand rubles at the people's commissariat and bought a full set of tires for seven hundred. Not that it's such a disgrace to drive on lassoes. But just take a peek at them great tires, eh?"

I laughed. What a man wouldn't do for love! Until then, Neposedov had purchased only small spare parts and gas for his car with his own money; but so little was officially allotted, he didn't think twice about spending his bonus on the car. That's an obsession for you!

All-Union Grease

About two months after the factory had sharply raised productivity, the technical director was concerned that we had too few saws left. He had long ago placed an order for saws, and since then he had sent several reminders. Moscow was silent, and the factory had only enough saws left for two or three weeks. We were faced with dire consequences: The plant could be brought to a standstill while in the full swing of production, just when we had begun to extricate ourselves from severe crisis.

The technical director reported to Neposedov that Moscow had not sent the saws. His report backfired when Neposedov flared up, which rarely happened with him. "Why didn't you speak up sooner? Don't you know what is going on right under your nose? This is not your first day on the job. How could you rely on an order? You have to wait a year for Moscow!" This explosion was justified, as saws were always in extremely short supply. What wasn't *defitsitny*, with us?

"Call Moscow, get Vasilev on the line," ordered Neposedov.

Vasilev was our supply agent in Moscow. We paid him a total of three hundred rubles a month, and he squandered no less than a thousand on drink. He was a bitter drunkard and reeked of vodka at all hours of the day and night. But this did not prevent his being an essential fellow, since Vasilev possessed one invaluable trait: He could get almost anything, unearth even the scarcest items "under the table," as they say. So we forgave him both his drunkenness and his boorishness, as well as the fact that he clearly lived not on his own means but by using various devices to pocket factory funds allotted to him for business purchases and expenses.

Neposedov picked up the telephone and ordered a travel voucher sent at once to Vasilev, stating that he was being commissioned to visit a saw manufacturing plant in Gorky, and providing him with a 300-ruble cash advance for his expenses.

Several days later a telegram arrived from Vasilev: "Confirm your consent to ship two train cars of lumber. Details in a letter. Vasilev." We sent our confirmation immediately. After another week Vasilev had obtained 150 brand-new saws and presented his bill of 600–800 rubles for travel, per diem expenses, accommodations, delivery of the saws to the train station, loading and unloading, everything as it ought to be, confirmed by documents. A master like Vasilev could obtain or compose any document! Without demurring, we paid him—Vasilev's cunning would come in handy again more than once.

According to a letter from the factory that manufactured the saws, we should also ship two train-car loads of timber without demur. That obligation had to be fulfilled since it was very possible that we would again have to turn to that factory for saws. If we deceived them, they would not give us the saws next time. We had to play fair.

According to the Plan, the saws that Vasilev acquired from the Gorky factory undoubtedly should have been shipped to some other factory, which thus would not receive its allocation. This did not bother us. As Neposedov put it, "Don't be a fool; just be careful. If you rely on the Plan, you will sit idle. And even though we got them by questionable means, we now have saws and can calmly await the saws allocated to us by the Plan."

If the mechanic announced that there was not enough babbitt to lubricate the bearings, through some mysterious method Vasilev procured babbitt. If there were no nails, Vasilev obtained nails, which were likewise unattainable through ordinary methods. Everything was in short supply, everything was in demand. But we could get almost anything because we also had a very scarce material: lumber. Lumber, like the air we breathed, was essential to builders and factories. We gave them lumber and in return received materials as essential to us as the air. If you don't grease the wheels, you won't budge. In the meantime, our requests for materials "allocated according to the Plan" were lying in Moscow, to be filled at some point, perhaps after being cut in half. If we'd waited for their fulfillment, then the factory also would be working at half capacity. Like it or not, we had to "show initiative."

All Soviet industry operated by combining what was acquired "by the book" with what was obtained by hook or by crook. It could not have been done any other way: Without personal initiative, it seems that even a socialist economy cannot exist if it wants to function and not merely to vegetate.

But what can an enterprise do if it produces nothing that can be bartered or used to "grease the wheels?" What about those who are employed, as we say, as servants of the people? They are left to rely solely on supplies allotted according to the Plan, to live in constant expectation of a dressing down or even arrest because of the poor performance of an enterprise that is unable to function better because "supply by Plan" invariably lets them down. Or else they have to exert colossal energy in order to satisfy their essential needs.

More than once, our town's director of municipal services—a nervous, worn-out old fellow and a member of the Party—appeared at the factory. "Be a friend, extend a hand," he beseeched Neposedov. "What would it cost you?"

"I'm not running a Department of Social Services here," Neposedov retorted. "I operate according to plan, my every plank is accounted for. Why don't you have a requisition?"

"I have one, of course, but I still haven't been able to get even one stick of wood with it since spring. And it's my busy season. Don't we have to repair the electric power station? Of course we do. Don't we have to get the public baths ready for winter? Don't we have to put the apartments in order? Don't we have to replank the bridge? Horses are breaking their legs on it. Where can I get the lumber? Be a friend."

"I am not obligated to supply you; go to the devil!" Neposedov barked, greatly annoyed.

"And you, where do you live—in Moscow?" The director attacked him on the other flank. "You go to the baths yourself in winter; you yourself will be sitting in the dark, and you'll be using the bridge."

"I bathe in the factory and get light from the factory," Neposedov brushed him off. But the municipal director did not leave, and finally his lament so wearied Neposedov that he asked: "How much do you need?"

"Hardly anything: about fifty cubic meters, all told," replied the director in a deliberately casual tone.

Neposedov started. "What, have you gone balmy? Two train-car loads? Have you come to joke?"

The pleas and bargaining began again. They settled on half of the amount the director had originally requested, and the happy director, who had of course initially overstated his needs, ran into town in order to send conveyances for the lumber.

After the director of municipal services there came the director of health services, who had to repair the hospital and the children's day nursery. Then the director of the cattle-breeding technical school appeared; and after him, the director of the technical school for mechanics, the director of the theater, and many, many others. After long entreaties, curses, and disputes, each one left the factory with a load or more of precious lumber.

Life went on imposing its demands; people were born, got sick, married, studied, died. They needed to rest, enjoy themselves, dance a little. They all had to have a roof over their heads, a floor, and four walls. "A planned socialist economy" does not have the wherewithal to serve the population. Therefore, willy-nilly, one comes somehow to shift and dodge, thus outflanking the obstacles of socialism and actually operating, not according to the Plan, but according to a freakish "dialectical combination" of the planned and unplanned, in essence by constant violation of the Plan. This practice was officially referred to as "manifesting a healthy initiative."

The chief bookkeeper at our plant sometimes ran out of patience with the health of this initiative. A mild and tolerant sort in general, he usually didn't mind letting Vasilev get away with his tricks. But occasionally when checking the agent's reports, the bookkeeper would stumble on such a brazenly fictitious account that he could not tolerate it. Flinging the report at Vasilev, he would scream: "At least make an effort to cover your tracks! I wouldn't accept this useless scrap of paper if my life depended on it!"

Placidly, with the air of an innocent victim, Vasilev would go to Neposedov. The director would call in the head bookkeeper and patiently explain that yes, the report was fictitious, but it enabled the factory to procure absolutely essential materials that could not be obtained by more honest methods. What would he have us do?

Sighing, the chief bookkeeper in most cases would acquiesce, and using methods known only to him, he would draw up the necessary documentation. But it sometimes happened that, brought to the boiling point by Vasilev's schemes, the head bookkeeper would not budge. Then a cozy gathering, which included Neposedov, Vasilev, the technical director, and me, would arrive at another method to pay Vasilev's bills and hide the traces, such as by drawing up an order for some kind of unfinished work. Vasilev, a master at forging signatures, would hurriedly sign it; the technical director would cosign; I would okay it; and then Neposedov would add an order to "release the funds." The accounting department thus received a properly composed document that not even the most exacting inspector could fault.

Admittedly, this was forgery, but how could we otherwise have continued to function? Either we resorted to forgeries in violation of established state laws and regulations, or we would not be able to operate. In the final analysis, the government itself did the very same thing. At least we were doing it for good reason rather than for our own personal gain—despite the fact that the personal risk to each of us was high, should the forgery be disclosed. Fortunately, experience taught us how to go about it so that it remained undiscovered.

After one such meeting, Vasilev came to see me in the planning department. A big, heavy man with a ruddy face, he sprawled in the chair opposite mine. I smelled the strong stench of wine on his breath as he rasped: "Are you still making up plans? Still writing? Why don't you take a break from that dirty business? Who needs your plans? We can manage without them. Better let's go and have a drink."

I did not condemn Vasilev. When I visited him and his family in Moscow, I learned that he was actually a pretty big-hearted fellow. In another system he no doubt would have been a resourceful businessman. Was Vasilev really guilty because he dirtied his hands in scheming to get around impossible circumstances? Our entire economic system was nothing but continuous dirty scheming, a kind of "universal grease," and it forced even the most irreproachable people occasionally to become excellent manipulators.

Big and Little Schemers

The depth of some people's hope and credulity is unfathomable. While working in the camps, I saw incredible *kombinatsii*, cheating, and deception that could hardly be imagined under normal conditions. When I was first released from the camps and went to work, I had hopeful delusions that I would encounter no more such incidents. For example, I imagined that our lumber factory would operate according to a strictly calculated plan, that each cubic yard of production would be accounted for and could be procured only by requisition of the Lumber Executive Board in Moscow and with the proper warrants. Everything would be calculated, weighed, and counted, with no room for scheming.

But reality was entirely different. No matter how strictly the plan was drawn up, in reality it could not provide for everything, and enterprises usually kept some type of reserves. According to the plan we were supposed to produce 67 percent of finished product from our raw materials, but we contrived to obtain 68, 69, even 70 percent. This surplus constituted our reserves. It, too, was accounted for, but we could be more flexible in disposing of it.

For example, we had a crate-making shop that processed scrap materials for extra, nonbudgetary income. We soon found that crates made from scraps were expensive and a bother to produce. It was better to saw the scraps into regular boards of one to two meters in length and sell those separately. The boards were "grabbed up" as eagerly as the finished crates had been and at the same prices. The cost to us was very low, and we sold them at five to six times the production cost—so this was a highly profitable operation for our plant.

The Central Board looked the other way. They understood that without *kombinirovanie* we could not survive and continue to operate. They only issued occasional reproofs, when we let ourselves go too far and sold too much lumber without the proper warrants.

Dozens of representatives of various construction projects and factories flew to our reserves like flies to honey. Each one had his own plan to fulfill. But not every one of these representatives would receive an allotment; we were selective, and endowed only those who could give us something in return. Thanks to deals like these, we were able to keep our dining room, factory cooperative, and thus our own workers pretty well supplied with food and manufactured goods even when these became especially scarce, as happened toward 1939.

Once I dropped in on Neposedov and found an unfamiliar, impressive looking man in a leather coat in his office. Neposedov was enjoying himself: "Well, what do you propose? A tank? Or machine guns? Those we do not need; we are peaceful people. Cannons we don't need either. Or maybe we could organize an army in the factory?" Laughing, Neposedov turned to me.

The man in the leather coat was the representative of a large munitions plant near Moscow. They had a shortfall in lumber and needed several train-car loads in order to complete an important construction job. They had sent dozens of couriers to various factories. Perhaps one of them would get lucky.

"Why a tank or bullets?" retorted leather-coat. "We can give you *makhorka* [cheap tobacco], manufactured items. We have them."

This representative concluded an agreement to the effect that we would give them two or three carloads of lumber in return for several crates of *makhorka,* a cask of vegetable oil for the dining room, and other products. Our deal with the munitions plant was quite providential.

Another factory, which made parachutes, balloons, and dirigibles for the military, gave us several hundred yards of percale—a silky, thin, and surprisingly durable fabric used in balloon making—in exchange for lumber. The bolt was so wide that you could get a whole man's shirt out of little more than a yard of fabric. Everyone in the factory was supplied with percale shirts and blouses.

Neposedov once returned from a business trip, bragging: "It's a pity you're not married. Look what I brought this time!" He removed some elegant ladies' pumps from his briefcase. These pumps, *model'nye* [designer items] from Moscow, cost between 250 and 400 rubles at the time.

"Do you know how much I paid? Seventy rubles. One artel proposed to give us fifty pair in return for a carload of lumber. They manufacture only for export, and these pumps are considered defective. But just look them over. Do you see any defects?"

We found no defects in the pumps. Our ladies disclosed barely noticeable scratches on a heel here, an entirely undetectable blotch there—enough for the pumps to be seized as defective by an export controller but no hindrance at all to their being worn. We sent the artel a carload of lumber, and our fashionable ladies, who before then could only dream about expensive pumps, began to prance around in them.

The most colorful figure among these visitors was Yakov Abramovich Ginzburg, who sometimes lived at the factory for weeks at a time. A loud old fellow of about sixty-five, with a huge mane of gray hair, Ginzburg never wore a hat and was distinguished by his robustness and good nature. Before the revolution he was a wholesale broker in the lumber business. He had known my father, who worked for a firm with which Ginzburg did business, and this circumstance drew us closer.

Once I happened to go with Yakov Abramovich to the warehouse where we kept the finished lumber. Ginzburg lifted up one of the boards, which made a slapping noise when it was thrown on a stack. "Look, it's all water! Squeeze it, and it oozes. What do you get for this board? Could your father ever sell even one such board? And we call this an economy!"

In years past, lumber had been cured before it was released for sale; but by this time, we were shipping boards directly from the frames, with no time to spare. Roofs were covered with damp boards. Ceilings and floors, doors and window frames were made from them. As the boards dried, they warped and split, creating cracks. *Krokodil*[3] once printed an amusing story about a woman who dropped a scissors on the floor of her new third-floor apartment and later found it in an apartment on the first floor: The scissors had slipped through the cracks in all the apartments below hers.

Ginzburg worked for five or six Moscow manufacturing artels, procuring wood for them from our factory and others. He received a small payment or "recompense" from each artel, essentially a commission for lumber supplied, although working for several enterprises simultaneously and paying such "recompenses" was strictly forbidden by law. Ginzburg lived in Moscow, on the Arbat, in a building of an original construction. After we got acquainted, Ginzburg invited me over, saying, "Come visit us in the crypt." I did not understand. He explained. "Yes, yes, I live in a crypt. Drop in and you will be convinced."

And so it was. Some housing cooperative had transformed a huge stone barn into a residence. Ginzburg had an interior room with no windows to the outside. Instead, it had a skylight in the ceiling—which made it look exactly like a crypt. Ginzburg lived there with his wife, who invited us over many a Sunday for an abundant and magnificent dinner of Jewish dishes. The Ginzburgs loved to eat.

Ginzburg was mainly interested in our crating boards, although he sometimes came looking for a carload or a half of top-grade lumber. In return, he supplied us with products from his artels. Arriving at the plant, Ginzburg would remove a parcel from his briefcase, twirl about, and kissing the ends of his fingers, remark: "This is so delicious, tasty! Smoked fish! They go crazy over these in Moscow: tender; rich; melt in your mouth. I can get a ton!"

Neposedov would frown: "You're forever full of all kinds of rubbish! We need to feed our workers. What the devil do we need a ton of smoked fish for? Give us something a little more substantial."

"And what do you need? Macaroni, cereals, candy? I can give you marmalade, candy, jam, pastila, canned fish. How much?" Yakov Abramovich was an irreplaceable help to us in obtaining groceries.

He stayed at Neposedov's or my place, importuning us to entertain him in the evenings. Even during the day, at the plant, he would pester us: "Can we play preference this evening? Quit working, listen to an old man. Horses drop dead from too much work! This evening it will be preference, and not a word out of either of you!" He was an avid but extremely reckless preference player, and so in spite of his enormous experience, he often lost to us. Neposedov was also a clever player.

Ginzburg's *kombinatsii* were completely irreproachable. He honestly earned his 1000–1500 rubles a month, maneuvering along the complicated channels of the "planned economy" and getting through its logjams. There were schemers, and then there were *schemers*.

Once when we were in Moscow, Neposedov told me that someone had invited us to dine at the Hotel Europe that day. I knew their restaurant: More modest and sedate than the Metropolis, the Moscow, or the Savoy, where procurement agents like our Vasilev often went carousing, it was distinguished by a fine kitchen and equally good service. The white, formal china looked to be pre-NEP, if not prerevolutionary. I also knew that the prices at the Europe were not ones we could afford. Thus our host had to be an important person.

That evening, the two of us went to dinner at the Europe. Our new acquaintance really looked like an important fellow: He was Georgian, tall and, like Chichikov,[4] inclined to corpulence, with an imposing bearing and friendly manner, around fifty years old. He spent about 150 rubles on a dinner that reflected his own personal style—fine but not extravagant. During dinner we talked about the weather, about the theater, about films. Our new acquaintance seemed to be striving to establish an impression of himself as a respectable and congenial fellow.

We sat at dinner about two hours and I still did not understand who we were dining with and why he was entertaining us. I asked Neposedov. "Wait—I do not know, myself, yet," replied Neposedov. "It will become clear."

Several days later, the Georgian came to our plant. He brought candy for Neposedov's wife and children and charmed us all completely. In the evening, after a supper at Neposedov's, we gathered in the office, which was simultaneously serving as our visitor's bedroom. There the Georgian revealed that he was an agent in charge of out-of-plan procurements for the management of a Georgian building firm. They had much construction to do but not enough lumber, so they did not fulfill their plan. He obtained some lumber, but it only partially satisfied their construction needs. He lived in Moscow but frequently traveled around in lumbering regions. The price was immaterial; he was ready to pay any amount, just so the lumber was available. As evidence the guest opened a bulky briefcase: One of its compartments was crammed full with bundles of money.

"Here's a hundred thousand," said our guest, with an ingratiating smile. "I can pay cash, or I can pay you through the bank, in the customary manner. It can also be done another way: We can pay through the bank according to list price, while I pay the difference between that and a negotiated price in cash. I am authorized to purchase lumber without a bill of sale, at any price you choose—we have lots of money. A load of lumber normally costs 2,000–2,500 rubles; I can pay you 10 or 15 or 20 thousand."

Familiar as we were with deals of that kind, the sheer scale of his proposal stunned us. Under the circumstances, with cash payments strictly forbidden by law, it was really too much to have on your person 100,000 rubles, and moreover, to suggest paying any price without a bill of sale! Our scheming in order to pay Vasilev something like 200–300 rubles according to some fictitious account, for the absolute necessities of the factory, seemed pitiful by comparison! To be sure, our guest also was seeking only what was essential for his firm's construction, but one could imagine how much stuck to his hands! No wonder he could pay 150 rubles for dinner!

We informed our guest that, regrettably, we could not be useful to him because we did not have any out-of-plan lumber. Apparently deciding from our changed tone that he was doing business with hopelessly backward provincials, our guest bowed and departed, still smiling politely and respectfully. We saw no more of him.

"What sort of odd duck was that?" remarked Neposedov in amazement when we were alone. "What a number! Compared to him, you and I are Little Octobrists![5] The only thing we're missing is the red neckerchiefs!"

The closer we came to wartime, the more frequently such "numbers" were repeated. Military construction swallowed up more and more of the lumber—and the state of civilian construction thus worsened. People were even resorting to outright robbery. Neposedov once told me about a procurement agent, possibly from Odessa, who had purchased a small raft of logs, about 300 cubic meters, from a foreman of the Volga Construction Trust for 10,000 rubles. He asked Neposedov to accept it for unloading via our plant's log conveyor and then to load it onto train cars for shipment to Odessa. The factory representative agreed to pay whatever we asked for the job on our bill of sale and proposed a separate "gratuity" for Neposedov, also 10,000 rubles. Neposedov chased the agent away, still not knowing where he had obtained the lumber. Shortly afterward, the Volga Construction foreman composed a loss report to the effect that the lumber had been scattered during a storm; but he got caught on some detail, and the story came out. The Odessa representative had to leave his lumber and flee.

Another fellow, from some construction office or other in the Don region, begged Neposedov to accept lumber likewise suspiciously obtained from somewhere or other, saw it up, and ship it to the Donbass—in return for a bribe of 5,000 rubles above the usual payment to the factory for work recorded on a bill of sale.

"I wanted to phone the procurator and have him arrested right then," said Neposedov, "but I just threw him out. Who the hell knows, perhaps he is a decent fellow too? Everyone needs lumber."

There were other, similar instances. It was often impossible to sort out the swindlers and scoundrels from the good people who were obliged by vicious necessity to resort to scheming. Neposedov was revolted by them all, finding this situation distasteful; but each time he ended up merely throwing the agents out of our plant.

The chief *kombinator*, who had organized and was stubbornly upholding this system, remained far beyond our reach. He sat in the Kremlin and schemed—and not on the scale of our little enterprises but on the much grander scale of the nation and the globe.

5 ✍

The Art of
Socialist Accounting

Riding the Peaks and Troughs

This is how I spent my mornings, mid-month: Work began at eight o'clock, but I was in no hurry and would arrive at 8:30.[1] En route I would ponder futilely about how I should spend my day, and conjure up nothing special. As a result, I would be in no hurry to get there—boring, wearying, empty hours stretched ahead.

I would enter my office, greet my coworkers, spread out some papers, and continue to ponder, agonize: What could I dream up? I dragged out the previous day's production computations in every way I conceivably could, until my assistant Valya picked them up. I would kill an hour on that, then joke around a little with Valya. I entertained her by demonstrating the fine art of calculating on the abacus and the adding machine. This could come in handy for her, but why bother when I was so familiar with all of it that it made me sick to death?

In anguish, I would stare at the clock: only ten. Two hours until lunch break, then sit it out until five. Excruciating! Go chat with Neposedov? That would be no fun, either—we had already talked everything over. Sighing, I would get up and go outside. If the weather was good, I would wander among the supplies of raw materials or sit on the bank for hours, watching while the conveyer belts endlessly dragged logs out of the water, one after the other. In bad weather, I would visit the shops, drop in at the mechanic's office, or hang around the supply warehouses, joking with the stockers.

A casual observer would say that we worked hard; but a large part of the time, I was bored, with nothing to do. I had a full-time job about four months out of the year. The rest of the time I spent mostly on dreaming up little projects to keep myself busy. I spent about one or two hours each day going over the accounts, but there was no more for me to do there. I also took on the responsibilities of a legal consultant, carrying on correspondence with our suppliers and purchasers and concluding agreements with them; but even this did not fill up my working day.

Nonetheless, I had two full-time assistants—statistician Valya and planner Nina Mikhailovna. Valya was a wholesome, healthy country girl from one of our workers' families, not very literate, but zealous and conscientious. She managed with considerable effort to learn the principles of planning and bookkeeping, finally achieving a solid mastery over them that no doubt would last her forever. Cheerful and merry, Valya was a member of the Komsomol, but if another organization for youth had existed in its place, she would have belonged to it. For her, as for almost all of our young people, the Komsomol was practically the only outlet for surplus energy and for socializing with their peers.

Valya also had only enough work for three or four hours. There she sat, spoiling my mood even more, demanding that I find her a job. Nothing is more boring and wearisome than sitting behind a desk for a prescribed number of hours: It's even harder for someone like Valya. Sometimes I got rid of her by giving her to the accounting department "on loan." An accounting department always has some snarl or other to be untangled or a few details that need cleaning up.

Nina Mikhailovna, to my delight, was another sort of person altogether. The wife of an electrician who worked at the town electrical power station, she was a graceful, fragile young blonde of average height. Although she, too, came from a worker's family, Nina Mikhailovna was not partial to work. She readily spent the day behind her desk near the stove, reading a novel. Her personality was unusually placid; she seemed to want nothing more than to be left alone with her reading. I tried not to bother her.

Despite the slack periods in our workday, I could not have let my assistants go and taken on their duties myself, because at the end of the month, our work would begin in earnest. At the end of the first day of each month, we had to send Moscow the initial data on the previous month's production. The second day, we had to send follow-up data, and the third day, we had to send a complete statistical report consisting of dozens of complicated tables. On those three days we worked until midnight or one o'clock in the morning.

Delaying or neglecting to send this information was out of the question. Our head office *[glavnoe upravlenie]*, which received data from dozens of factories, had to quickly compose a summary report and present it to the people's commissariat within a prescribed period. The people's commissariat had to give a summary report on all its branch industries to the Central Statistical Board and Gosplan,[2] also strictly on schedule. The Central Statistical Board had to present a summary about the enterprises of the entire country to the Council of People's Commissars, the Politburo, and Stalin himself, also by a specific deadline.

All of the links in this chain are tightly intertwined, forming an essential, carefully structured ornament of the socialist facade. If some information or other is not available, then it has to be invented somehow out of thin air; God help you if it is omitted. The entire chain can be broken because of a single inadequate piece of information, and the thunder and lightning of orders, reproofs, and even arrests for "disruption of the accounting process" might shower down from on high. To avoid this, we even had to keep three full-time employees who were bored to death from lack of work during the rest of the month. Everyone was reconciled to this; so in accordance with the official schedule, we retained the three employees, although our head office knew full well that they were busy no more than a week to a week and a half per month, overall.

Another busy time for me occurred during the month and a half or two months when the annual plan was being composed. In mid- or late November, the head office would forward the planning figures for the coming year to me: how much raw material we should process; what we should produce; what our optimal cost and productivity levels ought to be. The head office received these figures from the people's commissariat, the latter having received them from Gosplan. They were then incorporated into the government's plans for the following year of the Five-Year Plan.

On the basis of these figures as well as the obligatory norms, prices, and regulations approved by the government, we composed work plans for each shop and a general plan for the factory for the coming year, all calculated down to the smallest detail. Every item was projected, right up to when, where, and how much we could spend on rags for wiping up the machines, or when and where we might need to hammer in a hundred grams of nails. You can understand, then, why we tried in any event to maintain reserves in the plan, to give ourselves more leeway to maneuver.

In its final form, the plan is a voluminous book with hundreds of tables, which agree exactly with each other and are harmoniously amalgamated into tables of the overall plan for the factory. The result is a very exact picture, not unlike a classical work of art, where everything is in its place and subordinate to a strict logic, with one thing leading into the next and reaching completion in a final product in which every detail has a purpose. We spent a month and a half to two months constructing this masterpiece, again working until midnight or one o'clock. The finished plan had to arrive in Moscow exactly on schedule.

In Moscow our head office would check the plan carefully and uncover our reserves—and then the bargaining began. Defending the factory's interests, I would explain why I was right. They would object, citing the interests of the head office, the people's commissariat, and the government. Our head office did want its indices to improve; but they needed even more to follow established regulations and to hold us to them as well. The disputes sometimes went on for weeks but almost always ended in compromise. Then I had to redo the plan. The smallest change in one table necessitated the reworking of many tables. Often I would have to rework the plan as many as three or four times.

At best, we received the approved annual plan toward the end of January, but more often it would arrive in February or even March. By that time, it had been confirmed and carried the strength of law: Officially, we were legally bound to operate only according to the plan. The bank could give us money only in the amount projected in the plan. We had the right to maintain a designated number of workers and white-collar employees and to pay them only at the wages specified in the plan. We could obtain materials, resources, and equipment only in the quantities designated by the plan and could pay for them only as strictly prescribed by the plan. The facade was unusually harmonious and precisely calculated. In reality, however, we more frequently resorted to the services of Vasilev or Ginzburg than to the plan. The factory's overall effort also was enhanced by the energy and fire of Neposedov, which could not have been accounted for by any plan.

Neposedov himself regarded the plan with respect. Although he occasionally violated it or circumvented it, for him the plan remained the gospel according to which the factory must live and operate. In actuality, though, while we were waiting for the approved plan to arrive at the beginning of each year, we functioned quite well without it for a couple of months. When I told Neposedov that we could manage without the plan, he played dumb: "What would we do without the plan?" he asked, perplexed. "We must be oriented toward something, and that's impossible without the plan. What would we be guided by?"

That was our Soviet economic planning, in a nutshell. In former times, the owner or manager of an enterprise had run a business according to profits, the state of the market, and the level of demand. Under socialism, if these economic principles were not entirely dropped, they no longer played much of a role either in the economy as a whole or in the management of any particular enterprise. The plan became the only measuring stick for managers—

those famous "planned results." Managers had nothing else to go by, except perhaps their own noses. Gradually, especially among young people, the idea emerged that it was impossible to operate any other way.

The need to fulfill the plan also dictated our maneuvering and scheming. In the final analysis, the plan was nothing other than a command from above, and the entire complicated socialist ornament was simply a mask for this command.

People Cannot Be Trusted

My planning department was located in a corner office. The accounting department occupied two large rooms next door, along with the cashier's office—a small cage in the corridor, with an iron door and a little window. This department was full of girls and women just like my Valya and Nina Mikhailovna, not very literate or able workers, but workers nonetheless. Their boss was the head bookkeeper, an elderly, generally complacent, heavy-set man, with a head as bald as a billiard ball and a round, comically wrinkled face. He constantly made cracks at their expense but had a fatherly affection for them. The head bookkeeper rarely lost his good disposition, although his job was not easy. If it was my duty to work out the statistics for a plan ordered from above and supervise its fulfillment, then to a considerable degree it was the chief bookkeeper and the factory director who together bore the responsibility for the state of the factory.

The director is the major figure in charge of the operations and facilities of the plant. He is also the "manager of the credits," the one who is held financially accountable. The chief bookkeeper is subordinate to him, but he also has a means of control over the director: The bookkeeper has the right not to fulfill the director's order to release funds, if for some reason he considers a given payment illegal. On these same grounds he can also refuse to sanction the release of products or materials. In the case of a repeated order from the director, the chief bookkeeper must carry out the command but then immediately inform the procurator and higher authorities about what has transpired. Thus, in financial matters, the head bookkeeper solidly controls his domain, functioning as a sort of commissar to the director.

In Soviet conditions, the bookkeeping department's responsibilities exceed the customary purview of accounting insofar as this department exerts control over the disposition of funds or objects of material value. Accounting, therefore, becomes complicated in the utmost extreme. For example, let's say a mechanic has to order a kilogram of cleaning rags from the supply warehouse for the machine department. He writes out an order for them, which goes to the planning department. I approve this request, noting that expenditures for rags were projected in the plan and thus the funds may be disbursed. The order goes to the bookkeeping office. First, the bookkeepers must verify that the mechanic has not overspent the amount allotted him for cleaning materials, after which the bookkeeping office draws up four copies of an order to the warehouse to release the rags. The stocker releases them, recording the details of the transaction in his inventory; then, as part of his ten-day report, he forwards a copy of the invoice with the recipient's receipt to the accounting department. The latter, in accord with the record of the stocker and the receipt, notes the release of the rags as an expense, and then holds onto the invoice copy for a predetermined period.

Rags are rags. They cost only fifteen or twenty kopecks, so naturally no one would steal them. Yet workdays are spent obtaining them and keeping records of the transaction. Everything must be handled in the same way, regardless of its value or the amount ordered.

Such a system clearly is based on a lack of faith in people. Whether in the area of ideology or in the area of economics, the Soviet system is first and foremost designed to facilitate surveillance over the populace. It could not be otherwise, since communism has a Hottentot morality: "The only thing that's moral is what is good for communism." Marxism rejects universal moral standards of human behavior, which are based on confidence in people. Communist leaders are thus compelled to regard each person as at least a potential thief who must be diligently supervised.

It takes a great many people and a great deal of time to implement this complicated accounting system. Every shop and warehouse has its own little accounting office. Personnel from the planning and accounting departments keep tabs on them. The head office, the bank, and the financial department keep tabs on us, while the people's commissariat watches over them in turn. The huge apparatus of bookkeeping and planning departments is everywhere. And the procurator and the NKVD are also watching from the sidelines.

If we had adhered to all the rules and orders that rained down from on high, then we really would not have been able to function, as we would have had neither enough time nor enough people. We would have been occupied solely with observing the rules of bookkeeping and would have had great difficulty producing anything. We thus observed the rules haphazardly, and once again arrived at a dichotomy—externally, exact, strict accounting, combined with subordination first of all to the demands of life, and only after that, to those of bookkeeping.

This is natural. To the Kremlin we are faceless individuals whom the authorities have never trusted and must watch carefully. But to us, our factory workers were not units of labor; they were people we knew well and trusted implicitly. For instance, we never would have suspected the director of our supply warehouse, an elderly fellow from the steppes, of peasant origin and very likely a former kulak, of stealing rags or anything else. He was a very decent person. The chief mechanic also knew his people. All the people in the factory were just people, with all the merits and inadequacies peculiar to people, and we had no reason to regard them with particular distrust. So we carried out orders about control only to the extent needed to keep up appearances.

However, in order to maintain this charade, we needed many employees. Our accounting department alone employed eighteen of the more than thirty white-collar and "engineering–technical workers" in the factory administration. This figure does not include white-collar employees in the shops. With a simpler accounting system, the plant would have needed a third that number, while a private operation would have managed with five or six people. But since "socialism is accounting,"[3] our thirty employees were an overhead cost of socialism.

The phenomenon had its positive effects, to be sure. Unemployment was eradicated, albeit largely at the cost of paying surplus workers to sit idle everywhere. From the perspective of economic expediency, they are unnecessary for production and a burden on it. At the same time, there are huge shortages of the most basic essentials, goods that these "surplus people" could be producing. The socialist system, however, is not equipped to handle all of these problems at the same time.

The accounting office also has its own "peak times," when the bookkeepers are preparing their quarterly, semi-annual, and especially annual reports. The accounting department spent about a month and a half or two months of intensive work on the annual report, just as I did on the annual plan. Overtime pay was forbidden, but the accounting staff usually received a salary premium "for successful composition of the annual report"—even though it had been composed very unsuccessfully, at the cost of more than a month's extra salary. My workers and I received the same premium for composing the annual plan. Perhaps these premiums replaced the bonuses that a boss formerly gave his workers at Easter or Christmas. Now they arrived before spring, were always impatiently awaited, and were relied on heavily.

When I started at the factory, my attention was drawn to the chief bookkeeper. I suspected that something about his past was not entirely in order. His gait, his manner of sitting or talking—I don't know just what, but something reminded me of the old imperial officers whom I had met in the camp. After a year or so, by which time we knew each other well, my hunch was confirmed. Once we were sitting over a bottle of wine and somehow got to talking about the army. Slightly inebriated, the head bookkeeper began to recall what type of uniform various regiments had worn in tsarist times, revealing his great knowledge of this topic. I threw fuel on the fire by recalling the last names of some of my officer acquaintances in camp. It turned out that the head book-keeper knew one of them well. He was so moved that he began to cry and re-vealed a carefully kept secret: He was a former cavalry officer. Wounded in the civil war, he had stayed behind in a city occupied by the Reds, where kind people had concealed him and obtained documents for him. Adopting an ordi-nary lifestyle, he had lived under an assumed name from then on. After this ac-cidental confession, we treated each other more guardedly.

Volkov, a local fellow and a former peasant, worked as an assistant to the head bookkeeper. Ungainly, of medium height and muscular build, with wide cheekbones and eyes like narrow slits, Volkov was a dull fellow who grasped things with difficulty but was an assiduous and conscientious worker. Because he had trouble with accounting, he often turned to me for advice and assistance. Whether because of my knowledge or my friendliness, I gained his complete confidence, and he began dropping in on me to chat about personal as well as business matters. One day, coughing and sniffling as usual, Volkov said that he wanted to apply for Party membership. The Party organizer had told him that he would be accepted. "We should be con-scientious builders of socialism," Volkov stated, smiling in embarrassment, perhaps because of the hypocrisy of these perfunctory words. "Why should I not join the Party? I'm a former peasant; I work honestly."

I replied that it was a personal matter for everyone and that I was unable to advise him. But I thought to myself, What is drawing him to the Party? It could not be communism or socialism, to which he was totally indifferent. The truth must lie elsewhere. Volkov had a young, feisty, pushy wife, who was the boss of the family. Perhaps she had decided that her dull husband would hardly advance higher than his present job while he remained outside the Party. If he were a Party member, he could count on becoming head bookkeeper because the Party needed its own people in responsible posts. Volkov would be entirely suited to this role. With his unsullied social back-ground, he could be the ideal, absolutely dedicated Party member.

Nothing would change in the factory, no matter who was made head bookkeeper: Both the former cavalry officer and the former peasant would have to submit to the same regulations and at least present the appearance of fulfilling them to the letter.

Against the Rules

One day, Neposedov summoned me to his office. With him sat Aunt Pasha, our cleaning woman. About forty-five years old, she already looked like an old woman—tiny and thin, with a shriveled, wrinkled face. Life did not coddle Aunt Pasha. She swept the office, tended the stoves, mopped the floors—she had plenty of work. A widow, Aunt Pasha had two children, ages thirteen and fourteen. Only God knows how she and the two children managed on a mere 110 rubles a month.

Neposedov was indignant: "No matter how many times I have told the accounting department that Aunt Pasha's wages should be raised, they stand stock-still! If you don't take it up with them yourself, no one will do a thing about it. How can they expect a mother of two who does so much work to live on such a pittance! Let's look at the plan and see what can be done."

Of course Aunt Pasha could not live on 110 rubles, but the pay scale for maids was maintained according to the plan and registered in the finance department, which saw to it that employees were not paid more than the established rates. It was not the accounting office's fault; it did not have the right to increase Aunt Pasha's wages. Nor did Neposedov have that right. But while a right is a right, a person is also a person, and the plan is not always merciless: With skillful manipulation, something can be extracted from it.

"For washing floors, then, in accordance with the pay scale for 'cleaning the premises,' you order a forty-ruble-a-month supplement, at ten rubles per week, for Aunt Pasha," said Neposedov, looking over the plan. "And what was projected for the planing shop? Two cleaning ladies? One can manage there. Add another fifty rubles on the planing shop's account. And have it paid out from the workers' payroll, not the administration's." I understood perfectly: Neposedov feared the finance department might find out about our violation of the regulations.

Aunt Pasha left, well satisfied. She now would be earning 200 rubles a month. Of course, we had committed a crime, but what was more important? To adhere to orders on paper or to help someone out?

Another time, an elderly, good, conscientious worker had a seriously ill child. Local doctors could not determine what was wrong with him, so the family decided to go to a famous professor at a hospital in Moscow. The medical treatment would be free, but a considerable amount of money would be needed for their trip and living expenses in Moscow. The worker came to us for help. The trade union had given him a little money, and he had received his share of the mutual aid fund through the factory committee; but this did not amount to much. Having thought it over, Neposedov summoned the man's boss, the overseer of the raw materials warehouse, and ordered him to draw up a pay voucher for his employee, for work that was never done. Of course this must be done on the sly. Another forgery—but the lad needed treatment, and his father had worked for us for several years and would continue to work in the plant. We had no choice in the matter.

Another instance: The factory had a day-care center. Many working mothers left their children there during working hours, paying about ten rubles a month. The day-care center's budget was very low, but the children had to be fed and cared for. Linens, toys, and dishes had to be acquired. One day the day-care center director started crying, "There is no money to buy provisions for the children!" I grabbed the plan, went to Neposedov's office, and together we hunted up a couple hundred rubles from some account, such as "costs for representation." After all, why couldn't the day-care center be considered our representative?

To the authorities we are faceless individuals merging into a mass, an indistinguishable crowd. But our factory employees are living people. In the past, a workforce usually formed a harmonious family with many common interests and needs. How can you ignore the needs of your family, how can you not try to help its members when they fully deserve help? The people are not to blame: They work, although admittedly they could work longer hours and more intensively. Given a chance, they wouldn't need any help, they'd do it all for themselves and on their own initiative. But the socialist economic system was not designed with people in mind. Its business is the "building of communism," cramming people into cubbyholes and not providing for their human needs. We had only one choice: to help people, to get around these limits where possible, not in the service of socialism but rather of those whom socialism plows under.

One evening, Neposedov, the head mechanic, the chief accountant, and I are sitting in the director's apartment discussing an upcoming matter in the plant. Neposedov's and the mechanic's wives are sitting at a table in the center of the room. Neposedov's wife wearies of our conversation. "Enough, you talk about the factory too much!" she interrupts us, half jokingly, half angrily. She approaches us, rakes some papers into a pile, and throws them down onto the desk.

"Stop that, stop," Neposedov protests, but it isn't so easy to bring his wife around. "You aren't going to accomplish anything that way," Neposedov remarks, to annoy her. "We'll just start playing preference."

"Honestly! You'll play preference, will you?" his wife retorts angrily. "It's the factory days, it's the factory evenings, then it's preference. And what about us? We're just supposed to sit here and watch you? No! Let's all play mouse together!" He is subdued, and we sit down to play mouse.

"You'll go balmy in this factory of yours before too long," Neposedov's wife grumbles good-naturedly. "Why not arrange an outing in the woods while it's still summer and the weather is fine?"

"That's right, we haven't had any group outings for a long time," the mechanic's wife says supportively. "Last year was so good, but this year . . . "

"This year we are wasting away in the wretched plant," Neposedov's wife finishes the sentence for her. "Director, when will we organize a *maevka?*"[4] she asks, turning to her husband. Neposedov laughs the matter off. He knows that a *maevka* would mean a further drain on the factory's funds. But the head bookkeeper cuts in, always chivalrously lending support to the ladies. "Quite right, why not provide a little amusement? It's hot now, so this is the best time to go into the forest."

The head mechanic also loves to toss down a glass or two in the bosom of nature. Everyone is united in a harmonious front, and the director has to give in. He turns to the head bookkeeper: "Okay, go get some paper and a pencil, and we'll do some figuring. But if we do organize something, then let's do it for the whole factory. Our plant is in first place again."

We begin to figure, estimating the number of workers participating in the forest outing at about 400 people, including wives. Snacks would be at the workers' own expense, everyone would bring something along. But the factory would have to provide beverages for them, nothing else would do. Not everyone could find the money for liquor, especially in those days, and a sortie into the forest just wouldn't be the same without liquid refreshment. We'd need a considerable amount for a crowd of four hundred people. Two, three barrels of beer? Not quite enough, we will order four. Vodka, even a smallish glass per person, would amount to a considerable sum. We must have music, too. The total cost would exceed a thousand rubles. Neposedov groans, the chief bookkeeper echoes him, but once you have given your word, you cannot go back on it. Anyway, people are not mannequins, and they need to have a little fun.

"We'll have to scratch some money out of the factory committee, from their account for mass cultural activities. This sort of thing is their responsibility," remarks Neposedov, not really hoping to get much from them. With its lean budget, the factory committee functions mostly on general factory funds.

The next Sunday, groups of factory people converge on a fragrant pine woods above the river. Near the riverbanks the pines change to dense thickets of alder, bird cherry, and osier. Carts carrying wine and beer squeak on the road. The brass instruments of the town orchestra glimmer. Until nightfall, waltzes, polkas, and *barynias*[5] resound throughout the forest. The young people dance with gusto in a huge clearing. Slightly older people also join in, and an intoxicated grandfather is thrown out of a *barynia* circle, from which shouts of delight rise to the sky. From the clearing come laughter and girlish shrieks. Further on in the forest, not wishing to be laughed at by the others, the more sedate delight themselves with quiet conversations in the bosom of nature. Complete democracy exists in the forest: The workers sweep up Neposedov, and he dances a *trepak* with them. Blue- and white-collar workers, engineering-technical workers (ITR), and junior service personnel (MOP)[6] commingle. In the forest are real equal rights, without socialist labels.

Toward evening the woods fall silent, but people will long recall how they enjoyed themselves at the *maevka*. The next day, we have headaches over where to ascribe the expenses for these "mass-cultural measures," which were not projected in the plan. However, remembering the happiness that the outing in the forest gave our people makes this task a little easier.

Tricks of Bookkeeping

To all appearances, Soviet accounting is extremely finespun. But as they say, where something is thin, that's where it will break. At each year's end, an inventory is taken—a full count of all tools, instruments, and materials. The data of the inventories is compared with the balances on the books, which invariably reveals huge discrepancies. The accounting department is perplexed. Where do the surpluses and shortages come from if the count was done carefully? This detail must be cleared up, that one erased or concealed; somehow, the differences must be smoothed over.

I remember how riled up our chief bookkeeper once got over one such discrepancy. It was no joke: According to the inventory, our raw materials showed a surplus of almost 1,500 cubic meters of logs, valued at approximately 300,000 rubles. That high a quantity and value are hard to conceal, and they made the flaws in our accounting painfully apparent.

Neposedov was taken by surprise, too. How could we have such a large surplus? Where had it come from? We didn't have that much raw material, almost every log was accounted for, but there was that 1,500 cubic meters! A miracle!

We checked, and found no miracle—but did find a simple explanation. For a number of years, raw material stocks had not actually been counted; but to preserve appearances, inventory records were still composed according to data on the books. In this way, over the course of five or six years, a surplus had accumulated. Actually, 200–300 cubic yard surpluses per year were quite common, in my experience.

Even as a child I had seen how log examiners in sawmills cheated their suppliers. Logs come down on the conveyor belt one right after the other. Without stopping the belt, the examiner would quickly place an arshin-ruler, along with his finger, on the top of a log. Almost imperceptibly, he would move the ruler inward from the edge of the log with his finger and thus underestimate its diameter, sometimes by almost an inch. The supplier often did not notice, and afterward the examiner would receive his reward from the owner.

I was not surprised to encounter the same tricks in our plant during the intake and measurement of logs from the People's Commissariat of Forestry, although perhaps I should have been. After all, our examiners were youths of about 18–20 years, educated under the socialist system. They could accept no gratuities, so they had nothing to gain by cheating the suppliers. Whence, then, this throwback to bygone days, this habit that seemed to be as deeply ingrained in them as it had been in their fathers and grandfathers? The technique they used was exactly the same, that strategic placement of the finger. I concluded that there was only one possible explanation: For the examiner, cheating is simply a sport, a chance to flaunt one's skill and bravado. In addition, the examiners were loyal above all to their own factories, compelled by a traditional instinct of ownership: The factory where I work is mine.

Neposedov's instincts were similarly proprietorial. When the suppliers protested to him about cheating in the intake area, he would not listen to their complaints: "And what are you there for?" Neposedov cursed out the complainers. "To catch butterflies? If this is going on, then you, yourselves, are to blame." Although he did not encourage our examiners to cheat, he did not scold them either, but laughingly told them to be a little more careful.

The log surplus worried Neposedov. Then an idea dawned on him. He summoned the chief accountant and proposed that we conceal the surplus, presenting the inventory according to data already on the books, as we had before. The chief bookkeeper hesitated.

"Here is what we'll do," urged Neposedov. "A hundred thousand rubles in our capital construction funds are designated for a new residence. We can build two buildings with that money because the lumber will be free due to the inventory surplus. Do you understand? I give you my word that this surplus will be used up in a year."

The chief accountant, also a factory loyalist, agreed. The true inventory records were thrust aside and new ones composed, showing the usual permissible surplus of about 200 cubic meters. Neposedov began bragging happily about the construction he would get rolling the following year. He obtained the standard blueprints for worker residences and enthusiastically began altering them to suit his taste.

But in the end, we were not allocated the money for this residential construction. The Council of People's Commissars vigorously resisted the release of funds for that purpose, as their first priorities were heavy industry and the military. So we had to find another solution to our problem of what to do with the surplus lumber. If our deception came to light, the positions of many in the factory would be in jeopardy.

Fate protected us, although in an unanticipated way. One warm April night I had gone to bed late, after sitting over a chessboard all evening with Neposedov. I had just managed to doze off when heart-stopping shouts rattled my windowpane: "Fire! The factory is burning!" I jumped up and dressed in a flash, buttoning up as I dashed out of the building. Neposedov had already come in his car to pick me up; the mechanic and chief bookkeeper joined us, and together we raced to the plant.

A glow rose above the houses in town. We were silent; this was no time for conversation. As we drove into the outskirts, red tongues of flame were licking purple puffs of smoke over the dark trees in the distance. The fire appeared to be right inside the factory. But what was burning—the shops, the stoker, the lumber warehouse, or the living quarters? Neposedov drove so fast that the air hissed past us.

When we got beyond the trees, Neposedov began laughing. I looked at him as if he were crazy: How strange, when flames were roaring nearby.

"The ship is burning!" yelled Neposedov joyously. The tension eased. The dilapidated living quarters stood at a safe distance from the factory.

An excited crowd was rushing about, and some workers were still running around inside the building, removing belongings from the lower floor. The upper floor was wreathed in flames that looked like a red cloak billowing in the wind, with little streams of fire spurting downward from it. The factory and town firemen were racing around like madmen, aiming streams of water at the fire, but it was evident that the building could not be saved.

Nor was it worth saving. Once we were certain that no deaths had occurred, we calmed down. All the inhabitants were evacuated from the building, and except for those living on the top floor, who escaped with nothing but what they were wearing, the majority had even removed their own belongings.

"I suppose they will try to save the barn," Neposedov remarked. After running around the blazing residence, he had returned to the car and was watching with satisfaction as the flames licked at the building, reaching out toward a long log shed in which the residents kept firewood, livestock, and fowl. "Where the devil are they going? Let the barn burn!"

The chief accountant did not understand: Why should they let the barn burn?

"It's very simple," winked Neposedov. "How much is the residence worth, according to our records? One hundred fifty thousand? The barn is worth another ten. That's one hundred and sixty thousand, in all—just about the sum we'd receive from our insurance. And the kind of building we will put up—you can't imagine. The more it burns, the better!"

The residence soon crashed down, throwing up huge puffs of sparks, smoke, and flames. They had barely reached the roof of the barn when, to Neposedov's delight, the firemen pulled the building apart with hooks.

After settling the evacuees in the dining hall and the club for the night, we left for home. Now it was Neposedov who was on fire. "Write Moscow in the morning," he ordered. "The living quarters have burned, and a hundred families are left without shelter, creating a catastrophic situation. Write forcefully in order to get through to them. We request permission to begin building a new residence in anticipation of receiving an insurance premium of such-and-such an amount. Tomorrow I will deliver this letter to Moscow in person."

Over the summer we constructed two large, twenty-four-unit apartment buildings, more than a hundred apartments in all. Whole families had been cooped up in a single tiny room in our burned-out hull, and now we could give as much as two rooms to big families and an entire apartment with separate kitchen to several families living together.

Neposedov was completely engrossed in the building project. Work in the plant was proceeding calmly, so for him the construction was occurring just in the nick of time. Otherwise he would not have known what to do with all his energy. The construction also gave him a chance to prove his mettle. The standard plans did not satisfy him, so he improvised, taking what was best from various models. He arranged for a kitchen, storeroom, washroom, and cupboards in every apartment. He wanted the residents to have maximum comfort. We could allow ourselves this because we could provide choice lumber for the construction at no cost, from our own surplus.

The building turned out fine, but this was not enough for Neposedov. He negotiated with a furniture factory, giving them about a dozen carloads of lumber, also from our surplus. In return they delivered about a hundred suites of furniture to us at a deep discount—tables, chairs, beds, cupboards, and wardrobes. Neposedov was exultant at providing the workers with proper furniture. He even dreamed of putting a divan in each apartment, but we lacked the funds for this luxury.

Neposedov personally helped the residents settle in. He walked around the apartments, offering to arrange the furniture himself so as to show them off to best effect. Later, he complained vexedly: "You know, those apartments were as pretty as a picture. But then the workers brought in their rags, hung them here, spread them about there, and spoiled the impression. Rags, rags; almost no one has a good blanket. Honestly, like we're supposed to provide them with blankets at our expense, too! . . . "

It so happened that a regional competition was held that summer for the best residential construction. Our buildings fell within the competition guidelines. They took first place and were written up in the district and regional papers, with Neposedovian construction being upheld as a model for others to follow. The committee of judges was unaware of the fact that we had spent 100,000 rubles more than had been allocated to us for construction, the cost of the lumber that we had "borrowed" from our surplus—a situation unlikely to be duplicated anywhere else or anytime soon. Nor would one be likely elsewhere to encounter another Neposedov, nursing a building project along as a mother would her child.

Tricks of accounting, combined with the unanticipated fire and the zeal of Neposedov, gave us a chance to provide our workers with good quarters. As for Neposedov, he too was well served: He had yet another occasion to experience satisfaction from the fruits of his labors. Once again he was walking around, beaming.

Stalin's Mistake

If need be, a person can live and work under any conditions, but this does not mean that he becomes reconciled or accustomed to them. The fundamental mistake made by Stalin and Marxists in general was to assume that inasmuch as "existence defines consciousness," a person can get used to any existence.

Stalin and his comrades in arms knew, of course, that unbelievable *kombinatorstvo* was concealed behind the strict socialist facade. Moreover, they even encouraged this scheming, calling for manifestations of "initiative in the workplace," when such "initiative," in a totally planned economy, could only take the form of unscrupulous scheming; they knew this initiative would aid the implementation of their orders. Anyway, the socialist exterior, not its ugly contents, was their main priority. This exterior, the basis of Soviet life, was maintained as the lifestyle of a "socialist existence." Soviet leaders believed that the present existence would instill in people a new, socialist consciousness, which would enable them to get used to their situation.

In reality, it was impossible to get used to this situation. No matter how many times we were forced to resort to scheming, we could not get used to it. Just the opposite: We began inwardly to rebel. Why were we compelled to involve ourselves in forgeries and in unscrupulous business deals? What kind of diabolical need necessitated all this abominable trouble? Why weren't we given the chance to work like human beings, honestly, without demeaning trickery? We felt humiliated and insulted by this scheming, and at times it became unbearably loathsome.

Granted, in certain individuals, a primordial, anarchic, destructive inclination prevails over the inclination toward creative work and to order. However, nearly everyone has an innate respect for official papers, regulations, and laws, regardless of their origin. So while we regularly broke laws without a moment's thought, as if we were already accustomed to doing so, at the same time our consciences gnawed at us: Such things were prohibited. Eventually, this situation leads to common depravity. Fortunately for us, Neposedov and our chief accountant were intrinsically decent people. In other enterprises, bribes, swindles, embezzlement, and fraud flourished in the soil of a casual attitude toward documents and rules. The courts were overburdened with such cases.

This contradiction nagged at many consciences in our factory. The technical director saved himself by retreating to the sidelines, seeking refuge in his own narrow affairs. For no apparent reason, the head bookkeeper would suddenly fall into a funk and walk around glowering like a storm cloud. Two or three times a year, the mechanic drank himself senseless, trying to release his pent-up frustrations. His terrified wife used to catch him and lock him up in a closet. These people seemed to be yearning for the chance to live and work like normal human beings, and without it they were foundering at sea.

An age-old desire for order compels a person to work conscientiously. But under Soviet conditions, a worker or a peasant could not see the fruits of his labor and got no satisfaction from his job, so he would waste time, dawdling on the job, for years. Then suddenly he would begin to work eagerly, animatedly, because he was fed up with wasting time and craved full-fledged work. And then he would cool off and gradually return to wasting time. So it went with us: No matter how scornfully we regarded our work and the tricks we played, we nonetheless tried to work like we were supposed to, subordinating ourselves to an instinctive yearning for order. We struggled to complete our plans and reports on time, not only to satisfy the demands of the authorities but also to assuage our own consciences. Why didn't the materialist Stalin rely more on this human need for order and, realizing that it eventually would win the day, organize his "socialism in content" as well as in form? Instead, his "order" only disorganized that content and corrupted people, so that when another order wins out, it certainly will not be Marxist socialism.

When I began working for him, Neposedov's attention was entirely taken up by technological and business matters and such questions seemed never to weigh much on his mind. Then about three years after we met, I began to notice that something was bothering him, as though our valiant scheming was becoming somewhat repellent to him. Maybe this realization came with maturity. In any case, he had begun to act a little strange. So occasionally, after some schemer or other with an especially base proposition came to our plant or after we had committed a series of violations of the rules and regulations, I would start a conversation with Neposedov on the theme, Why couldn't we find a way to do business without resorting to shady deals?

"What else can we do?" queried Neposedov, usually seeming puzzled at this question. He generally lacked the wherewithal to ask it, much less attempt an answer. Neposedov was too young to have experienced the olden days, and he wasn't even familiar with them from literature because he took little interest in anything beyond his own affairs and technology. The first time I asked this question, Neposedov tried to explain away the scandalous practices in the economy as bureaucratic red tape in the higher echelons and supply institutions, which would disappear with time, or else as due to individuals' shortcomings. Eventually, after pondering the matter, he guessed that the explanation went beyond all these issues; but he could not bring his conjectures to their logical conclusion because he lacked the necessary knowledge and breadth of experience.

Sometimes we quarreled vehemently, to the point that we did not speak to one another for several days. Instinctively trying to stifle a feeling of internal discord, Neposedov then threw himself into factory affairs, or if there was nothing to do there, he thought up something extraneous to occupy himself. Once, without rhyme or reason, he suddenly decided to reconstruct the water pipeline to the factory. The old pipe was coping with its job, the water supply for the plant and settlement was adequate, while new piping would require expenditures of 15,000 to 20,000 rubles. I protested resolutely: Why did we need a new water pipe? The ostensible reason for this brainstorm was absurd. Neposedov had discovered some kind of remarkable, powerful pump in the warehouse of the central board in Moscow and he was burning with the desire to try it out. The chief bookkeeper and I took a stand against this venture and categorically refused to finance Neposedov's folly. Neposedov blew up, we argued bitterly, and we did not speak to each other for about five days afterward.

In such situations, I generally dreamed up some business in Moscow and left. There I would drop in on Kolyshev, whose sympathy for the "working class" had so impressed me a year and a half earlier. We had become friends. Kolyshev lived in a settlement of dachas[7] that had long since ceased being suburban and had been included within the limits of "greater Moscow." Over a five-year period, Kolyshev and his fellow workers had built this little house, aided by our factory, which supplied the lumber at a discount. The house had two entrances leading into two separate apartments, each with two rooms and a small kitchen. Kolyshev lived in one of them with his wife and small daughter.

Kolyshev worked and studied a lot. Books were piled high on the shelves in his little room. On Sundays he made furniture. He had set up a workshop with a bench and a small woodworker's lathe. He dreamed of someday building a garret above his office-bedroom, when he had the money. Meanwhile, Kolyshev sawed, planed, and turned the lathe hour after hour, making shelves, whatnots, and frames to give his acquaintances. It was evident that this noble occupation provided him a respite from his factory work. We talked about this more than once.

"Just what are we supposed to do?" asked Kolyshev. "You and I cannot change this system. It is like a storm, a squall. Our job should be to preserve what can be termed inner decency and help others preserve it, at the same time creating something so that one's work is not entirely wasted. To preserve and create . . . that's all that's left us, in any case."

This was our only consolation, the North Star from which we took our bearings.

Humanity in Bedlam

I often went on business trips—to Moscow two or three times a month, or to Yaroslavl and Kalinin, where we also did business. This trips were mainly to get around the red tape in communications. If an urgent matter arose—and under Soviet socialism, as a rule, every matter is urgent, because the Kremlin tirelessly whips its subordinates into a frenzy—it was easier to go yourself than to write about something and wait weeks for a reply. But I also had other reasons for taking these trips. It was tedious to sit in the plant during slack periods. Moreover, after 1938, product shortages became even worse in the provinces, and business trips to Moscow were useful for replenishing supplies. During a business trip one received almost double pay, due to the per diem allowance and the allotment for living quarters. That was a big consideration.

But one also had to pay for this pleasure. Business trips were accompanied by major difficulties and were hard on the nerves. Only in the mid-twenties, in the NEP era, were the railroads able to cope with the passenger load. Later, the trains were crammed and a ticket could only be obtained with great difficulty. Millions of people were moving from place to place: one in search of better conditions; another on a business trip; a third going to a different job. Peasants went to the city to buy products; echelons of prisoners traveled under convoy to labor camps. Crowds besieged the train stations, and lines of hundreds or thousands stood at ticket windows. A certificate for a business trip conferred priority for procuring a ticket, but especially in Moscow, hundreds of people on business trips gathered at ticket windows and still spent hours standing in line. If you wanted to get around it, you had to strike a deal. Maybe you could give a railroad worker a tenner and he would buy you a ticket without standing in line, by going to the cashier directly, through the back entrance.

Finding a night's lodging in the cities presents another big problem. Having learned from more than one bitter experience, I was always ready immediately upon arrival in Kalinin or Yaroslavl. As soon as the train pulled in, I would jump out and rush headlong toward a hotel in order to show up first and grab a place. Often this didn't help, and I had to spend hours waiting for a room to be vacated. Kalinin had only two hotels, one then occupied by "Party activists," the other always overfilled. Yaroslavl also had two hotels, but one of them was half filled with permanent residents who worked for the regional Party committee. The socialist economy, which dispatched thousands of workers on business trips, could not possibly provide them all a night's lodging. People had to spend the night sitting on chairs in train stations or hotel corridors.

In Moscow, there was a Bureau for Allocation of Rooms for business travelers. It started out on Pushkin Street, then moved to Neglinnaya. Before I had acquaintances in Moscow, I used to rely on its services. I'd go straight from the train station to register there. A stamp and number, as high as 500 or 1,000, sometimes even higher, are put on your business trip certificate. Then you wait. If it takes half a day, or even all day, you're lucky; more often, you'll wait two or three days and still have no hotel room.

Approximately ten thousand people on business trips arrived in Moscow daily. Only about a thousand of them availed themselves of the services of the bureau, while the rest spread out among acquaintances. Hotels like the National, the Metropol, the Grand Hotel, the Savoy, and the Moscow were not under the bureau's aegis. Only foreigners, people in government service, or others with lots of money could get rooms there, as the average person could not afford their rates. Directors of big factories stayed at the Moscow, on the fifth or sixth floors, where a suite of two rooms, well furnished with rugs, soft furniture, and a bath cost 50 to 60 rubles a night. With luck and "knowing the ropes," you could sometimes arrange a stay in other hotels without using the bureau by slipping the doorman 15 or 20 rubles. Even under socialism, money remained a deciding factor.

People rushed about on business during the day, then pondered how to spend their evenings. They went to the theater or the movies, sat in restaurants until closing time. After this they dragged themselves to the Room Allocation Bureau, with its 150 chairs. People dozed off on those chairs or on the floor, and then went to work in the morning, unrested, with aching heads. Socialist Moscow would not coddle its workers who were building socialism in the provinces.

There was one other method of finding accommodation. I once returned to the bureau close to midnight, so tired that I dozed off. A fat fellow was seated next to me, struggling to stay awake but steadily nodding off. Leaning over so far that he almost fell off his chair, he moaned and turned to me: "I can't stand any more! Listen, why don't you accompany me? I need to sleep, but it's impossible. For two nights on the train I did not sleep. This is my second sleepless night in town, and I have no energy left. I am losing my mind. Shall we go arrange something?"

"Where?"

"To find some woman, just to have a good sleep." I declined. The fat fellow got up: "I am leaving. I can't stand it anymore."

Prostitution is of course forbidden, yet each periodic sweep of Moscow's streets nets more prostitutes, who are then dispatched to labor camps. Along Neglinnaya and farther down, along Teatralnyi, on Gorky Street and on Tverskoi Boulevard, you can't miss these female figures, some openly beckoning, some with embarrassed faces. Interspersed with the hardened professionals are petty laborers and service people with meager earnings, women who lack the resilience to live like paupers, constantly struggling with poverty. On the streets they make the supplementary earnings that the socialist government cannot provide for them. Among these streetwalkers one also encounters chic dressers, who generally target bigshots in responsible positions and go carousing with them in expensive restaurants. At the Bolshoi and other theaters one could also find fans with a keen appreciation for culture, who had no interest in the money for its own sake. A big city, even if it is termed socialist, remains a big city with all the ordinary urban defects, and you do not alter people through appellations and prohibitions alone. I do not know what category of woman my neighbor fell in with, but he did not return to the bureau that night.

There are two sides and two faces to everything. Soviet newspapers and lectures are full of bragging, self-satisfied declarations: "The Soviet people are conscious citizens of the country of socialism." "We lead cultured and prosperous lives." And the "conscious citizens," the youth, boozing and sucking on herrings in the evening, say in the morning, "Yesterday we got drunk in high style." How can these "conscious citizens" be "led to the recognition" that the expression "drunk in high style" is a monstrous, unheard-of profanation of culture?

The Kremlin's conductor urges, "Tempo, tempo!" while one waits for a tram, stands hours for a railroad ticket, and waits days for a room in a hotel. And inside the tram, which is crammed to overflowing, the female driver clambers onto a back bench in order to be visible over the heads of the passengers, vainly wailing: "Citizens, have a heart. Move a bit to the side, make way, I tell you. Oh, the devil take you, don't you have any shame at all?" But the bug-eyed citizens, packed together like sardines, cannot move a muscle to clear a path for her because they are exerting every effort to avoid being crushed altogether. Where can they go? They're stuck in the tram just as they are in the socialist cage, where even abuse no longer brings the desired reaction. Her nerves frayed by her job in that cage, the exhausted conductor, who may not be a bad person at all, is thus transformed into a socialist shrew.

The subway helps somewhat to relieve the congestion. However, when people are hurrying to work in the morning, sturdy police officers line up at the two entrances to the metro on Komsomol Square, using their elbows to channel the crowds through the doors. At this time of day, even the gigantic urban subway system cannot accommodate everyone. The socialist government cannot concern itself with giving its citizens adequate means of transportation, with providing them with the conveniences that would change people into "conscious citizens." It is too busy building socialism.

Meanwhile, the Kremlin summons thousands of "shock workers" and Stakhanovites to rallies. They live in the best hotels, with no need to worry for even a minute about food, lodging, or money. All this is provided them, and they actually live "prosperously." Be that as it may, they too are in a trap.

Even if you are not one of the Stakhanovites, you can still imagine yourself a citizen who does not feel trapped and can escape the abuse on the trams. For example, you can take a taxi—if you have the money, of course. Again, it turns out that only those with money can be citizens. But if this is the case, what kind of devil could term our life socialist!

One must also wait a half-hour or even an hour for dinner in an ordinary cafeteria. The waiters are rude and treat you as though you were their sworn enemy. But leave a good tip, and a rapid transformation occurs: The waiter will remember you, and should you return to that cafeteria, will throw everything aside and give you dinner immediately. In order to get a job in a busy cafeteria or restaurant, especially one where people drink a lot, Moscow waiters pay bribes as high as 2,000 or 3,000 rubles to the managers. Such is the underside of the socialist facade.

You can do nothing about it if you happen to live under socialism; you are stuck like the proverbial chicken in the soup pot. In the socialist bedlam, you must strive for just one thing: To hold onto a last shred, a semblance of humanity.

6

Sabotaged by Success

New Misfortunes

Before the revolution, my father worked for the same boss for almost forty years. He started as a youth and later became the owner's trusted agent, managing the firm's business independently for more than twenty years. Because of the way he did his job, he enjoyed unlimited confidence and respect, not only from the owner, but from his service personnel and workers. My father had never finished elementary school and was semiliterate. Later, he mastered fractions on his own. He became one of the outstanding experts in the lumber business in our region and was even recognized by the Soviet regime. To the old man's great embarrassment, the new authorities awarded him the honorary title of engineer—not knowing, of course, that he would not particularly welcome it.

My parents lived their entire lives in the city where they were born and where both sets of grandparents had lived till their deaths. In former times that's what almost everyone did: They were born and died near their ancestral burial ground, and they worked at the same jobs all their lives. People could live that way then because they submitted to the simple demands of integrity and conscientiousness. This is precisely what gave them the hope of living out their days calmly and in one place.

Living that way became impossible under socialism. Everything got confused and entangled, and as it turned out, the most important thing fell by the wayside—the knowledge of what it takes in order to greet each new day with confidence. How should one behave in order to gain that confidence? Integrity, conscientiousness, or even total submission to the authorities' every demand by no means guaranteed that on the next day you would not be fired from work for one reason or another, sent to work somewhere in the Urals or the Far East, or arrested, or face some other unexpected event that would pluck you from your locale, destroying your way of life along with all your plans, expectations, and hopes. Life lost its stability, its firm foundation. Everyone lived with constant, tormenting doubts: What would happen tomorrow, next week, next month? Making plans for the coming year was completely impossible.

Our plant functioned well for about a year and a half after we repaired the boiler, overfulfilling the monthly plans by 130–150 percent. Thanks to our great productivity, we accumulated about a million rubles of spare cash, and so we decided to create a small "director's fund." Although money could only be withdrawn from the fund according to precisely prescribed guidelines, it belonged entirely to the factory. The spare funds helped us to feel freer. The workers, receiving good wages, were heartened. The mood of everyone in the plant was pretty good, and it seemed that we need not worry about the future, which appeared cloudless. Yet more than once I caught myself wondering curiously about what fate might have in store for us. One could not believe that tomorrow would be the same as today, since we were living in a time that had lost all sense of permanence.

And so it happened. In 1938, at the end of the summer, we were notified by the People's Commissariat of Forestry that due to a reallocation of materials by the Council of People's Commissars, they would cease delivering timber to us the next year. As he read the notice, Neposedov's face fell. He rushed off to Moscow the same day, while I remained behind, feeling as though they had already slammed the door shut on our factory and our efforts. Our timber supply wouldn't last beyond January, and in our area no one besides the People's Commissariat of Forestry could deliver us the necessary raw materials. The factory might well have to close at the end of January. All our prosperity, built on the shifting sands of socialism, was being swept away by the wind.

Neposedov returned from Moscow as alarmed as when he had left. To keep the plant from closing, our superiors in the capital had decided to try to procure permission from the Council of People's Commissars for us to conduct our own logging operations. A plan was drawn up: We would harvest about 150,000 cubic meters of timber, which would include about 100,000 cubic meters of usable lumber and 50,000 of firewood—although good timber usually provided no more than 30 percent firewood.

I was beside myself. I had learned in the camps what a complicated, labor-intensive business logging was in our conditions. We had only two or three months left before the season started and no workers, horses, equipment, or funds whatsoever for logging. Only a child could expect all this to appear within the next two months. We did not even know where we would be logging because no specific territory had yet been assigned us for our operations. I voiced my doubts to Neposedov.

"We'll accomplish nothing if we give in to such thoughts," Neposedov objected, displeased. "You'd have us shut down the factory, then?! Either we start logging or we cease operating altogether, we've no other choice. So needless to say, we'll be logging."

"There is no fortress that the Bolsheviks cannot storm?" I grinned. Neposedov only shrugged his shoulders. I knew there was no way out; but it was equally clear to me that the prosperous little factory we had created, no thanks to the regime, would be destroyed. Now we too would be subject to the stresses, negligence, and shortages generally endemic to the Soviet system, and it would be a miracle if they didn't wind up suffocating us. As for Neposedov, he was still hopeful that better times would return to our factory someday.

Contrary to expectations, for once we received a quick decision from high channels, and within a couple of months we had been assigned an area to log. Unfortunately, the territory allocated to us was in two separate sections, half in Yaroslavl oblast on the Vilyuika River, about 90 kilometers from the factory, and half in a different direction, in Kalinin oblast on the Volchikha River, about 100 kilometers away. This complicated the situation because two separate sites demanded more service personnel, workers, and horses, and meant more trouble and operational expenditures. We still had none of the resources we needed in order to carry out logging operations.

We sent a request to the regional executive committee for workers and transport facilities, and Neposedov and I went to inspect our allocation on the Vilyuika. A forester led us deep into the woods to a thicket, the very appearance of which sent shivers down our spines. For as far as the eye could see on all sides, the forest was entangled and twisted in a sort of primeval chaos. Fragments of the tops of destroyed trees were wedged against other trees; others, cut off from their roots, either hung from their neighbors or lay on the ground, creating entanglements and barriers; young unbridled shoots embraced both healthy and dead trees. The resulting tangle resembled a wall in many places. To cap it all off, the thicket had many deciduous trees, which were entirely useless to us.

"Here's your section of the forest," the forester remarked. "Several years ago a storm came through here, so now this woods has to be completely cleared. Then we'll plant a new one."

Frowning, Neposedov was silent for a long time, then asked: "How much usable timber can we get from this mess? Ten to fifteen percent?"

"More than that," the forester objected. "If you take short, two- to three-yard pieces, as much as fifty percent."

"We'll be logging for a factory, and we don't need your short pieces."

"It's no concern of mine what you'll be logging for," replied the forester. "This is all I can give you."

It turned out that good timber, also designated for felling, was also available, but the Forest Protection Department was pursuing its own interests in this case: It had to get rid of the windfall. Later, with much exertion, again through Moscow, we managed to obtain another small logging plot with about 10,000 cubic meters, provided we remove the windfall. Neposedov cursed: "Let them remove it themselves. We'll fell what we need and then see."

The other section, on the Volchikha, had good timber, but there was another problem: On the Volchikha only selective felling of trees designated by a forestry agency was permitted. Out of twenty to thirty trees, only five or six could be cut down, so the logging had to be conducted over a huge area. We could not expect high productivity from our work force.

Our requests to the regional executive committee for workers were only half satisfied, while transport facilities were denied us entirely. Most horses and workers had already been assigned to the People's Commissariat of Forestry. "Supply your own means," the heads of both oblasts told us. But we did not have even a single horse for logging.

As to the warrants for a work force, we would be lucky if we got half of the workers "guaranteed" us: There was no labor surplus on the kolkhozes. We'd be lucky to have a quarter of the workers we had requested. Under these conditions, we hadn't a hope of supplying the plant with timber for the following year.

Neposedov wandered around, as tense and gloomy as a thundercloud. Summoning us to a meeting, he barely restrained a curse. "Well, here's the deal. We'll roll up our sleeves and squeeze out everything that we can. We are up against a wall, but we will be logging. We won't have saws, as their teeth will crack, and they won't give us horses. We'll take the whole job upon ourselves, with no refusals. And if this doesn't work, then . . . " He spread his hands wide and said no more.

Useless Agonizing

According to my plan for the logging operations, the timber would cost us three times more than that supplied by the People's Commissariat of Forestry.

This was understandable: The commissariat operated at huge losses, which were concealed by government loans. As self-producers, we would have no such subsidies. Where would we get the money for our logging operations?

We needed about four million rubles in order to purchase seventy horses, sleighs, equipment, riggings, and many other materials. We turned to Moscow with our demands, which the central board found justifiable but could not satisfy. It lacked the means to do so because, according to the regulations about accumulation, all spare monies of both the central board and the People's Commissariat of Forestry had to be quickly turned over to the People's Commissariat of Finance, which directed them to other branches of the economy. It was useless to turn to the Council of People's Commissars or the People's Commissariat of Finance with requests for the release of funds in the last quarter of the fiscal year, when all available resources had long since been distributed. No one would consider such a request. We could only hope to be allotted the necessary funds in February or March of the next year, as the logging season was coming to an end.

"Operate with what you have at the plant; mobilize all your resources," advised the central board. "We promise not to take even a kopeck from your factory."

This meant that we would be spending the factory's last cent, putting ourselves in a lousy position, and most likely winding up high and dry.

The snow was already falling, and we still had not a single worker in the forests. The kolkhozes would not release any people. Neposedov dispatched the factory's Komsomol members to recruit workers. At the same time, we sent Ginzburg requests for cheap tobacco, candy, and manufactured goods to be delivered to the forest, to entice people to work. Unable to count on the *kolkhozniki,* we pulled one shift from the plant and formed two brigades of loggers using our own workforce. We had no saws or axes, but Vasilev promised to get us some in two to three weeks. We collected all we could at the factory, from both blue- and white-collar employees. We went to the homes of local residents and bought saws, paying an exorbitant price for them. With all these efforts combined, we collected several dozen old, bent, worn saws, and sent the workers into the forest.

The cutting got off to a so-so start. But what was to be done about the hauling? We could not legally purchase horses because the acquisition of the means of production is financed through a bank from a special account, according to a special procedure that cannot be circumvented. Scheming in this case would be rapidly detected.

The central board tried to help, coming up with a Caterpillar tractor from one of its own factories. A skid was hurriedly constructed to transport it, and it was dispatched to the forest. About ten kilometers from the city, it got stuck: The block and tackle had ruptured due to heavy snow on the road. We scoured Moscow and the entire central region for a spare part, even tried a tractor factory in Chelyabinsk, but came up empty-handed. It turned out that the factory made no such spare parts. So our tractor spent the rest of the winter in a field, covered with snow.

Managing to get us six three-ton trucks from somewhere, the central board dispatched them to us with the order that we haul all our felled timber out within two weeks, which meant hiring two shifts of truckers. First, we had to find a dozen truckers, but truckers were extremely scarce. With great difficulty we located eight, but one look at them left us in despair: Two were juveniles, and another three were obviously confirmed drunkards who most likely had been fired from their previous jobs. As for the other three, we couldn't be sure, but they looked like a shifty bunch. Every enterprise valued its good drivers, so it was generally impossible to find good ones. You had to train your own, from your own workforce.

None of the drivers we found knew how to handle the wood-powered gas-generator trucks. More than a month passed while we trained the drivers, located other specialists, prepared a set of skids, and made a drying apparatus for the truck fuel.

A good six feet of snow lay blanketing the ground, so the roads were suitable only as paths for horse-drawn sleighs. The first truck we sent into the forest got stuck in the snow about three kilometers from town. We made a snowplow and sent it with a second truck. It, too, got stuck, because it was much too light for such deep snow. We sent a second snowplow with exactly the same result. We dispatched a brigade of workers from the factory to help out; they struggled with snow and metal for three days and moved the trucks all of three or four kilometers. It wasn't hard to figure out that spring would be upon us by the time our trucks reached the logging sites.

Neposedov ordered the trucks to return to the factory, once it became obvious that the ninety kilometers of snowdrifts could only be surmounted by building new roadways, which we were unprepared to do. It was evident that our trucks would not make it into the forest until summer.

Half of the season passed with our logging somehow limping along, although we had not hauled a single log out of the forest. It looked as though we might have to carry the timber out on our backs. We were saved from this by happenstance: In a regional office of the Horse Supply Bureau, Neposedov found twenty horses that were somehow unaccounted for in that year's plan. The bureau could not allocate them until the next year's plan took effect in spring, so it gave us the horses for temporary use, thus sparing the suppliers the expense of their winter upkeep.

The horses were emaciated and weak. It was obvious that the Horse Supply Bureau had fed them just enough to keep them from dropping in their traces. They had to be fed, but we had no fodder. Without the appropriate orders, one couldn't get so much as a gram of oats or hay, while a request for fodder had to have been sent in a half-year earlier, when we could not have anticipated having these horses. We were forced to buy hay at local markets from neighboring kolkhoz stocks, from individual *kolkhozniki,* or from various enterprises, wheedling them out of every cart load yet paying about ten times the official rate. The central board sent us several train-car loads of baled hay from one of its southern factories, and Ginzburg came up with two carloads of oats. We thus managed to feed the horses, while also acquiring harnesses and sleighs for hauling timber. After sending everything off into the forest, we heaved a sigh of relief. We had done what we could.

That winter, we exhausted ourselves and wore out both the foremen and the workers who were on the job in the forest. Neposedov's nose had shrunken to a blackened stump, and his eyes shone feverishly. Where his cheeks had been, he now had a taut, frostbitten rind. We forgot about preference, about all leisure. We rushed constantly from one timber site to the other, to neighboring villages and kolkhozes, to Moscow, Kalinin, and Yaroslavl, even forgetting regular mealtimes. We tried as hard as we could, but our efforts yielded pitiful results.

By spring, 12,000 cubic meters of logs lay on the upper reaches of the Vilyuika, and another 6,000 lay on the Volchikha, for a grand total of 18,000 cubic meters instead of the 150,000 projected in the plan. Only a miracle could have produced more. We were operating with less than one-fifth the necessary workforce and with twenty horses instead of seventy. The workers had not put in a full season, the horses less than half a season. Even with all our zeal, we could not accomplish more.

Drama on the Vilyuika

Eighteen thousand cubic meters of harvested timber would not save the factory, but we had to see the work through to the end. The logging season ended, the roads became impassable, yet the felled logs still had to be floated. Our requests for flotation workers were refused because field work had already begun on the kolkhozes. We enlisted about twenty fellows who were utter misfits in the workers' paradise and again mobilized our own factory workers.

The fact that we were not operating alone on either river complicated the flotation process. The Kalinin Forest Agency, which was operating on the Volchikha, had more than 100,000 cubic meters ready to go, and it was given priority on the river. From the Kalinin Forest Agency came the word that they would float their logs first. Ours would follow as a matter of course, and we would pay them for the work, thus freeing us from the trouble of floating our 6,000 cubic meters.

Things turned out to be more complicated on the Vilyuika. For a number of years the Moscow office of the Meat and Milk Production Trust had been logging near our site. It had felled about 20,000 cubic meters upstream from us and dumped this timber on the bank of the Vilyuika for shipment from the river's mouth to Moscow by rail. In contrast, we had to float our timber to the mouth of the Vilyuika and then build rafts for moving it an additional five kilometers along another waterway to our factory.

According to logic, the flotation ought to have proceeded as follows: We float our wood to the river's mouth first. Then the Meat and Milk Production Trust floats its logs and deposits them at the right place. That way, the logs would not get hung up along the river and both organizations would be satisfied. We proposed this to the trust but ran into unexpected intractability. Having been the only operator on the river in previous years, the trust declared that it did not wish to enter into discussions with anyone about floating and would conduct its flotation as it deemed necessary.

This was an absurd response that defied a time-honored tradition of conducting flotations according to logical sequence. If each operator conducts floating as he chooses, chaos ensues. In this case the river would get a jumble of 150,000 logs that could not be separated. Who would be able to tell which logs were ours and which were the Meat and Milk Production Trust's? Besides that, the Vilyuika [from the verb *vilyat'*, to wag] justifies its name: It winds in a spiral, tracing arcs and zigzags every two or three kilometers. Along the zigzags stood several mills and bridges that could easily be wrecked. Who would be held responsible for such damage? Since deciding whose timber had broken a bridge or a mill would be impossible in this case, a single operator ought to take on full responsibility for the flotation.

We tried to reason with the Meat and Milk Production Trust, but nothing came of our efforts. The trust refused to negotiate, plainly sabotaging us. Neposedov, who had several acquaintances in neighboring villages by then, had learned on the q.t. that the director of the Meat Trust's timber section once bragged in a drunken state that he planned to drag us novices on the river around by the nose. By taking advantage of the mixed flotation, he hoped to seize part of our timber.

We were furious. From an intractable partner the Meat and Milk Production Trust had turned into a bitter enemy that was encroaching on timber we had acquired by superhuman efforts! Obviously we were up against real schemers in the Meat and Milk Production Trust. We had to do something. Neposedov rushed to Yaroslavl and obtained a decree from the presidium of the regional executive committee stating that our factory was the main floater on the Vilyuika and that other organizations had to subordinate their flotations to us. The decree was sent to the Meat and Milk Production Trust at its main address in Moscow and at the timber site. As "Muscovites," the people at the trust must have considered themselves beyond the jurisdiction of regional institutions; they did not respond to this order. Neposedov obtained a second decree—with exactly the same result.

Spring would not wait, and the ice had begun to swell on the river. There was no time for another appeal to the regional executive committee. We sent workers to the river's upper reaches and placed others farther along its course. The Meat and Milk Production Trust also put their workers in place. Neposedov became furious and dragged in the district procurator, who sent several telegrams to the trust, ordering it to stop its arbitrary action and accept our conditions for the flotation. Neither we nor the procurator received an answer to the telegrams. Such blatant disregard was unheard-of even in Soviet conditions. The director of the Meat and Milk Trust's timber site was hiding out somewhere. His workers claimed that he had gone to Moscow and they could do nothing against his orders. Because the timber site overseer would never have left at such a busy time, it was obvious that we were dealing with malicious sabotage of our efforts to negotiate. The flotation would have to be conducted at random.

Using foresight, Neposedov ordered the measurement of all our timber by representatives of the local authorities, who would sign documents about the matter as disinterested parties. The ice thawed, the water rose, and we threw in our timber. The Meat and Milk Trust threw theirs in at the same time, and after several hours the logs were intermingled in a general muddle.

Detained at the plant, I left for the flotation only on the following day. Due to muddy roads, it was almost evening when we got to the Vilyuika. We stopped midway downriver, at a bridge just across from a large village. There a group of people blocked our way, warning us to proceed no farther because the bridge might collapse at any moment. I jumped down from the cart and ran toward the structure.

Nearly topping the high, hilly bank, the turbid, foaming waters of the swollen river rushed angrily past. Logs floating by in bunches and singly were hung up at the wooden bridge, forming a log jam. Hundreds of logs, entangled in a chaotic mass, rested against the bridge's pilings; the water, rumbling and turbulent, was beating against them. The bridge shook, trembling from the pressure. A crowd of curious onlookers stood on the opposite bank. Neposedov was gesturing wildly at the crowd, trying to explain something to a group of local authorities who had gathered around him.

I did not want to remain on my side, since if the bridge collapsed it would be impossible to get to the other side. I decided to cross on the bridge before it was too late. So as not to risk destroying a government horse, I told my driver to return to the factory, and then I ran full tilt to the other side. I felt very uneasy, running those fifty meters across the bridge as it swayed underfoot like some living thing.

Full of curiosity, the district authorities had all gathered around Neposedov. The president of the executive committee, the procurator, an NKVD agent, the police chief, and the secretary of the Party committee were all present. The workers of the Meat and Milk Production Trust were standing nearby, hooks in hand. Neposedov had warned our workers not to stand too near the bridge, explaining that we had enough workers there for now. One of the trust's foremen was also on the spot—people were pressing on the poor fellow from all sides. How could he permit the jam? Why hadn't he obeyed the authorities' order that our factory carry out the flotation? Completely at a loss, the foreman did not even try to defend himself, although he was only a subordinate and thus not responsible for this turn of events. Meanwhile, Neposedov was preparing the soil for the future, skillfully stirring up the district authorities against the Meat and Milk Production Trust.

Efforts to break up the log jam failed because it had formed in such a tightly enclosed space. The logs were so entwined with the bridge pilings that it was impossible to separate them out. Hundreds more were piling up by the minute, forming a monstrous pile at the bridge which only dynamite could dislodge. Cursing the foreman, everyone waited for the bridge to give way. It held about fifteen minutes longer. Then suddenly, with crashes and cracks like gunshots, it fell into the water and headed downstream. A pile of logs, its ends rising high into the air like the rigid proboscises of ugly monsters, crawled lugubriously downstream, crushing what was left of the pilings. Within minutes, nothing remained of either the jam or the bridge apart from the miserable wreckage spread along the bank.

"You'll disrupt the spring sowing campaign!" shouted the head of the district executive committee, deflecting the blame from himself and onto the foreman of the Meat and Milk Production Trust. "How will I get my deliveries of seed? Fertilizer?! A person can get himself shot for such goings-on!

Our district is remote, and the bridge was our only connection to the outside world. We'll be completely isolated, now!"

Neposedov was able to calm him somewhat by telling him that our factory, as the major floater on the river, would quickly pay the cost of restoring the bridge. All he need do was draw up a report. We went to the district executive committee, and the chief instantly drew up a document stating that the bridge had been destroyed during the flotation through the fault of the Meat and Milk Production Trust. The district authorities signed the document, and the Meat Trust foreman was thrown into a panic. By then, he was imagining all sorts of nightmarish scenarios.

The bridge cost 40,000 rubles. Neposedov phoned our plant and requested that this sum be sent to the district executive committee. We also sent a telegram confirming Neposedov's order in writing, following the chief bookkeeper's instructions.

That night Neposedov announced that two mills, farther downstream, also had been wrecked. We drew up reports showing that the Meat and Milk Production Trust was also responsible for the damage at the mills. Neposedov gave me heaps of documents: reports, copies of telegrams, and decrees with a multitude of stamps and the signatures of the local authorities—priceless material for convicting the trust and contributing to its future destruction. I sensed that despite the difficult battles over the flotation, Neposedov enjoyed gathering these papers together. His cheerfulness bespoke both his love of red tape and his thirst for vengeance.

In the morning came news of further trouble. Our foreman phoned from the mouth of the river to inform us that the Meat and Milk Production Trust had built holding booms, keeping our timber from reaching the river's mouth. Meanwhile, the first logs were already arriving at our holding booms, but as yet they totaled only 150–200 cubic meters. We rushed downriver, arriving at the mouth only toward morning of the second day because of the rough roads. By then, about 1,000 cubic meters had accumulated at our holding booms, but the great mass of logs, which was just beginning to approach the lower reaches, was being held back by the Meat and Milk Trust's holding booms. Neposedov flew into a rage. How dare they hold back our timber! Mustering dozens of workers and the flotation foreman, we raced to the trust's holding booms. One of our employees, Matveev, a broad-shouldered, energetic, able fellow of great physical strength and a fine forester, ordered the workers to bring their axes.

The Meat and Milk Production Trust had already established a complete system of holding booms. The main one, wide and strong, composed of eight logs, was so durable that it looked as though it had always spanned the river. Additional holding booms and pocket booms stood further upstream. The river was so choked with logs, it appeared that the Meat Trust had no intention of letting a single log drift downstream. Their workforce was already preparing to start hauling the trust's logs, while ours had not yet been stacked at the hauling area. The trust's holding booms had to be smashed. If we let too much time slip by, the river would dry up and flotation would be impossible. Our timber would be left sitting about five kilometers from the river's mouth, until autumn if we were lucky, or possibly into the next year. Meanwhile, how much of our timber would fall into the hands of the Meat and Milk Trust?

A few of the trust's workers and a foreman (not the fellow who had guarded the bridge) were standing on the riverbank. This foreman was an insolent fellow who fancied himself his own boss. Dispatching Matveev and some workers to the main holding boom, Neposedov flung himself at the foreman. "Why don't you release our timber?"

The tall foreman looked down on Neposedov and idly replied: "Oh, was it your lumber? We didn't know that. Your name wasn't written on the logs."

Neposedov almost croaked in rage and looked ready to box the foreman's ears. Turning, his face contorted, Neposedov yelled in despair, "Matveev! Chop up the holding booms!"

The foreman had not expected this: "Wait, stop! How can you chop up the holding booms? You have no right to chop up someone else's booms!" he protested in bewilderment.

"But you have a right to hold back someone else's timber? Chop, Matveev!"

Matveev and three workers were already busy destroying the thick hemp and bast ropes with axes. Sharing our excitement and indignation, our workers fulfilled their mission with ardor.

"Stop!" wailed the foreman of the Meat and Milk Production Trust, bursting to do something but at a loss in these unexpected circumstances. "Boys, over here!" he summoned his workers. About ten of them approached; carrying hooks, they appeared to temporize, ostensibly ready to support their boss yet seeming undecided. Our side also had hooks, and it was evident from our workers' faces that they would not mind throwing themselves into a fight, using the hooks to defend the property and honor of the factory. Perhaps the resoluteness on their faces explained the indecisiveness of the trust's workers.

Matveev had made quick work of the ropes, meanwhile. Opening like a gate, the holding booms moved aside, releasing a mass of logs downstream.

"Will you let out the timber from the upper holding booms?" Neposedov demanded of the foreman, who was still objecting. "If you don't, we will hack everything to hell! Matveev! Go to the upper booms!" Armed with hooks and axes, we moved toward them as a unified cohort.

The destruction of the main holding booms and our resoluteness had impressed the foreman, and his haughtiness deserted him. He ran after Neposedov, sniveling obsequiously that he was just a little fellow who had to do what his boss ordered. He asked us to hold up a bit. He would phone his boss and the holding booms would be opened. Neposedov was adamant: "I tried long enough to persuade your boss. You did not want to talk amicably; you wanted to take our timber high-handedly, to swindle us. You didn't come up against dummies. Against bandits we are bandits, too. Either release our logs or your holding booms will go flying to the devil right now."

The foreman had no choice but to start releasing the wood. That day, 8,000–9,000 cubic meters arrived downstream, but the trust's holding booms still had the rest tied up. At night they closed the booms again. A day later they raised a rumpus, turning to the NKVD and to the procurator whom they had not wished to recognize a week earlier, with a complaint against Neposedov for criminal destruction of their property. The district authorities knew that the Meat and Milk Production Trust was the original perpetrator and therefore did not call Neposedov to account. However, we were forbidden to destroy the holding booms a second time.

The trust finally agreed to delegate a representative for a joint inventory of the timber at the mouth and to supplement the inadequate amount it had released to us from its own holding booms. But we had other plans. While the talks were going on, Matveev gathered up about 500 cubic meters of logs and secretly floated them to the factory, so that they would not fall into the joint inventory. The trust thus lost hundreds of cubic meters of its own timber. We refused to feel guilty about our cheating: Let them pay for their despicable conduct and their dishonest intentions! They meant to steal from us; instead, we stole from them.

We managed at great expense and with huge difficulty to float our remaining logs to the river's mouth—about 1,500 cubic meters of them. The water had receded, leaving the timber stranded, so we had to drag it with hooks, log by log, five kilometers down the shallow stream. Floating these 1,500 cubic meters thus cost us more than had the previous 10,500.

We had similar bad luck on the Volchikha. After floating its own timber, the Kalinin Forest Agency neglected to fulfill its agreement with us, letting the water level drop so that half of our timber was drying up in the riverbed about 15–20 kilometers from the mouth. We fooled around with this wood all summer, floating it with the help of small dams that we had to build. It was difficult and expensive labor, and the 3,000 cubic meters of logs floated by this method were thus worth their weight in gold.

An Expensive Proposal

Having more or less completed the flotation, we took stock. Our situation was pitiable. The factory had no raw materials, the logging and flotation had eaten up all our funds, and we had nothing but debts. Something had to be done.

Our first step was to settle accounts with the Meat and Milk Production Trust. It would have to pay us the more than 100,000 rubles we had spent repairing the broken bridge and mills. We presented our demand, but the trust refused to pay, blaming us for the wreckage. We took the matter to court. Because we had well compiled reports, there was no doubt that we would get the money from the trust. But this seemed insignificant to Neposedov.

"According to an order of the regional executive committee we were the main floaters. Didn't we direct the floating?" he asked. "We did. So let the Meat Trust pay us for floating their timber. Present them a bill for flotation. If they don't pay, we will take this to the arbitration bureau. Didn't they hold back our wood and cause us extra expenses? They did. Let them compensate us for these extra expenses. And we still have to get a court order to get them to give up the rest of our timber, we mustn't let them stall and pocket the proceeds. Then, too, they might dig up the fact that we made off with their 500 cubic meters. In that case, we'll catch it from the arbitration bureau—you play tricks, my darlings, and you will most surely pay!"

Pointing out the logical inconsistencies in his argumentation, I took exception to all of these points save the last. If we had conducted the flotation and were responsible for it, then we were also to blame for destroying the bridge and the mills. In that case, we had no legal basis to demand repayment from the Meat and Milk Production Trust. As for verifying why and by how much we had overspent our funds, the arbitration bureau ought not to be involved in that matter. Including that factor would only complicate our suit and we might lose it. Furthermore, we would pay a huge court fee and could lose that as well.

It proved impossible to change Neposedov's mind: He thirsted for revenge and intended to deal the Meat and Milk Trust a heavy blow. Paying about 15,000 in court costs, we sought damages for more than 300,000 rubles. Knowing the system at the arbitration bureau, I drew up a one-page claim form and attached numerous estimates, reports, and copies of other documents to it. An arbitrator could see the basis for our figures and claims from the form without reviewing the documents, turning to them only for clarification.

The Meat and Milk Production Trust sent a five-page rejoinder. I was amazed: this from Muscovites, supposedly skilled in business matters and familiar with the system! The rejoinder was so long and written in such confusing language that no arbitrator would read it. And we would be appearing before the arbitration bureau of the Council of People's Commissars of the Soviet Union, the country's highest legal organ for deciding property disputes.

Property disputes between different institutions involving sums up to 1,000 rubles were reviewed in the regular people's courts. Departmental arbitration bureaus in each people's commissariat reviewed disputes between enterprises under their jurisdiction. Disputes involving 1,000–5,000 rubles between enterprises subordinate to various commissariats were decided in state arbitration bureaus of the regional soviet executive committees; disputes involving 5,000–25,000 rubles (later, up to 50,000) were reviewed in arbitration bureaus of the union republics; and disputes in excess of these amounts, in arbitration bureaus of the USSR Council of People's Commissars.

We had appeared before our departmental and regional arbitration bureaus on more than one occasion. Given the general disorder in the economy, many disputes arose. The typical institutional atmosphere existed in these arbitration bureaus. You could respond directly to an opponent or an arbitrator without constraint, defending your own interests and demonstrating that you were right. The arbitrators would not interrupt these arguments and they frequently investigated all the details. The atmosphere in the Council of People's Commissars of the Russian Soviet Federated Socialist Republic (RSFSR) is more official, and no one is expected to say much. Anyone should have been able to predict that in a higher court like the arbitration bureau of the USSR Council of People's Commissars, the loftiest of attitudes would reign; so we were prepared to be relatively quiet and unassuming.

Our hearing was scheduled for two o'clock. It was not without trepidation that we entered the waiting room of the state arbitration bureau, located in a wing of the GUM building[1] on Red Square that was occupied by the Council of People's Commissars. The office was silent and semi-dark, without the usual clatter of typewriters and multitude of employees. There was only a lone legal consultant to greet us. The representatives of the Meat and Milk Production Trust, headed by a slightly red-faced, middle-aged counselor-at-law from their Moscow office, were already there. Solidly built, with a paunch and a pince-nez, the legal counselor resembled an old-fashioned advocate or an actor made up to look young.

At exactly two o'clock we were invited into the arbitrator's office. Unpretentiously, with the air of the innocently suffering virtuous, Neposedov and I let the representatives from the trust go before us. They walked with an air of independence, holding their heads high. Neposedov nudged me in the side and almost burst out laughing, since he was aware that highly raised heads were inappropriate in that place.

The large office of the arbitrator was also dimly lit. A lamp with a green shade burned on a massive desk. Everything in the office was massive: the heavy leather chairs, the high-backed divan, and the inkstand on the desk; the big picture in a heavy gilt frame, which almost covered the wall behind the arbitrator's back; and the arbitrator himself, a flabby, bald man with a wide, oily face and large tortoiseshell glasses. He sat sipping tea and perusing the newspaper that lay before him, without even a glance at us. His face was sculptured in the mold of a Buddha—haughty, scornful, and tired at the same time. He looked as though he longed to be somewhere else, at some unattainable height, while his present surroundings were repugnant and bored him to death.

Soft, shaggy rugs muffled our footsteps as the consultant directed us toward chairs some distance from the desk, while he himself remained standing nearby. Looking intently at the arbitrator, he somehow divined that he could begin, and in a detached tone, he briefly laid out the matter. When he had finished speaking, he placed several papers before the arbitrator that evidently proposed a resolution to our case.

The arbitrator moved his glass of tea aside with one chubby white hand. Finally, he raised his indifferent face. Lingering a moment, he disdainfully inquired: "Why didn't the Meat and Milk Production Trust subordinate itself to the decision of the regional executive committee?"

The trust's legal counselor jumped up hurriedly and adjusted his pince-nez with a theatrical gesture. I had the feeling that this gesture would not please the Buddha. "We were unable to fulfill the order of the regional executive committee because the conditions of flotation on the river Vilyuika—" began the legal counsel, evidently prepared to speak for a long time.

The Buddha stopped him with a slight wave of his chubby hand: "Your arguments about the flotation do not interest me. I am asking why you failed to submit to the decision of the regional executive committee."

"We would gladly have obeyed if we had been able to obey," the legal counselor again proffered, smiling for some reason. "The flotation conditions made it impossible, since on the river—" With a displeased grimace and an impatient gesture, the arbitrator interrupted the trust's legal counselor. Evidently, he had no liking for the man.

"Enough. Write it up." Without turning his head, he addressed his consultant, who was scanning a piece of paper in front of him. "Damages for the destroyed mills and bridge are granted in full."

"But comrade arbitrator, we are asking you to look at the issue in all of its ramifications," the legal counsel said aggrievedly. "The documents presented against us are inaccurate and need to be qualified."

Extreme contempt, mingled with pain, appeared on the Buddha's face. His consultant then cut off the legal counsel with a warning gesture and a look, as if to say, "You must not provoke the deity."

"Fine the Meat and Milk Production Trust 25,000 rubles payable to the state for insubordination before an organ of Soviet power. Is there anything else?" the arbitrator mumbled indistinctly. The trust's representatives were stunned. Their legal counsel rose from his chair, attempting to say something, but with a stern look the consultant compelled him to return to his seat and proceeded to state our claims for the flotation fee and our other expenses.

"This does not concern me," objected the arbitrator. "Both were operating, both made the mess, so let both bear the expense."

Neposedov moved forward respectfully in his chair and asked meekly, "Will you permit me?" The arbitrator looked at him with dissatisfaction. Softly, as if speaking to a sick person, Neposedov continued: "We incurred heavy losses, comrade senior arbitrator, and not because we were at fault. Furthermore, the Meat Trust prevented us from getting our lumber, which lies in their harbor. Thus—"

The arbitrator interrupted Neposedov just as he had the trust's counselor: "You were delegated to direct the affair, so you also are answerable for your losses. I am unable to help you cut those losses. You should know how to operate." He then turned to his legal consultant, asking, "What about the timber?" The consultant explained.

"Write this down," said the arbitrator when the consultant had finished. "The Meat and Milk Production Trust shall turn the timber over to the factory, every cubic yard of it. Fine the trust an additional 25,000 rubles payable to the state for *partizanshchina*.[2] That's all." The arbitrator moved his cold tea closer and buried himself in his newspaper, instantly forgetting us. The consultant rose inaudibly from his chair, and with a gesture invited us to withdraw.

The trust's delegation left, perplexed and depressed, their legal counsel wiping the sweat from his brow. In the waiting room he recovered his senses and protested loudly: "We do not agree with this decision! We will appeal to the Council of People's Commissars!"

The consultant politely but firmly interrupted him, directing the group toward the exit: "I beg you to speak more quietly. We do not permit noise here."

Neposedov was bursting with suppressed laughter. Turning aside, he laughed into his hand, nudging me in the side and pointing to the Meat and Milk Production Trust representatives. When we exited onto Red Square, he gave full vent to his laughter. "Well, what a performance, a real performance!" he roared. "No need to go to the theater! 'Your arguments don't interest me,'" Neposedov mimicked the arbitrator.

"This performance cost us more than 10,000 rubles," I reminded him. "We only won one-third of our suit, so we will receive only a third of the amount we demanded from the Meat and Milk Production Trust. You and I paid the remaining 10,000 for the performance. Pretty dear, at 5,000 a ticket!"

"The devil take it," Neposedov brushed the matter aside. "A thousand more, a thousand less, it's all the same when we still have money coming to us. You saw how he burned the trust: fifty thousand! They got it in the back of the neck, my friend! Fifty thousand, as fast as a cow can lick you! Their business skills are weak at the trust. They're high handed, they don't see reality clearly. They really ought to take a lesson from that arbitrator—he grasps a matter and makes a decision instantly. He can handle anything!"

Old Acquaintances

During those years of my second life, the past occasionally was brought to mind by unexpected encounters. I was returning from a business trip once, dozing on the night train, when in the aisle opposite me a fellow stopped at the window and lit a cigarette. Through my stupor I sensed that there was something interesting about him. The round face, the beard—I felt that I had known him long ago and far away. But I could not be certain. I tried to imagine him without the beard, and my drowsiness vanished. I got up and approached him. Staring at me, the bearded man also seemed intent on retrieving a distant memory.

Many days have passed since the day when they arrested me, but I remember my arrest as if it were yesterday. It happened in the evening, so I spent the night in the GPU commandant's headquarters. In the morning, they took me to the train station and seated me in the compartment of some train or other. Only my two escorts and I were in the compartment. I was glad because I had not slept for three nights, and it looked like I might even be able to lie down on a bench and get a good rest. Nothing could have interested me more at the time. Just a minute before the train's departure, another fellow and his two escorts entered the compartment, which was now so crowded that I knew my dream of sleeping would not come true. They sat the second arrestee next to me and handcuffed us together, his right hand to my left. This done, the senior escort left and locked the compartment from the outside.

We were not allowed to converse but could only exchange sympathetic glances and smiles. My traveling companion also wanted desperately to sleep. Trying various positions, we found it best to rotate, taking turns sleeping on each other's knees, while the other fellow would rest his head against the back of the person in his lap. Companions in handcuffs, we rode in this way for about twenty-four hours to the capital. Once in prison there, we were uncuffed and lost sight of each other. A year later, I bumped into my traveling companion in a camp, then again lost track of him. Now here we were, near neighbors once more: The fellow who stood smoking at the window was none other than my companion in handcuffs. He had been released from camp at almost the same time as I and since then had knocked about from place to place, unable to find permanent work. I brought him to my place and helped him get established.

Another time, in Moscow, I left my hotel in the evening and headed down to take a walk along Gorky Street. I noticed a good-looking, stately military man near the Central Telegraph Building and approached him: "Comrade Bobrov?"

He was peering at me, too: "You look familiar, but I can't recall where I know you from. . . . "

"Remember Blue River? Camp Director Khrulev? I was your prisoner, but I escaped from there."

"Can it really be you?!" exclaimed the officer.

He had been the chief of the security forces at a camp that I had once escaped from. Not a bad fellow at heart, Bobrov had done much for the camp. In those remote places there was almost no work for the security forces, and he willingly helped with the economic situation, obtaining food, clothing, and shoes for the prisoners. Fortunately, this happened in one of the more liberal periods. I became well acquainted with him through this work.

We went into a restaurant and drank a bottle of wine, reminiscing about old times. "To this day I do not know how you managed to escape," remarked Bobrov. "You know, I mobilized as many of the local residents as I could for the search, and I myself walked for two weeks with two dogs in the taiga, in the mountains. I got into a hunter's frenzy, and you would have had a bad time of it if I had caught you! Where did you go?"

I told him.

"Yes, I was still in that area! I climbed around in those mountains for five days!"

"Now I remember," I smiled. "Once I noticed that there appeared to be a fellow with dogs on the opposite mountain, about eight to ten kilometers away. I thought I might be mistaken, but just in case, I began to hurry to put more distance between us."

"Where did they catch you?"

I told him I'd been apprehended in Siberia due to my lack of appropriate identification papers.

"Yes," corroborated Bobrov, "you can run, but you can't get away. There's nowhere to escape to."

"Well, at least we can drink a bottle of wine, and maybe more," I replied, extending my hands. Bobrov laughed, understanding.

We sat for about an hour, chatting like old acquaintances. I thought about how he would have shot me if he had spotted me back then and been unable to catch up with me. Now he was working with the security forces at another camp, in the Urals, and was away on leave in Moscow. In the new camp he guarded others exactly like me and pursued them when they escaped. Later he might meet up with them, too, as he had with me, and share a bottle of wine. He was exactly the same kind of worker and functionary as I, with no free will. He was unable to leave his job, just as I was unable to leave mine; a multitude of circumstances prevented it. Neither of us wished the other evil, as we realized that neither of us had control over any of these matters.

I had yet another such encounter with a person from my past, this time at the factory, which made it difficult for both of us.

Our factory had one foot in the grave. Processing the next 18,000 cubic meters of timber, even if it all came at once with no problems in flotation, would take no fewer than three months. We could afford to operate only with one shift, and that with breaks. There was no money. The central board had ordered us to "spare no effort to obtain windfall resources." We tried to intercept every hundred cubic meters from other organizations operating in our district, in order to increase the workload at our plant. A year ago, Neposedov had thrown representatives offering bribes for our services out of the factory; now, we were ready to offer bribes ourselves, if only the taker would supply us with timber. But "windfall suppliers" of timber yielded only about 200–300 cubic meters, enough for three or four days' work. And there were few windfall suppliers.

One day, Neposedov came to me and said: "Some rich traders have arrived; it smells like a major deal. Be on your guard. We can't afford to blunder. Get the plan and come on."

Some representatives from the NKVD's Volga Construction had come to negotiate about the factory's sawing up about 100,000 cubic meters of timber for them. They were sitting in Neposedov's office. One of them was Seletsky, a tall, puffy fellow who was the Director of the Lumber Division of Volga Construction. I had gotten to know him at the camp on the Solovetskii Islands. A former military officer, he also had been a prisoner there, and worked as director of lumbering. His name alone produced terror in the other prisoners, who knew that if they wound up working in lumbering operations it could mean their death. Seletsky never beat or killed anyone himself, but he often got drunk and indulged in debauchery, turning a blind eye at such times to the cruelty of guards and foremen, most of them criminals who mercilessly beat and killed the convicts working as loggers. If you could catch him sober, Seletsky at that time was a dashing fellow, in the prime of manhood.

Now a crumbling wreck, the nearly voiceless old man was sitting in the office, coughing. Seletsky sat there, bantering and cracking jokes like the good-natured, dissipated landowners of a previous era. His assistant, an assertive and boorish middle-aged fellow, dominated the business aspect of the conversation, making impossible demands. They could not supply us with timber for processing, and they would furnish their own personnel. The upshot was that almost nothing would remain for us to do in the factory, and we would have to let many of our workers go. We rejected their demands. Seletsky's assistant pressed us, not cajolingly but in a demanding and even threatening manner. Employees of the NKVD were accustomed to negotiating in commanding tones. Neposedov, not in the habit of subordinating himself to just anyone who came along, remained obdurate. A fight seemed imminent when the Volga Construction representatives announced that they would seize the plant. We were not easily frightened, and we felt we had nothing to lose because the negotiations clearly had failed.

We were not afraid of these fellows: They were only economic NKVD personnel, not political agents. They could give orders in their domain, in the camps, to prisoners who had no rights, but we did not see ourselves as subordinate to the demands they presented to us. Seizing a factory was not so easy. First, the Lumber Division of Volga Construction would have to bring a petition before the director of the camp; the latter, before the NKVD's General Directorate of the Camps [GULag]; and the GULag, before the Council of People's Commissars. This bureaucratic ladder had many rungs that were not easily surmounted. If they skipped even one, their attempt to seize our factory would fail.

A week later, Seletsky's assistant visited us again, this time with a more accommodating attitude but with the same unacceptable demands. We again refused. During his third visit a week later, he displayed a friendly attitude toward us and accepted our conditions. But it turned out that they would supply only 20,000 cubic meters instead of the anticipated 100,000. The NKVD bluffed like nobody's business.

We accepted the 20,000 cubic meters, but this too was insufficient. We had to let go an entire shift of workers and part of our white-collar personnel. Many could not find other work in our town and had to leave their homes of many years. Those who remained were again getting low wages, almost the same as two years before. There were no prospects; the factory was slowly dying. We had become a "kingdom of sleep," in Neposedov's words, with a despondent, hopeless mood pervading the place.

I asked Neposedov, "Maybe we should change jobs and transfer to another spot?" But Neposedov had become accustomed to the plant—it was his baby, and he could not imagine abandoning it. He was sad, but he had not lost the hope of better times ahead. "I will not detain you in this graveyard," he answered. "You want to go. Leave. I won't take it amiss." So I quit.

I had had enough of provincial life, and it was time to move. I decided to go to Moscow.

7

Storm Clouds
Gather

By this time, I already had many acquaintances in Moscow: There was Koly-shev, and my fellow employees at the central board and the People's Com-missariat of Forestry, and I had even run into two of my former school-mates. One of the latter, Lapshin, who was my age and had graduated from the military academy, was now a major and working at the Red Army's gen-eral staff headquarters. He had joined the Party five years earlier and was now unable to leave it; only a convict could quit the Party. Lean, restrained, and cautious, Lapshin knew Marxism-Leninism inside out and was regarded as an exemplary, even an active, member of the Party organization of the general staff. Internally, however, he was an anticommunist. His outward coolness concealed the same ardent seeker that I had known in my youth, and we were able easily to resume our fast friendship.

Lapshin had a small circle of close friends, brought together by their love of literature and their anticommunist leanings. This circle included his col-league at the general staff, a colonel; another colonel who taught at the mili-tary academy; and a military engineer from the same academy. All three were Party members. A couple of non-Party military men also came on occasion. They rarely all got together, but one often found a couple of them spending the evening at Lapshin's large three-room apartment in a huge building be-longing to the People's Commissariat of Defense.

This circle was by no means a group of conspirators, nor even of people with the same viewpoint. Yet it somehow happened that during our conver-sations on the most innocuous of topics, certain themes reappeared that united us in a single sentiment. An eavesdropping bystander might easily have accused us of anticommunism; our remarks and the tones of our voices were full of it.

My other former schoolmate, an engineer, worked in the People's Commissariat of Heavy Engineering Industries. He also had a group of friends, likewise drawn together by a common sentiment. A third group regularly gathered at the home of one of my cousins. Her husband was a film director, so theater and movie people, artists, and writers regularly visited them. I used to drop in on one or another of these circles, which were composed not so much of shapers of the mood in the country as of partakers of that mood and one or another of its vibrations. The circles did include a number of people who played a role in forming public opinion, but these individuals were merely following the orders of the authorities. These people did not belong to the narrow circle of plotters sitting in the Kremlin, seeking complete mastery over the country. They were, however, among the masters' administrators at the highest echelons of the Party and the government. Their role in the country was great, but at the same time it was insignificant.

The announcement of the pact between Stalin and Hitler struck us all like a thunderbolt. Out of four million Muscovites, perhaps only a thousand knew that Ribbentrop had flown to Moscow and was closeted in negotiations at the Kremlin. In stark contrast, everyone knew that representatives of England and France had visited the capital and that talks were going on with them about a union against Hitler, who was officially characterized as our primary and most evil enemy. What a shock suddenly to be informed that we had signed a pact of friendship with him! This turn of events stunned everyone. We were all so bewildered for the first few hours that no one could collect his thoughts. I spoke with Kolyshev that day. "They are concocting a big mess in the Kremlin," he observed. "I sense that we will have to tighten our belts." Alarm rang in the voice of this normally calm, collected person.

In the evening I met with Lapshin. Usually slow to react, he too was alarmed. "We are taking a final, decisive step. By betraying the 'capitalist countries,' Stalin is unleashing war in Europe. Meanwhile we will remain on the sidelines and arm ourselves. When the hour arrives, we will strike such a blow that Europe will never recover. An old strategy, based on the long-range view."

"We will strike against whom?"

"Against whomever happens along and turns out to be weakest. To us it doesn't matter because they are all our enemies."

"But will the blow be strong enough, given our frame of mind?"

"Time will tell. If we attack the weakest, any blow, regardless of our frame of mind, will be shattering."

The shift was so unexpected that the authorities decided not to use the customary method to explain it to the population. A propagandist from the regional Party committee came to our factory for this purpose. At a general factory meeting he simply, ably, and enticingly, without any shrill, propagandistic phrases, pulled aside the curtain that had screened the talks with Ribbentrop along with other current events in European diplomatic circles. Much of what he revealed was unknown to anyone apart from a small circle at the top and had not been mentioned in the press. He discussed Munich in more detail than did the newspapers, revealing to us that Ribbentrop had brought along a secret tape recording of conversations between Hitler and Chamberlain, even quoting to us from the transcript. The excerpts indicated that western Europe was giving Hitler a free hand in the east and would not protest the separation of the Ukraine from the USSR. The propagandist conveyed a number of other tidbits that supported this story. He drew no conclusions, leaving that to his listeners. His inference, however, was obvious: Stalin had no choice but to break off his negotiations with the western powers and sign an agreement with Hitler.

This presentation made a great impression. None of us could be certain how much of it was true and how much was fabricated; however, even those people who were not at all inclined to believe the authorities seemed completely incapable of disbelieving them in this case. The duplicitous, self-contradictory politics of Munich was staring us in the face: Austria and Czechoslovakia had been betrayed, so why would England and France observe any agreement with us? The ordinary person was inclined to believe what the Politburo was pushing on him—"English cunning," all over again.

Many in the audience were flattered by the ingratiatingly confidential nature of the information. Here was the Kremlin, communicating to the people about matters that were not even discussed in the newspapers! Given this confidentiality, people unversed in political subtleties and accustomed to being ignored felt as though they had brushed up against the invisible web of the powers that be, and as it were, even touched them. At decisive moments, when the fate of the motherland is at stake, the authorities turn to the people and take them into consideration. This confidential information was but an early foreshadowing of the appeals to the populace that the authorities would later resort to during World War II.

Hitler's attack on Poland and the outbreak of war in western Europe intensified this popular mood even more. Our march into Poland was evidence that Stalin was using this opportunity to initiate a grandiose plan of communist advancement, which could unfurl in various ways. At a time like that I did not want to remain in a dying factory, and I was drawn closer to "great politics." I talked it over with Kolyshev.

"Yes, just what is there for you to do in the factory?" he concurred. "Come to us. One of my employees was drafted; take his place."

"And what about registration, living quarters?" If one was not a Muscovite, moving to Moscow was an exceptionally difficult matter. Permission could only be obtained through special dispensation by the people's commissariat.

"We will arrange a transfer through the people's commissariat and register you in our factory in Losinka. For the time being you can live in our dormitory in Ostankino; somehow we will find you a room there. Then get situated and register in Ostankino. Agreed?"

Some time later, I left for Moscow.

Anticommunists Building Communism

In my life after the camps, I had met few Party members. Of five hundred people in the plant, only six belonged to the Party. The most visible of these was Neposedov: The Party organizer, the president of the factory committee, and the three others, all workers, were entirely ordinary people. Likewise, about two hundred people worked at the central board, eleven of whom were members of the Party. So while the percentage of Party membership was higher in Moscow, the small number of members meant that they could exert no particular influence over our affairs.

What is more, I almost never met members of the Party whose views and mood were sharply distinguishable from mine. For instance, I never chanced to meet anyone about whom I could say, "This is the ideal communist." You came across stupid bootlickers, like the director of the All-Union Fish Trust, who had fired me more than two years earlier "for concealing my past," but they were few. Many were careerists, openly grasping self-seekers. There were those who fell into Party membership more or less by chance. One often met young Komsomol members trotting about on their high horses. Not one of them could be described as above average. They were all prototypical Soviet professionals, or speaking in more general terms, *intelligenty*.[1] This average type was akin to the likes of Neposedov, Kolyshev, or Lapshin in that they shared an uncomplicated philosophy toward life and work in Soviet conditions: Subordinate yourself to the authorities, but do not forget to look out for yourself and insofar as possible, for your fellows. The ranking of these three principles could be changed: In certain cases, one of them could take on greater significance, with another being given less weight or none at all; then when circumstances changed again, the original ranking might be reinstated. Even among the frankly greedy and careerists one now and then encountered a desire to attend to the third principle, which even Bolshevism could not eradicate from the Russian breast.

Former counterrevolutionary and camp inmate that I was, I remained a staunch anticommunist. The attitudes and views of my friends were the same as mine. Meanwhile, we were under an authority that frankly declared its aim of establishing communism. We subordinated ourselves to that authority, fulfilled its orders, and thus gave it the chance to claim that it was "one with the people." The devil it was!

Russians always have understood that this "community of the Soviet power and the people" is just a facade under which popular opposition to the authorities is concealed. People have no choice but to submit: They need to work, and they must work for the state because everything is subordinated to the state, and beyond it, to the immensely powerful Politburo. Thus, by working, you already "support the authorities." You are connected to your people and your motherland by thousands of strands. You want to share the life of your community and help the country, but you can do so only through the state. Thus it turns out that you are connected by thousands of strands to a regime that is building communism. How can you escape it? How can you remove, break, or destroy this diabolical facade so that everyone can stand on his own two feet?

Fear was not the primary obstacle. Man cannot live by fear alone, and so we did not live in constant fear. We knew there were NKVD informers among us, but we usually recognized and avoided them, and they did not evoke much fear in us. Generally speaking, there was an unspoken taboo on several topics, and these were not raised among strangers. Everyone knew that the Lubyanka[2] was in Moscow—that was reason enough to conduct oneself cautiously and circumspectly.

Nonetheless, scathing anti-Soviet jokes would spread through Moscow within a mere two or three days and be heard in the offices of Party executives and others, in homes, in shops, and on the street. It seemed the all-powerful NKVD could not prevent this from happening. Never once did such an anecdote evoke indignation or revulsion in anyone. People merrily amused themselves at the expense of the authorities, again revealing a common sentiment. But while laughing, they proceeded to fulfill their orders.

Once, over Sunday dinner at Ginzburg's, we were discussing new literary works with his son, a *politruk*, or political leader for a company of the Moscow garrison.[3] I praised Kaverin's "Two Captains," which had just appeared in one of the larger literary journals. The *politruk* grinned: "Say, have you read Solovev's 'Indignant at the Calm'? It appeared in *Roman-gazeta (Novel-Gazette)*. Read it—it will amuse you!"

I obtained "Indignant at the Calm" and read it. Masked as a portrayal of Bukhara in the Middle Ages, Solovev presented such a clear satire on conditions in the Kremlin that I was simply amazed that a *politruk* who was responsible for indoctrinating Red Army men into the spirit of communism had recommended such a book!

The Soviet citizen lived as have citizens always and everywhere, quietly gloating, chuckling, or bristling with indignation, giving the authorities "the finger in the pocket." People might be frightened, but they never forgot about themselves or neglected their primary task of obtaining a crust of daily bread. The few who were capable of reflection as well as indignation were unable to answer the question: How can we change our way of life?

The cultural level of people in Kolyshev's and Lapshin's circles and of my other Moscow friends was immeasurably higher than Neposedov's, but they did not have the answers either. The ugliness and inhumanity of the socialist order were clear, but none of us wished to recognize it. We realized that the previous epoch was over and that life had been irrevocably displaced from its traditional foundations. What could, or should, happen next? The destruction of the past, in which we were not only witnesses but also direct participants, was instinctively and stubbornly opposed by millions. Peasants, workers, and the intelligentsia were defending their own existence as well as much of the past, and thousands, even millions of them, had given their lives for it. Obviously, much more was at stake than merely the old, the stale, and the obsolete. Eternal values, without which people cannot live, were under threat. What from our past was eternal and ought to be preserved, and what could or should be discarded as trash that impedes progress? In the new conditions, how should manufacturing and agriculture be organized so as not to revive the obsolete, while more fully satisfying both the requirements of the people and the needs of the state? How should the state be administered so that it would not be despotic, yet would still maintain order? What about public values? Which values should be modified and which preserved? A multitude of questions certainly demanded answers. Without those answers it would be impossible to move forward.

Some of these questions were formally resolved by the "Stalin constitution" and by Soviet regulations in general, which actually further obscured the reality—a reality that sharply diverged from the model. Who could guarantee that other institutions that we viewed as just would not turn out like those already in place in the Soviet system? How could fine words written on paper be converted into a decent system in their implementation?

Finding answers to such questions in tiny circles of three or four people was impossible. At best, each circle had its own answer. Although many similar thoughts and desires "were floating in the air," without a free exchange of opinions it was impossible to gather them together and reduce them to a system that could be put into effect. Apart from our dissatisfaction, criticism, and negation, we had no ideas that could become a driving force with which to oppose the authorities.

We tried to see beyond our borders but were unable to grasp what was happening outside the Soviet Union. We had no doubt that things were also bad there, having been convinced of this by renowned writers, scholars, and public figures who came to us on pilgrimages from the West and who—so we thought—could not be deceived by Soviet propaganda. If everything was fine in the West, why did they come here seeking something better?

Romain Rolland, Lion Feuchtwanger, the two Webbs, and many others frequently made enthusiastic comments about what they saw. We were puzzled as to what evoked such raptures. Was this captivation the result of an inexplicable blindness, or was there actually something bad in the West that was unknown to us, an evil that eclipsed even our own ugliness? It was hard to believe the latter, since accepting it created an obstacle to our faith in the West.

Yet we were unable not to believe in the honesty and sincerity of many of the visitors. When André Gide arrived, we hadn't the slightest reason to suspect him of bias. Upon his return, Gide came out with a book, *Return from the USSR,* after which the Politburo revised its view of him, from friend to bitter enemy. But only the few who had access to forbidden books could know what displeased André Gide. Once again, the majority had no criteria on which to arrive at independent judgments.

Discontent with the system was everywhere, but not enough links existed to utilize it to attack the authorities. In the name of what? Toward what kind of concrete order? What goal would suffice to arouse the people? However, even the absence of a guiding idea was not a deciding factor in our subordination to the authorities. Sometimes Lapshin and I conversed about such themes over a bottle of wine. "Imagine that an insurrection flared up in Moscow," I began.

Lapshin smiled scornfully and said: "Hm. And in just what form? Describe it."

"Insurrections have already occurred in the provinces. Why couldn't one happen in Moscow? Not an actual revolt, but let's project one in theory. The revolts in the provinces were put down with force after troops were dispatched from other districts. That's the official explanation. The incidents happened far from the center and could be explained as 'intrigues by enemies of the people.' But here in Moscow, if the workers of the Ball-Bearing Works or the Stalin Works rebelled and the populace joined them—would the Red Army fire on them?"

"Why not? An order would be issued and they would shoot."

"But what could be done to prevent them from shooting?"

"For a Red Army man to refuse to fire, he must know that others will not fire either. And all of them would need to know exactly why they risked disobeying an order. A leader is essential, a commander who also must understand the cause and believe that others will support him. But today a leader can neither turn to his own Red Army troops nor make contacts with other commanders, because he is surrounded by political soldiers, secret agents, and KGB operatives. Given these circumstances, why would any commander defy orders by refusing to issue an order to fire?"

"Does that mean it's hopeless?"

"Totally, while there is such lack of unity that we are unable to join together around a general aim. While there was still a Tukhachevsky,[4] a well-known and authoritative figure around whom people could unite, we could hope. But now we must wait for the chance to form an organization, or for some person, ideas, or events that could overcome the disunity and rally the people."

That was how all such conversations ended: We had to wait. We inveterate anticommunists talked the evening away in this fashion, while the next morning we were once again burdened by work routines that had the single aim of building communism.

The Communist Yoke

I once jokingly defined the tempo of our life as follows: Deep in the provinces, in the villages and towns, people stroll about sleepily, at the speed of turtles. In regional cities people walk, but in Moscow they run. Arriving in the capital from the provinces, one is amazed by and caught up in the noise and bustle. You run around frantically from morning until evening and only have a chance to catch your breath at night—unless you fall asleep immediately after throwing yourself on the bed, drained of all energy. The constant feverish activity in Moscow makes it seem that Muscovites never rest, by day or night.

Nevertheless, I am convinced that this frenetic activity is nothing but a fiction. Only the Kremlin worked feverishly, only the Kremlin had a clear goal, in the name of which it goaded us on. But our feverish haste was only a response to a fired-up Kremlin, not a genuine fervor.

On the surface there is a great deal of turmoil, business-like activity, and animation. You cannot arrange a meeting with anyone in a responsible position because they are always busy, constantly attending meetings, which frequently end after midnight. But people in responsible positions also show up at work as much as two or three hours late, sometimes arriving at their offices in the afternoon. People who don't have responsible positions do not hurry either, and it is a rare person who shows up for work on time. Moreover, with a little effort one's duties can be organized to allow plenty of free time. Over the course of the day it's possible to chat with one's coworkers, stroll the streets, or drop into a store. Feverish activity is also applied to non-work-related matters.

We had about a hundred plants, factories, and shops, and several all-Union bureaus that produced, manufactured, and distributed construction materials under our central board. It was our responsibility to manage and control the operation of these enterprises. However, they functioned under annual planning directives based on fixed periods, so we were merely an intermediate link between the factories and the higher authorities, carefully keeping records of the orders and responses that passed through us. This record keeping occupied several days at the beginning of each month and of each year. The rest of the time, we somehow "regulated" the enterprises under our jurisdiction, plugging the gaps that constantly appeared. Stopgap measures were also dependent on orders, such as allocations under the plan, and didn't take much time either. So it turned out that many people in Moscow were busy with productive labor approximately half of the time. The rest was spent in mindless busywork or outright idleness.

Such activity was nothing but concealed sabotage, a result of the fact that no one could answer the question, Why are we working? The Kremlin was working for communism, while for us communism had a hollow, negative resonance. The only stimulus for work was pay, material well-being, although many like Kolyshev made an additional effort to create something valuable in spite of everything. Because Soviet life is poor and unstable, allowing no hope for achieving material prosperity, this stimulus also turns out to be fragile.

Toward the end of the 1930s, tardiness at work, truancy, and instability took on disastrous proportions for the offenders, being characterized as "concealed sabotage." Many enterprises hired and fired many more workers than their operations warranted, turning over their staff two or three times in the course of a single year. In 1940, the regime issued decrees forbidding voluntary transfers from one enterprise to another and establishing penalties for tardiness and truancy. We had to sign in on special sheets upon arrival at work, and the sheets were collected promptly at ten o'clock. Latecomers could expect punishment, including imprisonment. The authorities had to compel us to work harder. But the decrees did not have much benefit: We began to come on time but to merely sit out the prescribed number of hours, giving the appearance of being busy.

There was no reason for enthusiasm. We were building plants, factories, new towns. But what were they giving to the population or to the country? And they could have been built by normal methods, without hysteria and sacrifices.

One of my closest coworkers was one Pospelov, a thin, withered fellow with a tired, sorrowful face. A remnant of a bygone era, Pospelov had graduated from Moscow University before the revolution, then had gone abroad for further study. He was a broadly educated and highly cultured man. For many years he had worked in the Central Statistical Bureau. Then almost its entire staff was arrested for "sabotage" connected with the 1936 census,[5] which had revealed a decrease in the population as well as a general lack of cognizance of socialist progress. Pospelov, too, was arrested, but he was a low-level employee in the Central Statistical Bureau and thus was released after half a year. Through his acquaintance with Kolyshev, he got a job with us as a statistician. Pospelov worked conscientiously but without the slightest interest, appearing to be subtly and sadly amused by his work and by Soviet life in general. He referred to himself as "doomed," having found no viable niche for himself in the Soviet system and having decided that the system itself could not be modified.

Pospelov lived in a large building on Novinsky Boulevard, where he had a closet-sized room. This building was slated for demolition in the plans to renovate Moscow. Pospelov had told us that he would not be provided new quarters when they started demolishing his building. Residents of the building had been given only about two thousand rubles each by way of compensation, although it took at least ten thousand rubles to rent a room in Moscow. Many of the displaced made arrangements to stay with relatives or acquaintances or left for the provinces. Some joined up with others and built shanties on land that had been allotted for private construction in the suburbs. None of the apartment building's former residents were assigned rooms in the new buildings, which were occupied instead by Party members, other "notable individuals," or people decorated with orders, frequently from the provinces. The authorities were inundating Moscow with people whom they considered more faithful. Large, new buildings on Gorky Street were almost entirely inhabited by the military, including participants in the battles at Khasan and Khalkin Gol.[6]

One summer day in 1940, Pospelov did not show up for work. At noon we learned that he had hung himself in his little room the evening before. When he arrived home from work that day, he had discovered a notice in his room containing an order to move from his building. Rather than be subjected to another ordeal, Pospelov had ended his life.

I was also close to another coworker, inspector Vinogradov. An elderly, educated, and cultivated man, Vinogradov was impulsive and easily carried away. His ardor led him to believe that there was still room for hope and that one could still work productively. He was often captivated by some project, and then he bustled around excitedly, giving it everything he had. Frequently his efforts were in vain or yielded such insignificant or distorted results that he fell into despondency. He lacked the calmness, patience, and persistence of a Kolyshev, or the agility of a Neposedov, that were so necessary in order occasionally to surmount or outflank the iron barriers thrown up by commands from above. Vinogradov would then cool down—until he was overtaken by his next obsession.

Watching him, I thought, he's our entire Soviet workforce in microcosm. Here and there, now and then, someone will suddenly break out of the pack, get lathered up, and work with a frenzy. After awhile, such impassioned workers will encounter an insurmountable barrier, which usually dampens their enthusiasm. The rest turn into bureaucrats, mechanically recording "hitches" and somehow patching up "defects" that cannot be eliminated. Regular, orderly work does not exist, but neither do the conditions conducive to creativity. A creative outburst unavoidably rams up against some command or other, or is countered by the desire of the authorities to squelch it and inevitably cools off.

Even Neposedov, whose vigor seemed inexhaustible, became mired in such troubles. During one of his frequent visits, I saw that he had changed beyond recognition: He was completely withered and had dark shadows under his eyes. The bantering and confident ardor in his glance had become an unpleasant, malicious smoldering. Affairs at the factory had gone from bad to worse. Once again, the plan for timber production was only half fulfilled and there was no money or workers. His car had long since broken down and he had stopped working on it. I sensed that Neposedov also had undergone an internal metamorphosis. Before, he had not exactly been a communist; now, he had become an anticommunist.

Neposedov had lost his faith in technology and no longer deified it. He seemed finally to have understood that more than technology was needed. And he was no exception. I often encountered people who had lost their faith in the omnipotence of technology. At the end of the 1920s and the beginning of the 1930s, most young people were captivated by technology, and many worshiped it. By the end of the 1930s, however, the love of many captives of the machine had turned to scorn. Perhaps people had become satiated with their infatuation and understood that they themselves could rule over technology instead of it over them. Possibly they felt dissatisfied or degraded by their love for the "inanimate mother." For example, I met a number of chauffeurs who knew their job well yet regarded their vehicles with total scorn. Yet, ten years earlier, these same people had been as much in love with these machines as Neposedov was with his "little M."

It was Neposedov's misfortune that he could not maintain a calm and even temper. Fearing he would end in disaster, Kolyshev and I were frankly worried about him, but our efforts to influence him were to no avail. Neposedov still believed in his own strengths. It seemed to him that he could still master complicated situations, and he was incapable of becoming just a bureaucrat. He was asking for trouble, risking expulsion from the Party, the loss of his job, and possibly a prison term. He refused to see the potential results of his actions: Surely his efforts to surmount established limits could not be criminal?

In the end, Neposedov's revolt had no visible impact on the system, while his own life was forever altered. They fired him and sent him to prison. Another Neposedov was found for his job. Millions of our people are endowed with abundant strength, talent, and knowledge. It is indefensible that this huge, inexhaustible fountain of ability was constantly being restrained and repressed by the deformed lid of the authorities' orders, and that all our energy was directed exclusively down the odious road to communism, which no one needed.

Engineers of Chattel

Life in the camps convinced me that the renowned "reforging through work and education" could only serve to corrupt people. Hungry, driven by the survival instinct, shifting and dodging, we learned to hate work and the knout instead of to love them. We learned to deceive the knout, feigning resignation to it, even praising it; but still we could not come to love work. You cannot command love.

To a certain extent this situation prevailed everywhere in the Soviet Union. People have an enormous craving for activity, but if such activity is directed toward an aim that they internally reject, the craving is arrested, warped, and extinguished. As a result, people begin to regard work as simply a painful duty, creating a situation where almost the entire population tries to work less in return for more. The socialist formula "From each according to his ability, to each according to his labors" was twisted into "Work less, try to snatch more!"

The second part of the formula threatened to stifle all sense of decency. As always, this phenomenon was more strikingly noticeable at the top, particularly among the Soviet "elite," Stalin's "engineers of the human spirit"—writers, artists, film producers, and others in the arts, who were being forced to help the Politburo reeducate the Russian people and indoctrinate them in socialism. In 1939–1940, these "engineers" revealed their own "Soviet spirit."

The Russian populace observed the Soviet seizure of western Ukraine and Belorussia with indifference, showing neither approval nor any upsurge in patriotic feeling. Many understood that Stalin was only advancing his outposts farther to the west. The regime's slogan about the need to "extend a helping hand to our brothers, the Ukrainians and Belorussians," who were languishing under capitalist oppression, met with popular skepticism, evoking a tragicomic one-liner that circulated widely at the time: "We will extend them a hand, and they will be lying at our feet." The acquisition of the Baltic states a bit later met with a somewhat different reaction. The masses were equally indifferent, but this time military circles and a part of the intelligentsia responded positively, obviously manifesting both patriotic and pro-regime sentiments. Russians had shed much blood annexing the Baltic region, which had twice belonged to Russia, and many saw the area as the nation's natural boundary and a much-needed outlet to the sea. Leningrad and Kronstadt, being situated on the Gulf of Finland, were icebound in winter. Thus, we were unable to fulfill the role in the Baltic that our geographic location and power would seem to have dictated, which in turn created an imbalance. Many Russians viewed the reincorporation of the Baltic states as a return to past normalcy, rectifying an abnormal situation, which sooner or later, by one path or another, was bound to be rectified. The subordination of the Baltic peoples to our regime was a minor factor in this reaction: If we Russians, one hundred seventy-five million strong, had to live under that regime, then why shouldn't the four or five million inhabitants of the Baltic states?

Our march into these countries evoked considerable confusion in the Red Army, especially among the young. For example, in Poland, which the Politburo's propagandists had described as a land of complete lawlessness and unheard-of poverty, it proved difficult to find a hungry, destitute proletariat. The well-dressed workers looked like "capitalists" to the amazed Red Army troops, who mistook peasants for rich land owners and ordinary townspeople for "the bourgeoisie." The stores proved to be heaped with goods. Where was the poverty and destitution of the capitalist world?

However, these discussions came later. First, the Red Army threw itself into shopping. At the sight of such low prices and such an array of western abundance, the troops, who were starved for goods, snatched up everything, whether they needed it or not, just for the sake of buying. Everyone with even a little money acquired heaps of underwear, shoes, and other items.

Fearing the Germans, the population initially greeted the Red Army benevolently. Merchants and tradesmen were happy to see Red Army troops, wondering only why they were buying so much at once. No need to rush, comrades: Shortages would not be a problem, since more goods could always be obtained from the factory if stocks were depleted. Recalling the tsarist era and completely unfamiliar with the Soviet system, the naive Poles could not comprehend at first that they were greeting a Soviet and not a Russian army.

It was easy to understand why Red Army troops were so greedy for things they had been deprived of for many years. However, a number of Soviet writers, journalists, and filmmakers had followed the Red Army into Poland, allegedly with the aim of enlightening their "liberated brothers." These individuals lived well at home and had enough money. However, upon seeing such fantastic abundance, they soon left the Red Army shoppers far behind.

Distinguished cameraman Dovzhenko brought several train-car loads back from Poland under the guise of film equipment. One car did indeed contain film equipment, but the rest held furniture and various other items that he had purchased for himself at bargain prices. The writer Avdeenko bought two vehicles: He himself drove a motorcar, while behind him came a truck crammed with clothes, shoes, and other manufactured goods. A jazz musician bought up all the accordions in Chernovtsy, where an accordion that would have cost five or six thousand rubles in Moscow was available for three or four hundred. Aleksey Tolstoy, one of the richest people in the Soviet Union, perhaps lacking, as they say, only pigeon's milk, bought an antique silver service for 60,000 rubles at a Polish estate. Tolstoy gained considerable notoriety for choosing rare items and paying for them without bargaining, so much so that Jewish traders in Bialystok said of him, "It's immediately evident that he is a genuine count!"

Artists, writers, and journalists bought up furniture, musical instruments, leather coats, shoes, and other manufactured products, frequently with the aim of *spekuliatsiia* [speculating, that is, selling at a profit, often a very high one]. An artist friend of mine once brought back sixty pairs of women's shoes from Bialystok, but unluckily for him, they had begun to prosecute people for speculation in western goods. Someone reported him to the NKVD, and one day agents turned up at his house. They asked him to show them what he had purchased abroad, then inquired why he needed so many shoes. My acquaintance replied that he bought the shoes for his wife; but they did not believe him, since the shoes ranged in size from 36 to 40. They confiscated all but two or three pairs.

At first, Muscovites spoke of these shopping orgies in western regions with condescending sneers at their "uninhibited" brothers. But as the orgies grew, their indignation increased. People were indignant because the "elite" was disgracing us in full view of the West and because our "engineers of the soul" turned out to be capable of such disgusting greed. Their indignation was combined with obvious bitterness: What had we come to?

The hue and cry eventually reached the Kremlin. The behavior of the "engineers of the soul" was a total disgrace, undermining the prestige of the regime. It had to be stopped. The presidents of the committees for art and film production, responsible individuals of the Soviet Writers' Union, prominent film people, and other "engineers" were summoned to a Kremlin meeting on "questions about Soviet creativity," with Stalin himself presiding. The theme of Soviet creativity was incidental. The main business of the meeting was a scathing rebuke, delivered by Stalin, of the "engineers of the soul" for their behavior in occupied western regions.

This meeting decided Avdeenko's fate. Not long after declaring his devotion to Stalin before the Congress of Soviets, Avdeenko had slipped up in his screenplay for the film *The Law of Life,* which was rejected for allegedly anti-Marxist tendencies. His greed and speculation in western goods finished him off. He was sent to the Urals and kicked out of the Soviet Writers' Union. On the other hand, no one else suffered. Either the "engineers of the soul" were not doing anything judged anticommunist, or Stalin still had need of them.

Learning about this meeting, Aleksey Tolstoy and the dramatist Vishnevsky, who lived in Leningrad, also rushed to Moscow. They arrived late, and the meeting had already ended. Tolstoy telephoned the Kremlin and asked that Stalin be informed of their desire to meet with him to get his "creative instructions." Stalin refused to receive them. A story later went around Moscow to the effect that Stalin ordered the following reply to Tolstoy: "Tell them I do not negotiate with speculators." One can well imagine such a retort coming from the Leader, who knew his elite inside out.

After the meeting, the shopping orgies eased up a little, but they had left a strong impression in Moscow. Even those who were inclined to deny that the system was morally rotten and had faith that "it would all come out right in the end" had to wonder. We were living in a situation of internal decay and corruption that could only be held in check by force, with the knout.

At an Impasse

The war with Finland further exposed the weaknesses in our country's fabric, providing proof that the knout alone could not sustain the state and ensure the triumph of communism.

No one was excited about this war. Rather, a certain disdain was evident. "The devil's in league with a child," people said. But in this case, the child unexpectedly put up a strong enough fight to stall the lumbering Soviet juggernaut.

Our warring country was in shambles. Almost all of our railroads were on military alert, but rail transport could not cope with the freight, even for this laughable front. Factories near Moscow had shut down because the railroads could not supply them with coal. Manufactured goods disappeared from the provinces. Measures equivalent to bread rationing were introduced, with limited quantities of loaves made available according to a particular schedule. All this because of an insignificant war with three million people!

Woolen yarn was distributed to homes in the central and northern regions for the women to knit mittens, socks, and scarfs for the troops. There were no mittens or socks left in military warehouses, and industry could not manufacture them quickly enough. A house-by-house collection of skis was conducted; the army had no skis either. The population was uncomprehending, indignant. For ten years we had been told over and over again that we had to bear hardships in order to equip the military. We were assured that the army was obtaining all that it needed. And now old women had to knit pairs of mittens overnight! Did this mean they had lied to us all along?

Officers returning from the front told of Red Army troops who slammed their rifles against trees in rage. The oil in the rifles froze, so they were generally useless against the Finns' automatics. We did not have automatics. The claims of our authorities that our army was equipped with the latest weapons proved hollow.

The medical services were abominably supplied. Thousands of Red Army troops froze; thousands more were frostbitten, and help for them inevitably came too late. More died from the cold than from Finnish bullets and shells.

Light wounds turned out to be fatal because the wounded could not be conveyed to medical aid stations before they froze. Terrible train convoys were already arriving in Moscow from the front, with thousands of people minus arms and legs that had been frostbitten on the front and amputated. Relatives were ordered to come and pick them up. There were heartrending scenes at the October Station, where these train cars stood on sidings. The relatives had not been informed in advance about the condition of their wounded, and now instead of whole persons they greeted limbless hulls. Some wives could not bring themselves to accept what remained of their husbands. Wives and mothers in the loading area were openly cursing Stalin, the Politburo, and Bolshevism before the benumbed NKVD troops. The atmosphere was such that no one laid a hand on the wives and mothers to arrest them.

The war dragged on, with one hundred seventy-five million unable to defeat three million. In actuality, only Stalin and his close associates were fighting the three million, while the rest of the populace had not the slightest desire to fight. There were a few volunteers of sorts. Shortly after the war began, Komsomol detachments were organized, including some who could be termed volunteers. However, the fact that they received full pay at their workplaces for the duration of their service in the military played no small part in their decision to volunteer.

The prolonged conflict evoked considerable bewilderment. How could the Finns continue to resist, with such a mountain being heaped upon them? Wouldn't they be better off to capitulate at once, thereby freeing themselves and us from a burdensome war? We were bound to bury them in the end, so what was the sense in resisting? The latter query reflected a general feeling that since open resistance to communism was hopeless, people could only resort to concealed methods against it. However, further prolongation of the struggle resulted in a growing resentment of the Finns and a desire to end their resistance more rapidly.

Stalin took no pity on a populace that had sustained losses of about a half-million in the conflict. At his orders, our troops stormed Vyborg in a predawn attack, although a Finnish delegation to Moscow had already accepted the Soviet conditions for a truce and the latter had been announced in the papers that very morning. At the cost of forty thousand casualties, the attack was Stalin's belated and misguided attempt to display the mettle of the Red Army.

The Finnish War inspired a reevaluation of priorities, and a retraining of our military was hastily begun. For the anticommunists among us a hope was born: The war showed that steadfast, organized opposition to communism could be victorious. The fact that the Soviet army had not overwhelmed Finland was in effect a victory for the Finns and a Soviet defeat. And if one day a stronger opponent appeared in place of Finland, might not our communist system collapse and we be freed?

While talking one day with Lapshin, I remarked that his theory of a crushing blow against the weakest had not been borne out. Finland was a weak opponent and we had not smashed her. Lapshin readily admitted his mistake: Now he, too, hoped for the collapse of communism in a war.

"Yes, the matter hinges only on our future opponent's withstanding the first blow," he said. "We cannot endure a prolonged effort and will fall apart ourselves. What else can Stalin find to prod people along? At some point, the army would probably seize control."

At that time, we did not even consider two other possibilities. The first was a Soviet alliance with the West against Hitler. In 1940 we were friends with Hitler, depicting his war with the "plutocrats" as justifiable and welcoming their every defeat. Because we could not have projected a new, 180-degree turn, all calculations had to be based on our waiting while our friend Hitler and the "plutocrats" exhausted their forces in a mutual struggle. Only then would our hour arrive. At the time it never entered our minds that an alliance with the West would provide Stalin both material and moral support.

The second possibility had become apparent during the Finnish War and had given rise to a vague unease. Disfigured corpses of Red Army troops had been found in Finnish forests. These men, who had been beaten or tormented to death, had their ears or noses cut off, their eyes gouged out. At first this caused deep bewilderment. The Finns were considered a cultured people; where could such barbarism have come from? The Finns had created many snares, scattering various items—such as pens, cameras, and bicycles—that were attached to land mines. Many Red Army men were killed or wounded trying to get these items. This Finnish technique evoked revulsion. The war was clearly "unchivalrous": People were not being killed in honorable battle but by the dirty tricks of a base people. This explains much of the embitterment in the Soviet army against the Finns in the second half of the war, when Red Army troops began to fight ferociously.

This new, unfamiliar, antihuman face of war evoked indignation. How could the Finns not know that we were fighting them against our will? We understood that they had to defend themselves, but why else would they torture our brothers and degrade them so brutally? We did not desire their deaths, so why did they crave ours, planting mines even in locales that we had already lost and were abandoning anyway? The soldier wearing a red star on his cap remained a Russian human being, who did not think of himself as the enemy of another people and did not at all expect others to consider him a sworn enemy. He could understand neither the behavior of the Finns nor the new character of war, which led to such senseless destruction.

We were accustomed to thinking of western peoples as cultured and humane and thus we viewed instances of atrocities in the Finnish War as atypical, most likely provoked by excess animosity. We had not yet realized that a thin envelope of culture did not make people truly humane and that western peoples could be capable of refined and savage barbarism. Similarly, we never could have conjured up the mindless racism of Hitler, his savage hatred of Russia and of all Slavs, nor foreseen that it would create a solder for welding the people together in a single sentiment—Russian patriotism. And we could not then have imagined that the West, both fascist and democratic, would compel our people to help maintain Stalin's power and preserve his system.

These events happened much later. Meanwhile we took one day at a time, sensing that we had fallen into a period of stifling deadlock, from which there could be only one exit: war.

After the civil war ended, the Bolsheviks had to recoup their losses, so they introduced the New Economic Policy (NEP). Given some leeway for individual initiative, the people rushed to improve their material well-being. Then, during the First Five-Year Plan, the country was preoccupied by a struggle both for and against collectivization and industrialization. In the mid-thirties the populace again fell into a short period of comparative prosperity. Even Stalin felt compelled to proclaim, "Life has become better, life has become gayer," and to promise that the Second Five-Year Plan would be conducted at a slower tempo. At the same time, Stalin's dreadful liquidation of all opposition, both "right" and "left," was going on at the top. Finishing up the "liquidation," Stalin had already conclusively proved himself a personal dictator. And from this time on, people's lives were devoid of all purpose, beyond simply making it through each day and preserving their own existence. The daily routine of "constructing socialism" brought people no satisfaction. However, gripped at that time in a vise, the people could wage no active struggle against these routine activities. Lacking any dynamic goal, they could only dodge, accommodate, and act out—that is, carry on a concealed, passive struggle. One could not even strive for material well-being: Initiative of any kind ceased. There was an intense shortage of manufactured goods throughout the country, due to the rearmament effort and to Soviet exports to Hitler's Germany. The authorities could not come up with any overarching goal except the one that had forever faded from public consciousness: "building socialism." Meanwhile, for more than twenty years since the revolution, the pace of life had been stormy and feverish. The sudden suspension of that total dynamism created an impression of stagnation.

A general slowdown in tempo occurred toward the end of the 1930s in many countries besides ours. At this time, the "popular front" was on shaky ground in the West. The USSR had exited the League of Nations, despite some modest gains made by Litvinov. One could sense that our country was becoming more and more isolated from the rest of the world.

The slowdown could also be explained by Stalin's excessive bloodletting throughout the power apparatus and the army during the *Yezhovshchina,* which the authorities had halted in order to gather their forces for a new start. Given events in the West, it was imperative that we prepare for war. During the two or three years before the war's outbreak, tensions were in certain respects on the rise and the atmosphere was becoming heated. At the same time we were literally running in place, lapsing into a period of impasse and lack of vision. The nation could find no definite, concrete aim, either "for" or "against," as it had during the civil war or the First Five-Year Plan, when the authorities were "establishing the foundations of socialism." The regime was unable to come up with anything to mobilize support. We, meanwhile, could rot on the vine. The regime was also rotting on the vine, and could not even give its own Soviet or Party apparatus anything more than ineffective calls for "Soviet patriotism."

We envisioned two possible outcomes. The first was a victorious war. If Stalin seized part or all of Europe as a result of war with the West, communism would get new nourishment, the digestion of which would take more than a few years. This would also indirectly nourish the people. Communism would be saved for an indefinite period, with a chance of future growth.

The second prospect was more desirable to us: a non-victorious war, during which communism would be destroyed. We could not imagine how this might come about. We were certain only that given the rottenness of the Soviet regime, communism could not sustain a large military effort and that its defeat would favor our side.

Both variants boiled down to the same thing—war. The regime was making all-out preparations for it in the name of communism. While helping the regime, we could only wait passively, hoping the war would provide a means of liberation both from Stalin and from communism.

More Predators

Living on our hopes, we continued to supervise the work of our enterprises. Just before the war, I played a direct role in liquidating one example of the corruption endemic to Soviet society. One of our all-Union bureaus was responsible for overseeing a timber site in Rybinsk. Over the course of the previous two years it had become evident that things were not right there. The section was using up entirely too many resources and not producing much lumber. The office manager somehow defended the section, but negative reports continued to come in. In 1941, the manager—a Party member since 1919 and an important political worker—was called up from the reserves and sent to western Ukraine as the political commissar of a large army group. His deputy director, also a long-time Party member and a former worker in the Putilov Works, decided to check up on the unit. Not trusting his own employees, he asked that a controller be appointed from the central board. The head of the central board sent me, as someone who knew the lumber business.

I went to Rybinsk in spring 1941. This once rich trading and manufacturing center looked neglected: a chipped cobblestone bridge; a collapsing quay; a fence along the boulevard pulled asunder; homes that had not been repaired since the prerevolutionary era or the NEP. A theater that had burned during the revolution had still not been restored, and a streetcar system that had been projected before the revolution remained unbuilt. The town had two movie theaters. A new aircraft engine factory on the outskirts had a fine, large house of culture. City-dwellers rarely went there because transportation to the factory was available only by one busline.

While I was at the aircraft engine factory, a group of German officers and engineers came to look over the plant and discuss the supply of engines to Germany. The workers had been informed the day before that they should show up for work well dressed. Those who were unwilling or unable to obey this order would not be permitted to work the next day. About nine o'clock, a train of several first-class cars pulled into the station. Large ZIS [Stalin Motor Works] autos, which had been collected from almost every neighboring region, conveyed the visitors to the factory. They made the rounds of the shops and met with the plant managers and representatives from Moscow. One of the Germans noticed a grammatical mistake on a poster hanging in one of the shops, and to the embarrassment of the Russians who were accompanying him, he brought it to their attention. The workers grumbled and scoffed because they had been compelled to dress up for the Germans.

The NKVD's Volga Construction had built a bridge across the Volga at Rybinsk and a dam about ten kilometers upstream, near the tiny village of Perebor. A second dam and a hydroelectric power station had been built at the mouth of the Sheksna. Above the two dams, just before Cherepovets and Vesegonsk, a huge reservoir—the "Rybinsk Sea"—was created on the land between the Sheksna and the Mologa, two tributaries of the Volga. The Rybinsk Sea had flooded many villages and hamlets. Our lumbering unit processed timber felled in these flooded areas or from the dismantled homes of the villagers.

The manager of the power station was one Kravetz, a Jew from Odessa, about fifty years old. Before the revolution he had owned a lumber business. Kravetz had studied at a technical institute and become a civil engineer, then continued to work in the lumber industry, but not in construction. Having no doubt been forewarned of my arrival, Kravetz met me with an exaggerated welcome. Setting out a bottle of cognac and a dish of caviar, he tried in every way to ingratiate himself. I found him repugnant: His bulging, insolent eyes and stubborn chin and mouth gave him a coarse, aggressive appearance.

The next day, I got acquainted with his bookkeeper, Samuel Markovich, a sickly fellow who was practically invisible. He seemed upset, clearly fearing an audit. Until 1935 Samuel Markovich had lived in Leningrad. Why he left he did not say, but I conjectured that he had been expelled from the city along with thousands of other Leningraders in the aftermath of Kirov's murder. When I got to know him better, I found Samuel Markovich an outstanding fellow with a gentle, tender nature, although by then he was so suffocated by fears that he trusted nothing and no one. Kravetz terrorized him, brazenly taking advantage of Markovich's credulity and gentleness. Samuel Markovich was so intimidated by his boss that he could hardly keep from trembling in Kravetz's presence and unquestioningly fulfilled his every order. Because these orders often involved cover-ups, Samuel Markovich's job had become sheer torture. He was deathly afraid that he, too, would have to answer for the despot's fraud.

It took me awhile to uncover Kravetz's swindles. My initial review of the documents told me only that a closer inspection would be necessary. I noticed strange payments for work evidently not done, or done without visible results. In general, the records were in a horrifying muddle of seemingly deliberate creation. It was difficult to get to the bottom of the problem. I had to make certain that it did not simply originate in poor accounting practices. For two weeks I tried to untangle the confused figures, to fit them into some kind of systematic framework, but without result. Samuel Markovich could provide no explanation and referred me instead to Kravetz, who he claimed kept his affairs private. Kravetz, in turn, blamed everything on Samuel Markovich, calling him a confused, brainless fool.

Soon the suspicious sums added up to about a million rubles, and I had not yet checked even a third of the documents. Evidently I had stumbled onto a scandal of proportions that were unusual even under Soviet conditions. Several threads led me to Moscow, and gradually, after about two months, a picture began to emerge.

The director of the Moscow office of Volga Construction had worked abroad as a rather high-level diplomat for about ten years. In the early 1930s he had been suspected of some sort of deviation and recalled. With the help of friends in the Central Committee and the NKVD, he had managed to avoid arrest, but he was forced to resign from the People's Commissariat of Foreign Affairs. He switched to employment in the economic sector; but after living abroad, he found his Moscow lifestyle lacking. Since he felt unable to manage on the steady living and three-room apartment of a director, he had to think up a way of expanding his horizons. The director had already been acquainted with Kravetz when he was in Odessa, so the two of them decided to open up a lumbering unit, which in essence became their private enterprise.

In about three years on the job, Kravetz had embezzled more than three million rubles from the lumbering unit under the guise of payments for work that in fact was never completed. Some of this money went to a foreman who had helped him compose documents for this alleged work and who signed receipts for payments to nonexistent workers, but the lion's share fell to the director in the Moscow office and to Kravetz. Both men had outfitted fine apartments for themselves in Moscow and built dachas on the outskirts of the capital, the blueprints for which had been drawn up at the lumbering unit. The workers who outfitted the Moscow apartments and built the dachas were also hired in Rybinsk and paid at the expense of the lumbering unit.

I was enraged by the scope of what I had uncovered. These were no common Soviet schemers or ordinary thieves but typical manipulators of contemporary circumstances, bosses for whom nothing was sacred and whose motto was "grab as much as you can." The Moscow office director earned 2,000 rubles a month, had a car at his disposal, and enjoyed many other privileges. He lived a hundred times better than any blue- or white-collar employe, many of whom were superior to him even in business ability. But this situation was not good enough for the director. Like other representatives of his circle, he had to steal even more. Nonetheless, like other political workers and economic bosses, he was viewed as our "leader"—even our "molder"! Who gave this greedy beast such a right? Wasn't the right to exert force and exercise cunning exclusively that of the Party?

Kravetz lived ten times better than millions of other people, thanks to his 2,000 rubles a month, but he completely lacked human qualities. He brutalized and derided everyone who was weaker than he, including Samuel Markovich. Kravetz did not even try to mask this as a "struggle for the well-being of humanity," thus revealing the essence of our system, the chief qualities of which were brute force and brazen rapaciousness, all the more sharply.

Infuriated by these two scoundrels, I prepared my report with such care that there was no way they could evade responsibility. For a time Kravetz continued his tricks even in my presence, completely unshaken by the audit in progress. Heaping choice abuse on Samuel Markovich, he was again demanding that the latter authorize payments on the basis of suspicious-looking documents. I obtained an order from Moscow stating that during the auditing process, the unit's funds could be disbursed only with my prior approval. This enraged Kravetz but did not diminish his self-confidence.

Several days later, Medvedev, a senior foreman and Kravetz's right hand man, came to see me. A Herculean fellow with the ruddy face of a northerner, he made a good impression. He brought an order from Kravetz to pay a brigade of workers 30,000 rubles for rafting and floating timber. The documents, work reports, and records all had been compiled according to the rules and seemed well founded. But Kravetz previously had used documents just like these to steal three million rubles, so I had no faith in them.

I refused to pay out the money and told Medvedev that the workers themselves should come for it. He claimed that the workers were busy and unable to come. I replied that in that case I would go and pay them wherever they were working. Medvedev did not know what to say and left.

A half-hour later Kravetz came running in, shouting that I was disrupting his work flow. He could no longer be held responsible for supplying us with lumber because I was creating conditions under which it was impossible to operate. I declared that nothing stood in his way and I was ready to pay his workers on the spot. All I had to know was where they were so that I could take them their money. Kravetz had not expected this. He demanded that the money be given to Medvedev, saying that he could not work if he were not trusted.

The wrangling between us went on for two days. During this time I sent accountants into the country where the workers allegedly lived. It turned out that in general there were no such workers in that rural district. In order to catch the brazen fellows redhanded, I rented a horse on Sunday, rode to Medvedev's home, and invited him to accompany me to their lumbering site. Medvedev at first feigned confusion, then tried to come up with various excuses, but in the end thought better of this approach and consented. For a long time we searched for a raft along the banks of the Volga, as if it were a sliver that might have gotten lost. I was certain that the raft did not exist. But after a long search, Medvedev pointed out a raft that was moored along the riverbank. I called to two workers who were sitting on the raft, asking whose it was. It belonged to the Volga Construction Trust.

"What makes you think you can fool me?" I asked Medvedev. "Do you think that you and Kravetz are the only ones with brains and the rest of us are idiots?" Medvedev hung his head in seeming embarrassment. We stopped searching: Their raft was nowhere to be found.

In the evening Medvedev came to my place with a confession. He told me all about this affair and many other crooked doings and pleaded with me not to ruin him. He had a wife and three children, to whom he had only recently returned from a penal camp where he had served out five years "for agitation." It turned out that we were once in the same camp at the same time. Medvedev said that "the devil" had tempted him and that he never would have gotten involved in the fraud if Kravetz had not lured him into it.

Medvedev once again faced imprisonment in a penal camp because of his participation in Kravetz's crimes. I could not wish that on him. Kravetz might be a consummate predator, but nothing of the kind could be said of Medvedev. The conditions under which we lived, bestowed on us from the very summit of power, combined with Medvedev's instability and pressure from Kravetz, explained his conduct. Without Kravetz he would not have done this. However, I could do nothing to help him because I had already sent the results of my audit to Moscow. Medvedev had a head on his shoulders. He might evade a camp sentence due to extenuating circumstances. However, he could still be punished for his involvement in the swindle. He would have to move to some other place, perhaps in Siberia or the Far East, where economic criminals were not hounded so zealously.

I completed my audit in mid-June and returned to Moscow. On June 21, a Saturday, I went to see the new office director, the former deputy director, about the audit and the lumbering site. He shook his head in amazement. "Can you even conceive how they could do it?" he asked. I was not surprised at his incomprehension: He was a simple, likable fellow, unsuited to our times. This explained why even as a member of the Party with twenty-five years of service, he had remained in the modest post of deputy director for many long years.

We had collared the villains and now the case would be turned over to a procurator, who would sort out who was guilty and of what. We had liquidated the lumbering site. The matter was no longer my concern. I had completed my job and was glad to be free of Rybinsk.

8 ∽

The Invasion

The next day, a Sunday, I got up late and puttered around the house until around two o'clock, when I left for Kolyshev's. The first word I heard on the street was "war"!

Like any event awaited in agonized anticipation, the war came without warning. Although war seemed inevitable to me in Rybinsk, where I had access to every rumor, now the news stunned me. What would happen to us? On the streets, mobs of people crowded around loudspeakers that were repeating a communiqué from Molotov. Alarmed, groups of people milled about on the sidewalks with anxiety, depression, and fright etched on their faces. The stormclouds had opened and we were gripped by a strangling whirlwind that promised to twist, crumple, and reduce us to ashes. What would tomorrow bring?

Suspecting that the trains would be crammed, I set off for Lapshin's, but he was not at home. I could not bear to be alone, so I went to the Ginzburgs and found them in disarray. Mother Ginzburg was crying and a scowling Yakov Abramovich was walking around like he was in a funeral home. Minutes later, his political instructor son ran in, then left immediately. The Moscow garrison was already on a wartime footing. Their married daughter arrived in tears; her husband had been mobilized in the first call-up. Yakov Abramovich announced that they must leave for Novosibirsk.

"You are out of your mind!" I retorted angrily. "The war has just begun and you are already spreading panic!"

"You call *this* panic!" Ginzburg objected, laughing sarcastically. "Believe me, in two weeks Hitler will be in Moscow! Let me give it to you straight: Do you think that my son and my son-in-law will defend these scoundrels?" Ginzburg asked heatedly, referring to the regime. "You certainly aren't going to defend it, and neither is anyone else!"

"Fine, so no one will defend it, but what is the point of going to Novosibirsk?"

"Don't you get it?! Don't you know that Hitler is an anti-Semite? Don't you know that we have thugs here who are only waiting for some pretext to accuse the *zhidy* [Yids] of being behind it all?"

"Come on, you're exaggerating," I objected.

Ginzburg threw up his hands. "I am exaggerating, am I? Trust this old Jew: We'll see such horrors that even the Lubyanka will seem like child's play. You can do what you like, but I am going at least as far as Novosibirsk, and possibly a little farther." At the end of June, Ginzburg and his wife left for Siberia.

On Monday there was equal commotion at the central board. Many of our men had been served call-up notices and had come to collect their last paycheck and to bid us farewell. Everyone was bewildered and depressed. The usual malicious delight about the regime's perplexity had vanished. This was no time for wisecracks. We had no idea what lay in store for us. Many had been hoping that war would become a catalyst of freedom; but when the war came, it brought alarm instead of joy. What would happen?

I succeeded in locating Lapshin only on the fifth or sixth day of the war. Having been promoted to colonel shortly before, Lapshin had been at general staff headquarters around the clock since the war began, frequently sleeping there. He had lost weight; his cheeks were pinched and his eyes sunken from nights without sleep. He, too, was depressed and alarmed.

"Everything is going to hell," said Lapshin hurriedly. He was on his way to Red Army general staff headquarters again. "The army is disintegrating, the Germans have already taken hundreds of thousands of prisoners. Or rather, we can't tell how many they've taken—whole divisions and corps seem to have evaporated into thin air. We have lost masses of tanks, lost airplanes right on the ground, in the hangars. We have no artillery left. They are considering the possibility of abandoning Moscow. We might retreat to the Volga or the Urals."

"Maybe you won't have to retreat?" I said, alluding to the hope on which we had been relying.

Lapshin rubbed his forehead hard. "You know, something is going wrong. Something that isn't quite clear yet. But it's not like we expected. Just look here." He removed a folder from his briefcase, rummaged through some papers, and handed me a small sheet of yellow paper, folded into quarters.

It was a German leaflet with a sketch of strange, disgustingly ugly faces. I could not understand what they were supposed to portray. Underneath was an even more preposterous inscription, savage lines like those that later became widespread:

> Beat the Yids and political instructors,
> Their ugly mugs just beg for bricks.

"It's utter lunacy," I said, handing back the leaflet. "Perhaps it's just an isolated incident?"

"I don't know, maybe. But what if it isn't? What if this lunacy is Germany's wartime policy? Could it be that they think we are such idiots as to succumb to this trash? The very thought is enough to make me climb out of my skin! I don't think that's quite it, but at this point there's no way to know for sure what this means. We'll just have to wait and see what happens." Bidding me good-bye, he darted off to work.

They were expecting me again in Rybinsk: I had received an order to liquidate the lumbering unit that had been under investigation. There was no one else who could go. Of the entire central board staff, only fifteen or twenty had been given deferments, and these were mostly women and old men; the rest had been mobilized. I too had remained behind, as the bearer of a white ticket [that is, someone exempt from military service]. Due to poor health after my release from the camps, I had been relieved of the obligatory term of military service and removed from the draft registry. In late 1940, all those with white tickets were ordered to report for reconsideration, but I had not yet been summoned and was still exempt.

Obtaining a train ticket with considerable difficulty, I left Moscow on June 30. In our section of the overflowing car sat three young women in torn, disheveled clothes. One had a child in her arms, wrapped in a scrap of dirty blanket. She herself wore only a light jacket and a torn skirt, revealing bare knees. A little girl with frightened eyes, in a dirty, rumpled dress was pressed against the second woman. These were the first refugees: the wives of officers of the frontier guard, fleeing the hell of the first hours of the war.

One of them had been lucky. Just as shots were heard at the border, a watchman at a frontier outpost had gathered up all the women, put them in automobiles, and sent them to the interior. About a hundred kilometers from the border they had boarded another train, which took them farther. Not one of these women had seen her husband again.

Things had gone worse for the second woman, the one with the child pressed to her bosom. They likewise had escaped during the initial exchanges of fire, but because there was no vehicle at the frontier post, the women had left on foot with a Red Army chauffeur. The chauffeur had commandeered a bus by force in the nearest Lithuanian village, and they proceeded on their way; but without knowing the road, they were soon lost. Locals in one of the villages pointed out a route, but it took them back to the border, where they almost got caught by Germans, who fired at them. One woman was wounded in the shoulder, another was lacerated by glass splinters from the shattered bus window. The driver managed somehow to turn the vehicle around, and they escaped. On the way back he noticed the people who had pointed out the route, and cursed them out—the locals ran off. Bullets whizzed behind the bus as it left the village. I heard later that Baltic village residents who had been armed by the Germans before the war frequently shot Red Army men in the back. In this instance, they killed one woman and wounded another.

Toward evening, these refugees met up with an officer who had been separated from his unit and was wandering along the road. He led them to a highway and escorted them to the nearest military outpost. Early the next morning, they spotted a plane. A parachutist dropped from it and after several minutes landed in front of them, almost on the road itself. The officer and two or three women for some reason thought the parachutist was one of ours, and so they ran toward him. Freeing himself from the harness, the parachutist stood up and shot the officer with a revolver; a second shot hit a woman close by. Arriving just in time, the driver then shot the parachutist, who turned out to be a woman, no doubt a foreign spy.

"Tell me, citizen," interrupted a woman refugee, bewildered and shocked, in a voice that trembled with horror. "Can people really be so cold, so maniacal? She sees she is caught, so to avoid surrendering she opens fire. I can understand her shooting the officer—after all, he is a soldier; but why kill a woman? What kind of person would do that? That was no woman, it was Satan himself!"

Things were no better for the third woman, the one with the little girl. They had been living in a village almost on the border. The Germans had annihilated the frontier guards and had ridden through their village in the very first hour. The families of the commanders hid out. In the morning, the narrator made her way through backyards to a friend's house, but found that her friend had been killed. The frightened landlord said that some drunken German had forced his way in, spotted a photograph of her friend's husband in a commander's uniform on the dresser, declared in broken Russian that the man was a communist, and shot the wife on the spot. "We will massacre all the Yids and communists," he promised as he left. Despair had given strength to our traveling companion, who abandoned the village and left via the forests to join her own people. The three women had met in the station in Moscow and were now going to stay with their relatives, one to Kostroma, the two others to near Yaroslavl.

Silent and morose, the passengers listened to these tales. They all seemed to be thinking, What *is* this force that has risen against us? I too was seized by anxiety, as I had been earlier when I heard the tales about the Finnish War and in my last conversation with Lapshin. Fate had indeed brought us up against an unknown adversary.

What Awaits Us?

Rybinsk was transformed. The station and other white buildings had been painted a dark gray, almost black, for camouflage. The city was frowning and gloomy. I sensed confusion and not even a trace of enthusiasm or inspiration, just as I had in Moscow. As our train pulled in, I had caught sight of 155-millimeter guns on platforms on a siding. An artillery regiment that had been ordered to the front had stalled in Rybinsk. It never made it to the front or fired a shot; German bombers had crippled it en route.

Given the new situation, the Kravetz affair and the liquidation of the lumbering unit seemed completely insignificant. Kravetz had disappeared somewhere, as had Medvedev. I was glad for the latter's sake: In this time of war, they would not be able to call him into accountability.

All the same, I had to get busy with the liquidation. No dispatches of lumber and equipment were designated for our enterprises, and traincars were only available for military shipping. I sold the equipment, buildings, and other property to city organizations for a low price, but about 20,000 cubic meters of timber still remained, strewn about in rafts along the banks of the Rybinsk water reservoir. Who would get it? Who would transport it now, if absolutely no workers were left because the majority of males had been mobilized into the army?

Nonetheless I was able to find buyers. I went to a large defense plant in Yaroslavl, where I was greeted with open arms. They had to expand production because of the war. To do so they had to undertake some construction, but there was not a stick of lumber available, and it was entirely unrealistic then to count on obtaining it from the People's Commissariat of Forestry. Our timber fell on them like manna from heaven. Taking advantage of this, I named a figure almost two times higher than our costs. This helped us to conduct the liquidation at almost no expense to ourselves.

Selling off the property, delivering the timber, and settling the accounts for all of this took more than three months. Meanwhile, the Germans rolled toward Kharkov, Kalinin, and Leningrad. Streams of refugees from Latvia passed through Rybinsk. Arms, flour, and oddly enough, even vodka were evacuated from Riga. Barges with goods from Leningrad passed by, heading down the Mariinsky waterway. Piles of galoshes, which had not been available for years, unexpectedly appeared in all the Rybinsk stores. The barge they were on had sunk, but the several million pairs of galoshes were saved just in time and put up for sale.

In those first months, dozens of Rybinsk schools were converted to hospitals. The war had produced a horrifying number of wounded. It was decided that the locals should not be permitted to associate with them, but not everyone observed this rule, and local citizens often milled about near the hospitals. Rumors about what was happening at the front spread throughout the town, but there was nothing clear or definite in them. Reports from the official information bureau were much too vague, and frequently late besides. What was happening at the front was anybody's guess.

Many families in town had loved ones who were already dead or missing in action. I too received some unhappy news: Neposedov had been killed. Not long before the war, he had had some sort of major dispute with the regional Party committee. The committee insisted on his being fired, and he had left the factory. In the turmoil of the first days of war, the local military commissariat mobilized Neposedov, a lieutenant in the reserves, although it was later discovered from the draft registry in the people's commissariat that he should have been granted a deferment. Neposedov never made it to the front either. His echelon was bombed near Vitebsk, and Neposedov died in the bombardment.

Kolyshev was missing in action. He had been in command of a battalion of engineers and had fallen during a siege somewhere in the vicinity of Smolensk. A mix-up had also occurred in his case: He too should have received a deferment, but the military commissariat had mistakenly called him up and sent him to a unit at the front. The central board tried to rescue him, but it was too late. Neither Kolyshev's battalion nor Kolyshev himself was ever found.

The war had snatched away my best friends, and there was still no hint of what we had been hoping for. The Germans remained inscrutable, and not a single sign was evident that our prewar hopes might be justified. So the Germans were our enemy? But the regime was also an enemy to us. No one wanted to defend it, and so the Germans were closing in on Kalinin and Rostov. Just where was our side? Who was there to lead us? Why were people being killed without even understanding who and what they were supposed to be defending?

The Germans were not as mighty as the average person might think from following their successes. Rybinsk is a good case in point. Not far from the city is a bridge across the Volga, and there is another at Yaroslavl. These two bridges connect the country's important arteries from the north and east to the center and west, and these were the main arteries supplying the front. Alarming rumors circulated through the city that the bridges and Rybinsk, thanks to its large aviation motor works, would be bombed. People feared that the dams across the Volga and Sheksna would be destroyed and water from the Rybinsk Sea would flood the city. The fears proved groundless. German reconnaissance planes flew over the area only three or four times and at high altitude. One of them dropped three small bombs, which landed far away on the roadways at some supply depots; no one was wounded and no serious damage was done.

By order of the authorities, bomb shelters were excavated in every court-yard. We dug a trench shelter the depth of a person in the yard of the building where I lived. The trench was immediately flooded by groundwater. It was pointless to try to reinforce it, and it soon collapsed. Our neighbors had the exact same laughable "shelter." But at least we had carried out the order.

At night we patrolled the streets, looking for spies and saboteurs. It was stupid to imagine that a saboteur would walk openly down the street; but in every quarter, in every city, from sundown to sunup, changing shifts every two or three hours, residents, mostly women, patrolled their neighbor-hoods, staring at the rare passerby. Could he be a saboteur? There were no labels on the passersby to tell us whether they were spies or saboteurs; and even if they had been, we could not prevent them from calmly going about their business of sabotage. It made no difference: Again, the most important thing was that we carried out orders.

This was all child's play. The serious, the terrible, and the as yet incompre-hensible were taking place far away from us, on a huge expanse from the Arctic to the Black Sea. All eyes and minds were fastened on that drama, al-though we could still only guess at its outcome.

I hurried through the liquidation because I wanted to get to Moscow as soon as possible, to be at the center of what was happening. I finished my business in the beginning of October and paid off the remaining employees. Samuel Markovich had completed his report. He was truly a muddled-up fellow. At the very last minute, after I had already closed the bank account and sent all the remaining money to Moscow, Samuel Markovich suddenly announced that he still had about 20,000 rubles in his fund. In order to put them in the bank, it was necessary to reopen an account, since sending that large a sum by post was forbidden. This threatened to hold us up for several days, while rumors suddenly had reached us that the Germans were almost at Mozhaisk. I did not want to be detained for even a day, so I decided to take the 20,000 with me.

I found myself in a situation I had never before encountered. The road had been bombed somewhere between Yaroslavl and Moscow, and there were no trains to the capital. I felt as though the earth were burning beneath my feet. I dropped in at the regional executive committee to say good-bye to the chairman who had helped me with the liquidation. The chairman looked at me somewhat strangely and asked meaningfully, "Will you make it to Moscow, I wonder?" Unfortunately, I had no chance to find out what he was driving at, because his office was filled with an agitated crowd of other people.

Ships were still moving down the Volga and the Moscow–Volga canal to Khimki, so I decided to go by boat. No schedule existed, but at the wharf station agent's they knew that the ship *Josef Stalin* was leaving at noon the next day.

In the evening I put the folder containing my reports in a suitcase, packed my things in a rucksack and briefcase, and went to say good-bye to Samuel Markovich. The old man seemed doomed. I advised him to evacuate, as the Germans would soon be there. The old fellow shook his head: "I have lived out my time. Where would I go? It makes no difference what I endure."

I bid my landlady farewell on the morning of October 14, took my things, and walked down the hall. A siren sounded. Setting my things down near the wall, I donned mittens and climbed up into the attic. I was the only man in the building, and according to the schedule, I was supposed to be on watch in the attic during alarms in case of incendiary bombs. I always laughed when climbing to the attic, since I was firmly convinced that there would be no bombs, that my time had not yet come. An attic dormer window provided a long-range view of the main street, which had been hushed by the alarm: not a single person, not a rustle or a movement. High up in the sky, a German reconnaissance plane droned cheerlessly, like a mosquito, surveying our long-suffering land. From time to time, here and there, heads peeked out of doorways, attentively peering into the sky. Wasn't that what everyone was doing throughout our vast country, all holding their breaths, watching for something, fearfully assessing the damages? What was our prognosis?

In the West and the East

I shared a first-class cabin in the comfortable but run-down Moscow–Volga canal ship with a tall man in a leather coat, who wore a closed, gloomy expression. I tried to talk with him—it didn't work. He muttered something and turned away, clearly signaling that he had no wish to converse. I concluded that he was stuck up, and probably an important NKVD or Party functionary of "all-Union significance."

It was empty up on deck, in the saloons, and in the restaurant. There were almost no passengers because we were going west. The radio was not working, so after casting off from the pier, we found ourselves alone in the world, floating down the cheerless autumn river through a web of rain and snow. A ship approached from the west, then floated past us like an apparition, heeling heavily to the port side as though she had sustained a direct hit. Women and children covered with blankets, undoubtedly evacuees from Kalinin, were huddled on the upper decks, sitting on boxes, bundles, and suitcases. The ship moved past slowly, languishing in the foul, murky weather.

Occasionally we met tugs and barges, their decks full of vehicles and machines, with people packed between and atop them, sitting and standing, unmoving, drenched by the rain. The dark water lapped coldly at our bow, and an oily layer drifted on the surface of the river; it would soon turn to ice. The riverbanks looked dreary and sluggish through the dense downpour. The occasional hamlet or village was void of people and movement, as if they'd been condemned and abandoned. We stopped in vain at the piers: No passengers were waiting to board. Life seemed to have ground to a halt, to have gone into hiding, waiting for something.

We crept along. Near Uglich we had a long wait because something was wrong with the diesel engines. An elderly sailor on the lower deck was cursing: "They break down every time! I wish they were at the bottom of the sea." The diesels were a brand-new model, made especially for motorized vessels, but utterly worthless. The old Volga ships with diesels from the exact same Kolomenskoe factory came to my mind: Those engines worked for forty years without a hitch.

We approached the shoe manufacturing town of Kimry toward evening of the second day, and stopped again. About two hours later, when night had fallen, the captain announced that the ship would go no farther because the diesels had entirely shut down.

The passengers disembarked in pitch darkness onto land that was squishy underfoot and immediately went their separate ways. I was alone. Somewhere ahead, about three kilometers away, was Savelovo, where I could catch a train to Moscow. But where was the road to the station? The darkness was so thick, you couldn't see your fingers in front of your face. Swearing, I waded forward through the mud, going on sheer instinct. I passed what looked like houses and fences. I went around them, ended up in a field, and walked on, sinking up to the ankles in the sticky clay. The rustle of rain was tedious, the nasty, cold droplets crawled under my collar. I stopped to listen: not a sound, apart from the rustling rain. The darkness was like black cotton batting, containing not a glimmer or a whisper of life. It became terrifying. Would I ever emerge from this night or would it swallow me up?

I come across a lighter spot, looked around, and spotted a woman sitting on a suitcase, crying. Nestled against her on a sack sat a girl, also crying. Frightened by accounts of German atrocities from the information bureau, they were fleeing, but had no idea where they should go, except that they should be heading east. They had come on foot from Kimry and had strayed from the road, so they were waiting till sunup. I slung their sack onto my back, and the woman and I carried their suitcase between us. The little girl hung onto her mother's skirt. We had no time to be afraid, we had to get out of there. Suddenly we came upon the road, and we made better progress after that. We could hear the sound of other feet slapping the mud—there were others walking ahead of and behind us.

At the station, bathed in the reddish glow of darkened lamps, milled a motionless crowd of gloomy shadows with morose faces, hardened in an expression of apathy, as if nothing mattered. Just as everywhere else I had been since the war began, here there was not even a twinge of patriotic feeling or of bitterness. They had been ordered to evacuate, and so they were leaving; but their hearts were not in it.

Unexpectedly, my traveling companion in the leather coat turned up ahead of me in the line at the ticket window. He showed a little passbook at the window, and I managed to see the letters "NKVD." I was pleased to note that I had not been mistaken in my conjecture: I had acquired a good eye.

People in shabby, mud-spattered clothing crowded into our train compartment. They were stowing away bulky tripods, surveyors' stakes, and measuring rods on the shelves. In the flickering light of dawn I saw tired faces, frightened eyes. Who could these people be? Field surveyors fleeing from the front? I listened awhile to their cautious whispers, then dared to inquire. They had been on assignment near Kalinin and were overtaken by Germans. They had barely escaped, making their way through forests and ravines that were already behind German lines. It actually became funny for a minute, warmed the soul. Even while running for their lives, the fools had not thrown out their bulky tripods and measuring rods!

The mappers said there were practically no Soviet troops in Kalinin, and that today or tomorrow the Germans could be in Klin and Kimry. From there it was just a skip and a jump to Moscow. What would tomorrow bring?

The Breakdown of Order

We arrived in Moscow early the next morning, so I made it to the central board with time to spare and dropped into the snack bar for breakfast. There was as yet no visible alarm on the surface. Moscow was bustling as usual, with people hurrying to work, trams clanging, and trolley buses moving. However, I spied no taxis or buses, and people told me that for some reason the subway was not working that day. After a three-month absence, I stared greedily at the buildings and streets, as if they could tell me what had happened there while I was away. The streets appeared sterner, the poverty more sharply exposed by the shabbiness of the buildings, the litter on the sidewalks, and the worn, soiled clothes of the people. It seemed that everyone was dressed in dirty gray mourning garb.

The closer I got to the center, the more intense was the bustling and the tension, as if things were somehow not right. I hurried to my office. Climbing the stairs to the third floor, I found complete turmoil: The doors and windows were wide open and the wind was blowing papers around, strewing them about on the tables and the floor. My coworkers were hastily pulling binders out of huge cupboards and throwing their contents out the window. Loaded with a stack of folders that reached above his head, supply worker Vasyukov swooped down on me. A gangly fellow with a slight limp and a comically freckled pale face, he was a veteran of the civil war, in which he had served as a pilot. A heavy drinker, Vasyukov had twice been expelled from the Party for drunkenness. But both times the Central Control Committee reinstated him, taking into account his past service and proletarian origins. I liked his unsophisticated and straightforward manner, and he and I were good friends.

Vasyukov swore with relish as the folders tumbled about. Seeing me, he shouted: "Ah, the liquidator! You, brother, are just in time: We are also liquidating!"

"What is this a liquidation of?"

"We are obliterating stupid business forms as a category! Look." He dragged me to the window, out of which he passionately and with obvious satisfaction hurled the folders, which hitherto had been preserved with great care. I might have expected this, yet all I could do was rub my eyes: Could I be dreaming? They were throwing out the valuable cover vouchers and cherished reports on which our entire economic system was based! I looked out the window: White sheets of paper gleamed in the narrow courtyard. Out of the windows across from, above, below, and next to ours, other plump folders were likewise flying. Below us, two furnace men were shoveling papers into a stoker.

Secretaries, draftsmen, accountants, and typists were willingly devoting themselves to the demolition. It was as if they had been seized by the joy of destruction. Perhaps they were simply fed up with clacking away on their typewriters to produce those reams of financial reports, full of incomprehensible and boring figures.

I grabbed Vasyukov by the hand and sat down with him in the corner. "What's going on?"

"This is it, brother. We have been ordered to destroy all business records. They say that the Germans are just forty kilometers from Moscow."

"Is it really that bad?"

"It couldn't be any worse. We have almost no troops. Tomorrow the Germans will be in Moscow."

"Where is the chief bookkeeper? I need to give him some money."

Vasyukov grinned at me. "Look, don't be a fool. Who is there to give money to now? Keep it for yourself: We can go have a drink on it."

"Are you out of your mind? Where is Goryunov?"

"The devil knows where he is. And the chief bookkeeper is at the bank. He went to get money for a quick getaway. We are evacuating, the orders are to pay everyone a month's wages. Don't take it to heart, it will be enough to buy booze."

"No doubt you'll be drunk when the Germans come to hang you. Can't you think of anything besides drinking? The Germans are practically on top of us!"

"That's another matter, we can talk about that after. Meanwhile, we have to keep up appearances, don't we?"

The Germans might be in Moscow tomorrow! The news should not have surprised me, as Minsk, Kiev, Smolensk, and dozens of other cities already had been occupied. Given the course of events, one could surmise that the Germans would soon be near Moscow, in Moscow, even beyond Moscow. Things were moving in that direction. Had not I myself thought this would happen, that it would even be preferable? Without the war, we could never win out over the Soviet regime. But now, when the Germans were actually coming, the thought that they could occupy Moscow on the morrow seemed monstrous. Perhaps Vasyukov was only talking nonsense?

I saw the new director of the bureau, Goryunov, running into his office. His predecessor, who had sent me to Rybinsk, was already gone because the Central Committee had sent him to some other type of work that was important to the military effort. Previously Goryunov had headed one of the departments of the central board. He was a Party member of some standing and had a taste for leadership. Stout, built like a barrel, he had lost some weight and was sagging. I went after him.

After greeting him, I told him that I had finished my work, deposited some money, and brought the rest with me. I asked to whom I should give my report and the money. Goryunov looked bewildered, and his eyes darted about as he rummaged nervously in a desk drawer. "Finished? That's good. . . . Yes, excellent. . . . Report? That type of report . . . there's no one to give it to. They have all been conscripted, this one into the army, that one into the militia," he muttered, continuing his search.

"Anyway, we've been ordered to destroy all documents, so you can throw your report to the devil. That's it, just throw it out, now, literally, to the devil!" Goryunov raged, then immediately cooled down. "We have been ordered to evacuate, keep that in mind. You are going, too. . . . As for the money . . . You know, here's what you can do: Go far away, where nobody knows you. Keep the money for yourself. Yes, yes, don't give it up. Maybe it will be useful to you. Ah, here it is!" rejoiced the director. Fishing a scrap of paper out of the drawer, he grabbed his traveling cap and briefcase and impetuously raced out, leaving me standing agape.

Only then did the seriousness of the threat become clear to me. It was difficult enough for me to take in the fact that they were throwing away reports; but for the director himself to propose that I simply appropriate government funds rather than turn them over was mind-boggling! Clearly our order was shaken and collapsing. Whom was left to ask, and why? Nothing more need be said. . . . The money did indeed come in handy. Returning from the bank, the head bookkeeper announced in despair that he had obtained no funds for severance. Hundreds of bookkeepers and cashiers were gathered at the bank, but no funds were being disbursed because the bank employees had also been mobilized. Fearing havoc, the director of the bank telephoned the NKVD and asked it to send protection, but the NKVD was not yet at the bank, and no guards had been sent. The crowd was seething. Frightened, our elderly head bookkeeper left without any money, so as not to fall into an undesirable situation. He rejoiced at my 20,000 rubles as his salvation. If he failed to pay out the wages, he would not only be guilty of not following orders but he also would have to answer to the workers, the innocent victims of circumstance who so desperately needed this money.

I turned the money over to him. To be on the safe side, I then concealed my most important documents in my briefcase and flung the remaining contents of my suitcase out the window. Hundreds of tables and lists circled freely through the air. I thought of Samuel Markovich and his Rybinsk coworkers, zealously composing these papers, working night and day, out of conscientiousness more than fear. Somersaulting through the air, the papers fell at the feet of the furnace workers. I yelled "Watch out!" and flung the old suitcase, which I no longer needed, after the reports.

The bustle of destruction was still under way in the central accounting office. It gave me an unpleasant feeling: These documents were witness, however mute, to vast human labors. With nothing more to do there, I left to wander awhile around Moscow.

In Every Direction

The streets had changed during the couple of hours I had spent at the central board. Their frenetic, nervous bustle had escalated to sheer panic. Across the way, on New Square, and farther on, on Lubyanka Square, the trams were moving about with clusters of people hanging all over them. Vehicles rushed past, loaded with suitcases. The people in the vehicles concealed their faces in raised collars: They were abandoning their posts.

Paper and ashes were sifting down on Little Lubyanka and Kuznetsky Bridge streets: The state institutions were burning their archives. Rumor had it that even the NKVD was disposing of its files. Curious onlookers appeared out of nowhere, people who seemed to have nowhere to go and nothing to do. They stood at intersections and in doorways, as if aimlessly observing the fuss. On some of the faces there was alarm, bewilderment; but I thought I also saw a spark of satisfaction, even malicious joy, flickering here and there.

On Kuznetsky Bridge, books, notebooks, writing paper, and envelopes from the bookstores were lying in heaps on the sidewalk, although just the day before they had been unavailable at any price. I stopped to browse: fiction, scientific and technical books, many antique editions in rich bindings.

"We have been ordered to sell what we can and to destroy the rest," remarked a saleswoman, bundled up in a shawl. "You can have this twenty-volume set of Tolstoy for only fifty rubles. Don't you want it?"

My craving for books pressed me to grab them. This was a rare chance and I might not have another. I could acquire a fine library for a thousand rubles! My hands stretched out toward those books, but I stopped myself: This was not the right time. Where would I put them? How could I leave them in Moscow for the Germans? If we left, could I carry such a heavy load with me to somewhere in Siberia? I would need a miracle of God to get there even without such a load. I turn away, crushed, and wandered on.

I walked along Tverskaya, from there to Mokhovskaya and onward to the Arbat; from the Arbat to Sadovaya, then on to the Belorussian Station, to the Central Palace of the Red Army, along Samotechnaya Street, Tsvetnoy Boulevard, and Trubnaya, to Chistye Prudy. I wandered around Moscow in this roundabout fashion, aimlessly, following my nose, gazing around as avidly and as brokenheartedly as I had at those books on Kuznetsky Bridge. It was impossible to imagine the Germans striding masterfully down these streets tomorrow, the day after tomorrow, or next week. Although the French once had done so, that was long ago and all that remained of those events were literary accounts. Now we were facing the cold reality of Germans in Moscow, and I could not quite take it in.

I wandered in confusion, imbibing the mélange of contemporary buildings and ramshackle little homes, palaces and factories, crooked lanes and wide streets, squares and boulevards, until I ached for this familiar, plain, unpretentious Moscow whose charms were unequaled. The city was enveloped in bustle. I encountered people with suitcases and bundles, whose expressions told me to flee. Heavily loaded vehicles rolled through the gates of factories and plants, immediately prompting the thought that the trucks were hurrying east. Moscow was coming apart, and we were forsaking her like rats aboard a sinking ship. And this ship was going down without a blow, its inevitable destruction having been prepared throughout the entire course of our lives by those who had seized leadership over it and us. Eliminating its criminal leadership could only destroy the ship. Did that mean that we should welcome its destruction? No, the ship should not be destroyed; only its leadership ought to go. But with the Germans in Moscow, wouldn't it be destroyed, regardless?

I went to Lapshin's. The elevator operator told me that Lapshin's family had already left for the east a month before and that he himself only came home about once or twice a week. It was almost impossible to catch him in. I phoned my other friends, but none were in Moscow: One was in the army; others had left with the factories, moving east. All of them had left for some other place.

I headed home toward evening, tired from the previous sleepless night, from wandering around Moscow, and from the confusion of my thoughts and emotions. The apartment had a flat, unresponsive silence, as if the building were dead. The steam heat was not working, so my empty room was as cold and raw as a cellar. My head was in a muddle and my legs were giving out. I uncovered the damp bed, longing to burrow under the blanket, under a coat, under every warm thing I owned. Then all of a sudden, in burst Vasyukov, naturally accompanied by a liter of vodka.

"Don't scold, gramps," he said, playing the buffoon. "Let's hit the bottle! It's so cold in your place, wolves would freeze! Well, we'll warm up now!" He deftly removed the cork with his hand. There was nothing to do but get out glasses, and a bit of sausage left over from my wanderings. Vasyukov extracted French buns from the pockets of his short fur coat.

"The main thing is not to give in to fear. We'll have a drink to cheer ourselves. Leave the thinking to the horses; they have bigger heads."

"The devil we will!" I interrupted him. "We've got no time left to think, we have to act!"

"And what are you going to do? Well, what, tell me! Jump higher than your head?" snapped Vasyukov, staring at me with his suddenly snapping green eyes. With a wave of his hand, he poured vodka into a glass, drank up, frowned despairingly, sniffed at a roll, and said: "You know me. I gave up on things long ago. And if I hadn't, it wouldn't make a damn bit of difference. Those scoundrels of ours should have thought of this sooner." Our scoundrels, of course, were the Politburo, Central Committee, Council of People's Commissars, and the authorities in general. "And now it's too late to turn things around. You know it as well as I, we're a bunch of sheep: They order us to evacuate, and we go; if they order us to stay, we will stay. Turn this way, turn that way—it makes no difference, if you can't get out of the pen! Well, when you're a veteran, you know not to get involved in anything but this." Snapping the bottle with his fingernail, he again began to play the buffoon.

"Say, Novikov ought to be here," he remembered suddenly. "He arrived today on a mission from the front. I must have a chat with him."

After several minutes he returned with his apartment mate, a technician from our planning office, who had been mobilized on the first day of the war. Scrawny, with sunken cheeks, Novikov had aged greatly. Sorrowful wrinkles were sharply etched near his mouth. He had a dirty overcoat with khaki-colored tabs and a captain's insignia in indelible ink slung over his shoulders.

"What are you doing, feasting in the time of plague?" he said coldly, looking disapprovingly at the table.

"That's it precisely!" Vasyukov chimed in. "You, too, dear captain, have a little glass and then unbosom yourself to us, no arguments, now. How goes the fighting? Report to the working people," said Vasyukov, poking fun at him.

Downing his glass in a single gulp, Novikov sat down, took a little bite, and looked at us gloomily. "Get drunk, you devils, and refresh yourselves," he muttered. "They should send you to the front, to the Germans."

"Captain, no demagoguery, now." Vasyukov waved it aside. "Come on, relax a little and tell us what it's like out there."

"Exactly the same as it is here: one fellow fights while another drinks," said Novikov angrily. He poured another glass and drank hurriedly. His face reddened and became miserable. "There's just one thing I don't understand: How could they have expected us to hold out? The Germans should by rights have taken Moscow ages ago; they must have nothing but sawdust between their ears!" He pounded the table forcefully with his fist. The bottle shuddered and the glasses rang faintly.

"I just came from Smolensk, now there's a pretty picture for you. One unit fights like madmen to the death, chasing down German tanks with bottles and grenades, while another is taken prisoner with all its commanders. A third is scattered practically before it reaches the front. A fourth, when it smells a German, dashes off so fast that you can't catch up to it even on wheels. What's the matter? How could this happen? There is no front: Now the Germans are ahead, now on our flank, now in the rear. You have no way of knowing whether you're behind enemy lines, encircled, or what have you. We have no field communications, so we don't know which of us is supposed to be on the right flank, which on the left, not even the devil knows. How can you call that war? It's a madhouse, not a battlefield!"

"Could this be modern warfare?" interjected Vasyukov.

"What do you think we were preparing for, a war in the style of Peter the Great's era? For ten years they have been bellowing about our aviation, about our tanks, about our Voroshilov shells. So where are they? Instead we're fighting with rifles and bottles. The artillery's been abandoned. For weeks I have not heard one gunshot from our side. There are no tanks; where did they disappear to? Don't even mention airplanes. The Germans are laughing at us as they fly over, you see only German planes overhead. Sometimes they throw out empty barrels and metal rails over our heads. They fly with such a howling that you think, 'Well, it's the end; now we will go up in smoke!' Yes, train tracks were falling out of the sky! We're gasping in fury at the Germans' tricks. But what can you do with nothing but U-2 trainers, hidden on the ground, which are allowed to fly only on staff business? That's the extent of our air force, for you!" Novikov spat out in disdain.

"And the commanders!" he exclaimed after a minute. "I am from the reserves, and ours are okay, but you should see the regulars! What a laugh.

They're like little lost kids, you have to lead them around by the hand. Now they don't mind sending people to their deaths, but when they could have done something about it they wouldn't make a move till the order was given! You can't take a single step without an order; you can only retreat without an order. No plans, no sensible command, nothing but orders—and of course, executions! One is executed for failing to carry out a military assignment, although the assignment may have been impossible to fulfill. Another is shot for desertion, but how can you implement the punishment if the whole unit deserts? The third is executed for the devil knows what, just so there are executions! The Germans are beating us and we are beating ourselves. Who is willing to fight, if no matter what you do, you can get shot anyway? So just withdraw: We retreat to Mozhaisk. I go through a little forest and see them hiding in the bushes, a major and three or four more officers, staying behind to be taken prisoner! The thousands who are surrendering are not the rank and file, but the officers. The officers obviously prefer to give up and be captured! How can we fight under such conditions?"

"When we retreat, we destroy everything left behind, even warehouses full of valuables, even the crops, while the populace simply looks on. They beg, give it to us, don't burn it, we will die of starvation! But that would be going against orders. So we do what we must, and everything goes up in smoke! As for the people—let them be enraged. Are they really such blockheads that they can't understand what's going on? Red Army men are also dying of hunger, but when we retreat, we have to burn the foodstuffs. Of course, sometimes we fight fiercely, to the bitter end instead of retreating. But this is not by wish or by design, but out of despair and rage at the knowledge that we will perish just the same! Can wars really be won on rage alone?"

Growing silent, Novikov chewed morosely on a bun. His sunken eyes dulled and the wrinkles around his mouth grew even more distinct. Vasyukov thoughtfully fingered the edge of the oilcloth on the table. The wail of a siren suddenly burst into the silence of the room. Turning out the light, I pulled back the paper blackout curtain. It was a pitch black night, without a glimmer of moonlight. The window seemed to be facing a crumbling black wall inside which the siren was wailing in anguish.

The wailing suddenly stopped, while somewhere in the distance anti-aircraft guns were yapping. We could hear a muffled, insinuating buzz: *zhzhu-zhzhu-zhzhu.* People said that German planes made that sound. Invisible, the plane circled above us in the black night, over a terrified Moscow, compelling us to ask a hundred times those yet unanswered questions: What will happen to us? What will happen to Moscow?

Searchlights reached up into the sky like white pillars, and in the darkened spaces between them, starlets of antiaircraft fire exploded.

What Do the Germans Want?!

In the morning on my way to work, I stopped at all the tobacco shops and the kiosks, but was unable to buy cigarettes; they had disappeared. People seemed even more hurried and confused than the day before, and I spotted an even greater number of expectant and vacant faces, as if there by chance, steadfastly staring at something. Given that Moscow was near the front, it seemed odd that there were few military personnel in the streets. The police were lost somewhere; not a single one could be seen. I met a group, workers by the look of them, carrying sacks and baskets, with bunches of sausages and meat peeking out from them. Where was so much meat coming from?

I met Vasyukov at the entrance. He was hurrying out somewhere, his short sheepskin coat thrown open and his shabby little cap pushed to the back of his head.

"Hold it!" I stopped him. "Get me cigarettes. There are no cigarettes anywhere."

"So, cigarettes! Do you want some cheap tobacco? I got it from our warehouse," replied Vasyukov, holding out a package of *makhorka*. "Forget about cigarettes. They've destroyed the Ducat factory. All the warehouses have been evacuated, too, and the crates of cigarettes carried off, no lie. Even the stalls and the foodstore on Taganka were dismantled. And now they are destroying the Meat Trust. Our comrade workers learned that mines had been placed underground in order to blow up the place, so they figured everything would be gone anyway. They're hauling out hams and sausages in bags, making off with whole carcasses. It's as much fun as a revolution!" yelled Vasyukov, running.

"It's beginning," I thought to myself. But I could not really believe it, and I did not know whether to laugh or cry.

The offices were empty, but two or three of my coworkers were still carrying folders of "business matters" from cupboards and throwing them out the window. The chief of personnel, a woman with a mannish face, was typing out an order for her own evacuation: "... a resident of Moscow, is hereby authorized to evacuate to ... "

"To where?" I asked her.

"I don't know. Somewhere east, but exactly where I haven't decided," responded the chief of personnel, without looking up.

What did any of us in Moscow know? Life was seething around us, but it also had ground to a halt, as though it were preparing to take a leap into the future. Into what, was anybody's guess.

Blinov, the elderly engineer from the office next to ours stopped me in the hallway. Clutching a button of my coat, he said in alarm: "How am I to leave? Only three people are left in our office, and we cannot get authorization to evacuate. The situation is tragic. We will be left behind!"

"Well, you shouldn't be in any particular danger," I replied. "You aren't Jewish or a member of the Party. The Germans won't do anything to you."

Blinov recoiled, threw up his hands, and again grabbed my button. "How can you talk like that? Well, I'll not remain for a minute with the Germans! I will take my wife and my daughter and flee on foot!"

In the alarmed face of the engineer was something truly touching and tragic—and perhaps just a shade comical. I advised him to go to our personnel chief: Our offices were similar in function, and she might be able to do something for him.

About five minutes later Blinov ran out of the personnel office in a somewhat calmer mood. "It looks like things are settled, I'm registered now. But you know, I was in the Yaroslavl and Kazan Stations—no use! Crammed full. They are evacuating the people's commissariats and the military institutions. You can't get through. I went to the Nizhegorodskoe Highway, and the vehicles there are four abreast—all bound for the east! All full of people, machinery, cartons—you can't even hitch a ride. They say that there are NKVD checkpoints along the highway, set up to catch those who don't have permission to leave the city. All kinds of store managers who are fleeing with stolen goods are being shot right there on the spot. Serves them right! However, I'm making a run for it. Thanks for the advice!"

I dropped into an empty room and sat in someone else's chair, feeling muddled and agitated. I was compelled to do something, but there was nothing to do. I closed my eyes and envisioned Gorkovskoe Highway, with cars four abreast, moving eastward. I could hear the shouts, abuse, the noise of motors, vehicles colliding, could sense the people's feeling that this was the beginning of the end . . . of what?

From behind a thin partition I heard an indignant female voice. "They took us just outside Rzhev, to a forest where there were no barracks or houses. You make yourself comfortable on the ground, under the firs! The authorities put up a tent for themselves, but we were under the sky. Sure, we could build huts, but you can imagine how well we built them, having only ever seen it done in the movies. We put them up, and they tumbled down.

Rain poured through the branches; we were all wet—what a nightmare! They gave us shovels, sent us into a field, told us to dig! And we were in pumps and sheer stockings. Where I work I wear dress shoes. If I wear only dress shoes to work, why would I have a pair of everyday shoes? And if all I know is how to cook a meal and pound on a typewriter, how am I supposed to suddenly dig trenches? Well, we dug. That very first day, one came down with tonsillitis, another got the flu, and then dysentery set in—it was awful! The food situation was desperate, they gave us slop. We lived on bread. Imagine two thousand women from Moscow, in the rain, becoming so raggedy, sickly, and tormented that they cannot even be recognized. A real menagerie! Of two thousand, only half remained after two weeks: this one died; they put another in the hospital; another ran off. We dug anti-tank ditches. We were beginning to dig trenches when word came that the Germans were already at Rzhev, right behind us! We threw down our shovels and came home through the woods. Sixty kilometers on foot. How we got out of it alive I do not know, myself. We were just lucky, I guess. We met other women along the road. The Germans had bombed and strafed them, and many women from work detachments fell into German hands. What kind of devil would torture us like that for three weeks? And why? It's awful to go through such torment and for no good reason at all! Have our superiors completely lost their minds? What kind of war is it where women are used as cannon fodder? We have equal rights, all right! They kill us as recklessly as they kill our men!" The woman angrily pounded something heavy on the table, making a loud, cracking sound, like the discharge of a revolver. No one answered. Behind the partition there was dead silence.

Rybinsk women were also sent off to work on fortifications, and at a time when the first German detachments were shelling to the west of Bologoe. Half of the women were killed. More were slaughtered by a second detachment of Germans, and others were cut off, their children were left orphaned and abandoned in the city. The Germans, undeterred, crossed the land fortifications that had been erected in such haste and confusion and according to no coherent plan. And from Leningrad to the Black Sea, they continued to send hundreds of thousands of women out under German bombs, bullets, and shells. Tens of thousands of women had already been killed in this senseless, muddled, bloody, irrational waste of human lives. But what was so unusual about that, if the individual was nothing? To the authorities, we were worth even less than that: We had a negative value.

To escape dark thoughts like these, I went downstairs and walked outside in search of other people. At the door I caught up with our inspector, Zuyev.

A member of the Party since the first days of the revolution, Zuyev bore little resemblance to the typical Party member. He remained in the Party from inertia, having survived the purges—no doubt because he held an ordinary position and was not trying to make a name for himself. I got on friendly terms with him during the several business trips we made together, and we had since then talked openly with each other. In response to his question, I replied that I was going to wander about on the streets.

"I'll go with you, if you don't mind. I have nothing to do either. Are you being evacuated?" inquired Zuyev.

"Yes, if I can manage it."

"You will manage it. In my opinion the panic is groundless. The Germans can hardly take Moscow quickly. As far as I know, only one of their tank divisions has broken through, and they have no additional troops near Moscow."

"And do we have many troops?"

"They are in disarray, in a panic, but we can get enough together. Yesterday they added fresh troops in the subway, right from the train station. If headquarters is able to bring order, then we can hold out a week or two longer. Defend Moscow? It will hardly be defended. The mood at the top itself is already very panicky."

We went across New Square to the Polytechnic Museum, with the NKVD building frowning in the distance. What in the world was going on inside Vnutrennyaya Prison? Were they perhaps hurriedly executing prisoners under investigation, rushing from cell to cell? They would never evacuate them in this turmoil, and the regime would not wish to part with them by releasing them. Otherwise, it never would have had them arrested in the first place.

"It's a mess at the front. Our armed forces are letting themselves be captured, running off into the forests or into buildings," Zuyev said languidly. "If the Germans act intelligently, all of Russia can now be occupied without particular effort. Our system has no defenders. Strange as it may seem, the ones least inclined to defend it are the communists themselves. Yesterday someone at our district Party committee headquarters said that the Germans were already at the Vorobev Hills. If you saw what has become of our Party members! The district Party committee was prepared to flee east immediately. And the Kremlin is no better. Molotov and the other people's commissars are directing the evacuation instead of aiding in the defense. Molotov personally escorts the evacuees to Kazan station. Instead of being occupied with defense matters, they can think only of fleeing and saving what they can, somehow extricating themselves and perhaps surviving. The system is obviously bankrupt and yet they preserve the sham: They announce to us, for instance, that we members of the Party should stay and defend Moscow 'to the last drop of blood.' Of course, they weren't talking about themselves, the bosses—they will leave—but about the rank and file. I wish I knew who will be doing the defending. Actually, I will have the chance to find out: I'm supposed to remain behind as one of those appointed 'defenders.'"

Zuyev was in a talkative mood. It must have been a long time since he had bared his soul to anyone. His face was calm, but his eyes blazed feverishly.

"I realize that I do not want to flee from Moscow at all. Now only one question matters: What do the Germans want? If they only want to remove our regime and establish their own 'new order,' that's one thing. We could somehow manage with their system, the main thing is to get rid of our regime. But what if this is about the same old 'drive to the east'? Or the ravings in *Mein Kampf*? Or some other, similar lunacy? Then for us it's the end: We won't be delivered from Stalin. This is really a unique situation! Have you heard what is happening in the factories? Everyone is drawing an extra month's pay to keep them going during their evacuation, and almost everyone has already left their posts. Party members, Stakhanovites, activists, and administrators are evacuating—the workers don't want to leave and are evading evacuation orders. The Stalin Works is being transported to Gorky by truck. No one wanted to work at dismantling and loading the machinery, so they announced that the job would pay a hundred rubles a day; but they still didn't find many takers. Can you imagine such a mood? Everyone senses that the regime is reeling, that it's down for the count. And everyone is holding their breath!"

"And they won't exhale till the Germans arrive. Do you think people will be as happy to see the Germans as they are to say good-bye to the Soviet regime?"

"There's the rub. Once again, we find ourselves between a rock and a hard place. Of course, many people are eagerly awaiting the Germans: They may be Germans, but at least they are not communists! Most of us are in a quandary, though: We don't want the Bolsheviks any more than the other fellows do, but we're afraid of the Germans. No matter how you slice it, the Germans are foreign, they are the enemy. They are as alien to us as the Bolsheviks are. But what alternative do we have? We must choose between the two. So in the final analysis, perhaps we are as firmly bound to Stalin as a button is to a coat; even more firmly—we don't dare cut the threads. If only the Germans turn out to be sensible!" Zuyev exclaimed unrestrainedly, as his voice rose.

Conversing in this way, we arrived at one of the little side streets off Maroseyka. The lane was empty, not a soul in sight, with only a single car standing at the curb. The driver had the hood up and was fiddling with the engine. The car was loaded with suitcases and packages. In the back seat behind the glass partition we saw a chubby male face hidden in the corner and next to it that of a young woman with panic-stricken eyes. Parcels and little straw bags were piled in their laps. An elderly woman sat in the front seat, pressing a huge bundle to her breast. Zuyev and I exchanged knowing glances: They were bosses, fleeing. About twenty paces farther down the street, we met up with half a dozen fellows in greasy jackets and coveralls, coming around the corner. As they passed us, Zuyev drew me into the entryway of a nearby building and whispered, "Let's watch."

The workers stopped when they got to the car. "Bugging out, skunk!" one shouted loudly, and then they all laughed uproariously, maliciously, with no trace of humor.

"They gorged themselves, the swine, and now they are bugging out."

"Defend the fatherland, parasite!" Their shouts resounded, becoming steadily more heated. The workers seemed to be clenching verbal fists, as if the right word could send shreds of the bosses' straw bags and suitcases flying out of the car in all directions. That word remained unspoken: The driver slammed down the hood, said something to the workers, got into the car, and stepped on the gas. The car disappeared around the corner, and the workers moved on, talking loudly.

"Did you see that?" Zuyev asked heatedly. "Well, this is not like 1917! Our hands are untied, there are no more authorities! If you went around to the factories now, people would rise up immediately and dismantle the Kremlin rock by rock! This is a revolt—a revolution."

"So who's going to make the rounds of the factories?"

"You're right, nobody is," agreed Zuyev. "But that is not the issue. At this moment, one word would suffice to rouse the masses, and organizers could be found. The issue is—what for? In order to make it easier for the Germans to take Moscow? In any case, the government is in Kuybyshev, and Stalin is ready to flee the Kremlin at any minute. Can there be any thought of a revolution in Moscow if we don't know what the Germans are after? If they act against Russia and won't permit us to set up a new government, then a revolution would not only be unnecessary, it would even be harmful. If only the Germans understood that!"

Later that evening, I was groping my way home from a restaurant. It was pitch dark, so I had to proceed by touch and I constantly collided with other people. In order to adapt to the darkness, I stopped near the wall of the park on Theater Square. Darkened trams crept forward cautiously like lumbering ghosts, a faint light leaking from around their window frames into the darkness. There was no air alert, but an airplane was again monotonously droning high overhead. No antiaircraft fire rang out in response, but the red sparks of explosive shells blazed across in the dark sky. The pale tentacles of searchlights were groping about in the distance to the south. The footsteps of invisible pedestrians sounded on the pavement and an occasional car rustled past, with only its dim, darkened headlights visible as its dark body merged with the black night. It was a phantasmagoric Moscow night, full of invisible rustles, the alarming hum of airplanes, ghostly lights groping about the sky. What did this fantasy hold in store?

Away to the west, south, and north, Novikovs were beating off tank attacks in bitter despair, hanging onto their land by the skin of their teeth. They were moved by rage, irrational hatred for the enemy, and blind love for their motherland. Other Novikovs were slinking off under cover of night in order to give themselves up as prisoners. They, too, were moved by hatred—not for the Germans but for an enemy that had raped us for twenty-four years. Nearby, Zuyevs were racking their brains over the question of what the Germans would do when they came. Millions in the capital could not sleep: Would the morrow bring freedom or renewed serfdom? Would they have to defend the indefensible? Inside the Kremlin, their leaders were either trying to hold onto the power that was slipping from their grasp or else organizing their escape, trying to grab for themselves a few more people and vehicles the better to carry off the bulk of the country's wealth. Vehicles were scurrying eastward down back roads and country lanes in order to avoid the NKVD's highway checkpoints. The Kremlin's flimsy supports were deserting it and taking the public coffers along with them. The edifice was crumbling in all directions in the fantastic night—what would keep it standing? Could anything shore it up and hold it together?

At Their Posts

We walked on to Kazan Station. The huge, high-ceilinged waiting rooms hummed with thousands of voices, punctuated by the piercing cries of children. Men and women, young and old, many in unfamiliar dress, as though headed for the North Pole—felt boots, quilted jackets, sheepskin coats, sheets, and three-tiered fur hats, dragged out of God knows what closet. All this was scrambled up with parcels, bales, suitcases, boxes, trunks, and children's bathtubs. What if a bomb landed here? It was a terrifying thought—above us was only a glass roof. Goryunov approached, climbing over mountains of luggage, puffing and panting, looking like an Arctic explorer in his huge fur hat and shaggy fur coat.

"Comrades, don't wander around! The special train may be coming in at any minute. Don't walk around the city, stay together right here."

It was tedious to sit in the train station, and we had to purchase provisions for the journey. When a train would arrive no one knew; at a time like this, no one could be certain of anything. I had no faith in a rapid getaway, in any case: The people sitting next to us had been sitting there for two days. Vasyukov and I went outside.

A penetrating wind tore across Komsomolskaya Square (perhaps it would soon be called Kalanchevskaya again, as it had before the revolution?), bringing with it a sprinkle of dry snowflakes. It was cold: Winter had come early this year. Was that good or bad? The earth was frozen solid, so the Germans could advance as if they were dancing on parquet. But perhaps the Germans were not used to freezing temperatures? We went down into the subway and rode to Hunters' Row. The confusion and alarm on people's faces and in their movements had become so familiar that we no longer paid any attention to it. Evidently one could become accustomed to anything.

We entered a barber shop with a long row of chairs, standing there empty and forlorn as orphans, and two bored barbers. Wrapping a dirty sheet around my shoulders, an old barber shrugged when I asked where his coworkers were. "They left, melted away into thin air. Two were mobilized, and I would have to guess that the rest slipped away on their own initiative. That's it, in a nutshell. Have you heard what's happening at the front?"

"I haven't heard anything special. What's the information bureau saying?" I asked, pointing toward a radio in the corner.

"They're saying what they're told to say. That's their job. 'Red Army private Timokhin killed three Germans; Sergeant Nikudykhin blew up an enemy tank; Captain Pereplyuikin's unit completely routed a German unit.'" the barber mimicked the information bureau announcer. "And the Germans are at Moscow's doorstep. Just try to figure this out, comrade: We are winning, but we are getting it in the puss. They dish out whatever chatter they're made to."

Barbers are always garrulous, but I was unaccustomed to hearing them talk so freely.

"Didn't you hear what Pronin came out with on the radio? Called for calm as usual, for fulfillment of work obligations. The decision of the Moscow Soviet is that all public baths, barbershops, waterpipes, and the rest of the sewage system should continue to function as usual! You see, now we will beat the Germans without fail! We can steam them to death in the bathhouse or slash them with a razor. . . . They keep coming out with bright

ideas like that. The authorities have run off; most likely, the Moscow city soviet itself has taken to its heels; but here they're still appealing to us to stay
calm! Work honorably at your posts! They, themselves, understandably, will
run off as the Germans get closer, but what about us? Where will we hide?"

I looked at the agitated barber apprehensively. The razor was moving too
quickly in his hands.

"It is unfashionable to get agitated," he muttered, this time to himself.
"You be my example: Stand alongside me and die if it comes to that. Now
that's a hero, that I could understand. But no: You work at your posts, while I
have a small plane ready. You are in the jaws of the Germans, while I, *vroom*,
am off! Do you want eau-de-cologne?" the barber concluded, unexpectedly.

Leaving the aggrieved barber (how many aggrieved must there be now in
Moscow?), we went into the shops. Apart from the sales clerks, the shops
were empty. We couldn't even get cigarettes. But Vasyukov knew Moscow
like his own sheepskin coat, and he dragged me into an unfamiliar four-story
building on Neglinnaya. Wandering down the corridors, we ended up in the
buffet of an unfamiliar institution, where a pretty, middle-aged woman was
puttering around behind the counter.

"Grunyushka, dear, rescue me! Without smokes, my ears get puffy,"
Vasyukov said to the woman. "I'll take some of those Russian cigarettes."

"Then you do remember me, you flibbertigibbet," the woman laughed. "I
haven't seen you for a year. Now you need me all of a sudden?"

I sensed that I was witnessing a lovers' reunion. Nothing to be surprised
about. Vasyukov had had many such relationships in Moscow.

"Ah, so you've found the time to scold me!" Vasyukov joked. "You, as a
conscious citizen, ought to be sympathizing with me instead."

"The kind of sympathy you need is a shaft in the side. It was your good
fortune to find a good woman. Take these." The woman retrieved a package
of cigarettes from under the counter: Raketa, 35 kopecks. Vasyukov's brow
wrinkled.

"What do you take me for? You think I would smoke this rot?"

"You'll have to, that's all we've got. And we had to grease some palms to
get even these."

"That's really all you have? Well then, give me about twenty packages for
the road."

"You're bailing out?"

"What about you, Grunya? Staying to greet the Germans?"

"You're a notorious coward, like all of your kind. You run from woman
to woman, from these Germans to those Germans. Careful, running away
never did anybody any good," scoffed Grunya.

Vasyukov invited her to go with us. He would arrange for her to leave on
our train, as a relative. Grunya refused.

"No, dearie, thanks very much. I have run enough, have had enough.
Look, the Germans won't be any worse than you. It's not the first time. I'll
get by somehow, but I will not move from Moscow to anywhere else."

While they were talking, I looked at Grunya. In her slightly plump figure
with its supple lines, her oval face with its rather smooth features, and her
smiling eyes I saw warmth, softness, tenderness, as well as a certain recognition of self-worth, a firm confidence, a refusal to surrender. Where had I met
her before? Or had I simply seen these same characteristics in other women?

As we were leaving, Vasyukov waxed poetic. "Ah, brother, she's a good
woman! I was a fool to leave her: What more could I need? She is a country
girl from my native village. Her family had a big farm there. Then they were
dispossessed as kulaks and exiled to somewhere near Arkhangelsk. Her father and brothers died there, but she survived. She spent two years hiding
out in the woods, then escaped, and I met her quite by chance in Moscow.
She had just arrived and had neither documents nor money. She wanted to
go farther, but I held her back and arranged it so that she could live in
Moscow from then on. And you see how nothing has broken her—what a
queen! She has adapted with ease to city life. You would never even guess
that she is a country girl. Just try to 'reeducate' that kind. And we have millions of women like her!"

We had our smokes now, but finding food proved harder: There was nothing edible in the stores. They did have bread and canned crab (they say it's
considered a delicacy abroad), but we needed something more substantial.
After running around a long time in Soyuzryb, we found caviar: soft caviar
at one hundred rubles a kilo, red caviar at forty. We thought it over—it was a
luxury, but not in times like these. One has to eat on the road, and this was
no time to worry about money; so we took four kilos per head. We loaded
up with bread, Vasyukov provided the vodka, and we hurried to the station.

Making our way to our places, we stopped in puzzlement: Our fellow-
workers were gone. Their spots were occupied by unfamiliar people, while
our things had likewise disappeared. Our neighbors were also new, and they
knew nothing of where our friends had gone.

"Are they really gone?" Vasyukov worried. "Sit here. I'll run to find out;
maybe they are still on the platform."

Sitting on someone else's suitcase, I dozed off. My head was in a muddle.
Perhaps it was good that they had gone? I was fed up with the degrading
bustle of panic and evacuation. One stopped feeling like a human being be-

cause of it. Couldn't one stay in Moscow? I was less a defender of the authorities than the others. Officially I couldn't defend them because I had been exempted from military service. But I was greatly interested in what would happen when the Germans arrived. Would our hopes be justified? Zuyev thought so. Thousands of Muscovites were remaining; I would find a place among them. Would it not be better to go home, to wait for the Germans as others were doing, and thus to have done with all the fuss of evacuation? But would our hopes be justified? Would Moscow surrender? What was keeping the Germans? That thought really gave me pause. Then, what was I sticking around for? In Siberia or Central Asia it would be equally if not more interesting, observing what effect the war had there and how people were living deep in the hinterland. I could find a reason to go just about anywhere if I had the chance. Maybe I really should push on to the east. Yes, that's what I should do. I had the inexplicable feeling that what was happening was far from a finale, and time still stretched out before me.

"Ah, here he is!" a bass voice droned overhead, interrupting my thoughts. "Did you fall in somewhere?"

I raised my head. The mannish personnel director was looking at me suspiciously. She must have thought that I wanted to skip out of the evacuation.

"Where could I have fallen in? I thought you'd left."

"No, we have moved to another place, across the square. Come, I will show you."

When Vasyukov got back, we went across to the October Station. It seemed that our coworkers had adapted and occupied a basement under the customs section. Honor and praise to Goryunov, who had displayed unheard-of energy and obtained totally safe and tolerable premises for us. On the other hand, he seemed to have bustled about less on our account than to please his wife, a large-bosomed, very unproletarian-looking woman, who was temperamentally and demandingly leading our top brass around by the nose. That was very clear.

Under the heavy vaulted ceilings of the wide cellar, people were arranging themselves by families and by groups. It turned out that there was more baggage than people. Near each group were heaps of bags, bales, and suitcases. Our boss had outdone us all: Goryunov was entirely concealed behind a mountain of baggage, which would require at least a half-ton truck to transport it.

Judging from our rucksacks and briefcases, only Vasyukov and I were bachelors. As if having a premonition that henceforth I would be leading a nomadic life, I had already left some of my things in Rybinsk and some here in my room; on the road, even a needle is too heavy. Vasyukov held the same opinion. I spread my coat in the corner, Vasyukov spread out his sheepskin coat, and we lay down and watched life being organized. People were arranging beds from suitcases and sacks, rattling saucepans and teapots, preparing supper.

Vasyukov sighed: "And you want them to defend Moscow and Russia? They are saving their possessions. Look over there—they are taking kids' bathtubs and chamber pots to Siberia. What more could be said? Better let's drink up, eat our caviar, and call it a day." And he got a bottle of vodka out of his briefcase.

Farewell to Moscow

We spent two days in that basement, in the despondent mood of people fleeing for their lives. Only a few individuals, such as the engineer Blinov, were propelled by elemental patriotism, feeling that they could not bear to see Germans in the heart of their motherland. This same patriotic feeling led others to feel that their duty was to help defend their country, come what may. A few were leaving because they were compelled to under duress or by direct threats of force. The rest, the majority, both those who belonged to the Party and those who did not, were fleeing only out of fear for their own hides. For one reason or another, they were afraid that things would not go well for them when the Germans arrived. No one among this majority was thinking about helping to defend the country, and no one was leaving in order better to accomplish that goal in the new locale. They thought about just one thing: How to leave Moscow as quickly as possible in order to save themselves and as many of their belongings as possible. Goryunov and others kept going home and bringing back more and more suitcases: The basement had been transformed into a warehouse of goods and chattels. They also were establishing "reserves" in their apartments, in the event they returned home. Such concerns were dearer to them than either Moscow or Russia. The times had brought to light not only the human bestiality of Bolshevism's strongest supporters but also their lack of all the loftier human qualities and their petty, philistine baseness.

Vasyukov and I whiled away the time. He had no pretensions and was simply himself. Our sorties from the cellar into the city had already been transformed into "trips to Moscow." We felt as though we had already abandoned her and walked down her streets as mere onlookers.

The panic in the city had subsided, the confusion perceptibly diminished. Isolated individuals and groups who had appeared to be watching the turmoil from the sidelines, evidently only awaiting the chance to grab a rod or a crowbar to destroy whatever came to hand, had disappeared from the streets. Most plants and factories were still standing idle, although a few had managed somehow to get back to work. In general, the workers did not wish to leave Moscow, but they were no longer seen on the streets during the day. The destruction of stores and warehouses and the disorderly flight of the managers had ceased. The crisis point had passed. One sensed that some elemental strand of the people's moorings still held, and that the strong wind that had whipped them into a frenzy was now gradually calming down. The regime capitalized on this feeling. The police, who had previously been out of sight, reappeared on the streets. However, one still met few soldiers. Molotov went again to Kazan Station and personally "liquidated the congestion." The nervous muddleheadedness of the evacuation continued, but the wave of panic-stricken flight had subsided and taken on a more organized character.

The threat continued to hang over Moscow, as rumors circulated, each one more absurd than the last: The Germans had occupied Podolsk, the Germans were in Fili. But even without the rumors everyone understood that the situation verged on catastrophe. Fresh troops arrived that previously had never seen battle. They were quickly sent to the front, but no one could guarantee that they would not also scatter as had the regular units before them. Moscow stood in austere and gloomy silence.

We departed one evening from the dimly lit platform of Kazan Station, where echelons of passenger trains stretched into the distance. In the forward car was some academic institution or other; the People's Commissariat of River Transportation was in the next car; behind us was what looked to be some kind of theatrical society, or maybe it was an agricultural academy. We were a traveling Noah's ark, a tower of Babel, a motley crew. There were so many bags and so many people in each compartment that it was impossible either to get in or to sit down. The platforms at the backs of the cars were loaded with boxes, small bathtubs, and certain bucket-like pots—evidently, treasures with which it was impossible to part. Passing by, Vasyukov angrily kicked the pails with his good foot.

We sat together on seats in an upper berth—plenty of room there for the two of us. Below, they were so barricaded with bundles and suitcases that one could hardly breathe. Vasyukov used a few choice epithets against our neighbors, who likewise were swearing at one other over nothing.

"As soon as we start moving, I'll have a nice drink and then break up all these cozy arrangements of theirs," promised Vasyukov. "Red bourgeoisie!"

We left during the night. Shaded signal lights flashed past, as we entered the darkness and it was pitch-black once again. Trying somehow to peer into it, I observed once more the kind of sheer blackness that would one day taint my recollections of my last days in Moscow. From the hour when I had left the ship and gone to Savelovo, bound for Moscow, all the nights had been pitch-black, the days dark with foreboding and hopelessness.

The train moved slowly, as if threading its way with difficulty through the darkness. Switch signal lights again swam past—on to Tovarnoy and Okruzhnoy Stations, then again pitch-blackness. We suddenly stopped and stood still for a long while. It seemed that the entire train, even the cars and the steam engine, were listening, surely listening in alarm, extending a slim, smokestack ear to the sky. The breathing of a nearby passenger who was quieting down for the night became audible, covering up the dreary buzzing of an airplane hovering somewhere in the darkness: *zhzhu-zhzhu-zhzhu.*

The droning ceased, and we crept forward. Red fires were flickering ahead. We moved closer, and saw dozens of little fires in a nearby field. A tail of clear red flame reeled in the wind, stretched to the sky, and spread out along the earth. What had caused these fires? Had a German plane somehow mistakenly thrown incendiary bombs into an empty field? A train went by as I stretched out and peered through the window. The fires dancing in the black darkness seemed like secret sacrifices, of God only knew whom and to whom. Surely not of those left behind in Moscow, awaiting an unknown fate?

"Don't be sad, old man," remarked Vasyukov quietly, without his usual bantering tone. "Tears, as they say, won't help. Ah, Moscow, yes, what shall we do for Moscow? . . . Let us drink to her health, may she have better days ahead."

So we sat drinking on that stealthily rumbling train, moving eastward, away from our abandoned capital and across our suffering country, which held its breath as it waited and hoped. I drank fiery Moscow vodka with Vasyukov, bathing an unquenchable burning in my chest, and snacked on expensive caviar, scooping it up with a spoon, like kasha.

Biographical Sketch:
Gennady Andreev-Khomiakov

Gennady Andreev-Khomiakov grew up in Tsaritsyn, then a major river port and transshipment center on the lower Volga, in a house surrounded by lilacs and acacias. His father worked at the same lumber firm in Tsaritsyn for more than forty years. The largely self-educated Khomiakov senior had started at the company as a young man and eventually rose to become the trusted agent of the owner, and then the sole manager of the business for more than twenty years.

Tsaritsyn came under heavy fire during Andreev's boyhood, as a key point in civil war battles between Bolshevik forces and General Peter Krasnov's Don Cossacks. Josef Stalin, then a member of the Revolutionary Council of the Southern Front, played a central role in organizing supplies for Tsaritsyn's defense during the summer of 1918. The city was renamed Stalingrad in his honor in 1925, when Gennady Andreev was a student in one of the local secondary schools.

Andreev was still in high school at the time of his first brush with the authorities: "I was about fifteen when they called me a counterrevolutionary and expelled me from school. . . . I did not feel guilty. I knew that I was right. . . . For several months I walked along the banks of the Volga under the scorching summer sun, my mind in a fog."[1] Andreev did not explain the nature of the accusations then levied against him. Nor was he forthcoming about his own political activities during this period, assuming there were any. However, he later mentioned that his elder brother Sergey, who had fought with the White forces, had emigrated and was living in France.

Andreev finished secondary school in 1926 and went to work for a provincial newspaper, where he soon became an active member of a young people's literary circle. The budding writer had already published several short stories when he was arrested the following year and charged with "counterrevolutionary activities," the nature of which he did not specify. The OGPU (Unified State Political Administration) sentenced Andreev "to execution, commuted to ten years of confinement in a penal camp because he was a minor," under Article 58 of the Soviet criminal code. Barely out of secondary school, Andreev already found himself facing a "tenner"—according to Alexander Solzhenitsyn, the longest term then being meted out to those deemed enemies of the revolution. "From the day I passed through those prison gates, one thought never left me: I had to escape," Andreev recalled, adding that he was unable to reconcile himself to the loss of "ten long years" of his life.[2]

185

Various escape schemes are among the many details of labor-camp existence de-
picted in Andreev's 1948 "Solovetskie ostrova: 1927–1929" [Solovetskii Islands:
1927–1929], one of his earliest works written in emigration. While he spent some
time at backbreaking labor in the forests of those frigid White Sea islands, usually
Andreev was lucky enough to be assigned various office jobs, including bookkeeping
for the camp's department of accounting and finance. Ultimately he would direct
more than thirty subordinates: "At times, the thought came to me, . . . a prisoner
with a ten-year sentence, and I have an office as if I were an executive." While in that
position, Andreev had an unanticipated offer to join the staff of a fellow prisoner, a
former adjutant to a civil-war general, who had been appointed to manage the finance
department of a newly established camp on the mainland. With "eight years left to
serve out" Andreev grabbed the chance to leave "Solovki," the colloquial name for
the infamous "special-purpose camp" on the country's northern frontiers.[3]

A couple of years later, with more than six years in the camps still looming before
him, Andreev and another fellow prisoner embarked on a harrowing and futile escape attempt, recounted in vivid detail in *Trudnye dorogi* [Hard Roads], a companion
volume to this memoir. The attempt brought Andreev an additional three years at
corrective labor in the Solovetskii Islands—a welcome relief to a young man expecting the death sentence.

However, Andreev was no longer in Solovki at the time of his sudden release in
1935, after he had served eight years of his original ten-year sentence. Forbidden to
settle in some forty of the country's larger cities, Andreev elected a small county seat
(the name of which was withheld in his memoirs) in southeastern Russia. The year
and a half he spent in this peaceful steppe town were much to his liking. Then, when
the factory where he worked under the supervision of Grigory Neposedov (a main
protagonist in Andreev's memoirs) was shut down, Andreev opted to move to a
nearby regional center, which had a large university.

During the following year, most of which he spent in this larger urban center
(name again withheld), Andreev's hopes of working while attending the university
part-time began to fade. This was the era of the great purges (1936–1938), and with
his past record, Andreev was unable to find and keep suitable employment. Rescue
finally came when Neposedov summoned him to join his management team at a
sawmill in a small town in the lumbering region north of Moscow, Andreev's third
locale since leaving camp. Again he does not name the town, but we know that the
new job entailed frequent business trips to nearby Yaroslavl, Kalinin, and Moscow.
Andreev worked for Neposedov's new operation until mid-1939, when he decided to
leave provincial life and move to Moscow for employment with the central board of
the country's lumber industry. He arrived in the capital shortly before the August 23
announcement of Stalin's nonaggression pact with Adolf Hitler, which "struck us
like a thunderbolt."

Andreev concludes his memoir with a detailed and dramatic description of a bewildered nation in chaos after Hitler hurled 3.5 million troops, the largest invasion
force in history, across the Soviet border in late June 1941. That October, as the Ger-

mans approached Moscow, Andreev and his coworkers were hastily evacuated from the threatened capital along with thousands of their fellow-citizens. Andreev's unit in the lumber industry would eventually set up temporary wartime headquarters in Frunze, a large city in the Kirgiz republic.

During a business trip in late fall 1941, Andreev made a surprise visit to Stalingrad, in part because he had not heard from any family members since the German invasion. He found his younger brother, a lieutenant in the reserves, working in a former tractor factory, which was then turning out tanks. Exhausted, his brother often slept at the factory and rarely came home. Their worried father, eager for news, was unable to grasp the fact that with the Germans approaching Moscow and Rostov, fortifications were being dug from the Volga to the Don.

Soon after that brief visit it became apparent that Andreev could no longer avoid military service. Due to his camp background, his boss had opted not to request a deferment for him in spite of the unit's severe personnel shortage. However, Andreev prevailed upon his boss to send him on another business trip, which would permit a side excursion to "see my own people again before losing my head in the war." The second visit found his family living much the same, although they were hungrier and his father's mood had blackened deeply. "He seemed to feel as he had during the early years of the revolution," abandoning himself to despair and frequently cursing the "scoundrels," the Bolsheviks, for ruining Russia and his beloved home city. "The ravages of the revolution had become his personal sorrow," although gradually, with the passage of the first two Five-Year Plans, he had noticed in his father's attitude, if not "reconciliation, then perhaps resignation born of necessity" to the new situation. This change was accompanied by a return of his father's earlier pride in his city and even in its new appearance. But in 1942, Andreev's despairing father was certain that nothing could help: "Everything was being destroyed a second time. And this time it was not so clear who was to blame." Gripped by a fatalism that "what would be would be," his father paid no heed to Andreev's urging, endorsed by his mother, that they leave the Volga region at once. When Andreev left his home city and his family, he was certain that he had seen them for the last time.[4]

Shortly after that second visit, Andreev went to enlist in the army. A young doctor glanced at him and declared him fit for military service. The soldier on duty with her told him to report at nine o'clock the next morning. Most of Andreev's fellow recruits were likewise in their thirties. Reflecting a lowering in the standards of eligibility, many had been inmates of labor camps, and some of these, like Andreev, had lost their earlier medical exemptions.

Captured by the Germans in the Crimea in 1942, Andreev spent the remainder of the war years as a prisoner, first in occupied Norway, then in Berlin. By the time of his transfer to Berlin, Andreev was in such bad health that it was torture to drag himself up the two or three steps into a tram. He remained in Germany at the end of the war, never to return to his native land.

Life in emigration provided Andreev an opportunity to resume his delayed writing career. Once he began writing again, his long pent-up, unique experiences came flowing out. They continued in a steady stream for almost three decades. The Soviet labor camps, World War II, and provincial life in the 1930s provided the backdrop for many short stories and reminiscences. Although he never published an autobiography, many of his works were autobiographical in nature. All appeared in Russian émigré publications under one of two pseudonyms: G. Andreev and Otradin. He used the second pseudonym for his many political commentaries on events in the Soviet Union.

While pursuing his own literary endeavors, Andreev also helped many fellow émigré writers find an outlet for their works. In the mid-1970s he served briefly as coeditor of *Novyi Zhurnal* [New Journal]. He was the editor in chief of *Mosty* [Bridges] from 1965 until 1970, the final five years of its thirteen-year existence. As editor, he used his full name, G. A. Khomiakov, initially with a German spelling. Later, *Mosty* noted editor G. Homjakov's change of address, from Munich to New York, where Andreev and his wife, Elly Oskarovna, had moved the previous year. Chronic shortages of funds resulted in the journal's demise two years later.

Andreev continued his activities as writer and editor even after his retirement. He was still publishing occasional articles in *Novoe Russkoe Slovo* [New Russian Word] until just before his death in February 1984. His widow continued to live in their cozy oceanside home in Bayville, New Jersey, until she followed him in death in 1993.

Ann M. Healy

Notes

Introduction

1. Gennady Andreev, "Minometchiki" [Mortar Men], *Novyi zhurnal* (New Journal), 1978, 131:59. A brief biographical sketch about Gennady Andreev (Khomiakov) appeared in the anthology *Literaturnoe zarubezhe: sbornik-antologiia* [Literature in Emigration: An Anthology], published in Munich in 1958 (p. 213).

2. Gennady Andreev, "Solovetskie ostrova: 1927–1929" [Solovetskii Islands], *Literaturnoe zarubezhe: sbornik-antologiia*, pp. 215, 227.

3. J. Arch Getty, "The Politics of Repression Revisited," in J. Arch Getty and Roberta Manning, eds., *Stalinist Terror: New Perspectives* (Cambridge: Cambridge University Press, 1993), p. 51.

4. Alec Nove, *An Economic History of the USSR*, 2d ed. (Middlesex: Penguin, 1989), p. 211.

5. George M. Enteen, *The Soviet Scholar-Bureaucrat: M. N. Pokrovskii and the Society of Marxist Historians* (University Park, Pa.: Pennsylvania State University Press, 1978), pp. 151–152.

6. Martin McCauley, *The Soviet Union Since 1917* (London: Longman, 1981), p. 66.

7. Nove, *Economic History*, pp. 135–137, 180.

8. Janos Kornai reiterated many of these earlier conclusions in capsule form in his 1989 "Preface to the Soviet Edition of *Economics of Shortage*" (Kornai's major 1980 work, which appeared in English translation in 1981). Janos Kornai, *Vision and Reality, Market and State: Contradictions and Dilemmas Revisited* (New York: Routledge, 1990), pp. 205–207.

9. Nove, *Economic History*, pp. 213–214.

10. Naum Jasny, *Soviet Industrialization: 1928–1952* (Chicago: University of Chicago Press, 1961), pp. 119–121.

11. Michael Kort, *The Soviet Colossus*, 2d ed. (London: Routledge, 1990), pp. 177–178.

12. Roberta T. Manning, "The Soviet Economic Crisis of 1936–1940 and the Great Purges," in Getty and Manning, eds., *Stalinist Terror*, pp. 133, 128, 125.

13. Ibid., pp. 116–119, 127.

14. Ibid., pp. 117, 125, 136–138.

15. Ibid., pp. 136–137.

16. Ibid., pp. 125–127, 129.

17. Moshe Lewin, *The Gorbachev Phenomenon: A Historical Interpretation,* expanded ed. (Berkeley: University of California Press, 1991), pp. 22–23, 59.

18. Boris Yeltsin, *Against the Grain: An Autobiography,* translated by Michael Glenny (New York: Summit Books, 1990), p. 71.

Chapter 1

1. Andreev's aside: Regrettably, I must refrain from giving the exact names of people and places and the exact dates in these sketches. Such superfluous information might tempt the MVD [Ministry of Internal Affairs] to search for some of the people that I have frequently mentioned. [Andreev here used the initials MVD for the internal security police; later, he would use NKVD. The name of that institution changed several times. More familiar to Western readers are the initials KGB.—Tr.]

2. In prerevolutionary Russia, an *artel* was an association of persons formed to carry out work in common. In Soviet Russia it was a cooperative organization of producers under government supervision.

3. The White officers fought on the side of the White forces and opposed the Bolsheviks (Reds) during the civil war that followed the Bolshevik revolution.

4. *Dekulakizatsiia* was the term for taking land and livestock away from peasants during the collectivization drive of the 1930s. The more prosperous peasants in tsarist Russia were called kulaks (from the Russian word for fist), since they allegedly hung on to their wealth and squeezed their fellow peasants. While *kulak* was a term of political opprobrium, its definition was loose enough to allow the Bolshevik regime to repress any peasants who opposed giving up their property and joining collective farms.

5. Preference and mouse were popular card games in tsarist Russia.

6. Neposedov, a coined name, means "one who cannot sit still."

7. The Komsomol was the communist youth organization for teenagers and young adults. Its members ranged from about 14 to 27 years of age.

8. People's commissariats: After the Bolshevik revolution, government ministers were called people's commissars. The Council of People's Commissars was the highest executive–administrative organ of state power. It was renamed the Council of Ministers in March 1946.

9. A book, compulsory for all Soviet citizens, which contained their employment record.

10. In a footnote Andreev explained *blat* as a word in thieves' jargon, strongly entrenched in Soviet usage, used here in the sense of "protection" or "who you know."

11. *Yezhovshchina* was the peak period of political show trials and mass arrests of "class enemies and anti-Soviet wreckers" in the 1930s. It took its name from Nikolai I. Yezhov, a central Party secretary and the head of the NKVD from 1936 to 1938, who argued that "enemy forces" seriously endangered the regime.

12. *Defitsitnyi* (in short supply) is a term commonly employed for scarce items in the USSR.

Chapter 2

1. A reading of Peter Blandon's detailed study, *The Soviet Forest Industries* (Boulder: Westview, 1983), suggests that Andreev might have painted too rosy a picture of the prerevolutionary forestry industry. According to Blandon, the lumbering areas around Moscow had a "long history of overexploitation" of forest resources. One of the most backward industrial sectors in tsarist Russia, the lumber industry traditionally relied on manual labor and concentrated its activities in winter, thus permitting the use of peasant labor during times when farm work was not available. These part-time loggers worked under very difficult conditions for low wages. The forestry industry began to acquire a permanent workforce only during the late 1930s, and significant efforts to modernize the industry did not occur until after World War II (pp. 31, 92–94, 158).

2. In 1921 Lenin introduced the New Economic Policy (NEP), a temporary retreat on the road to socialism, which allowed some private enterprises in retail trade and in small industries employing fewer than twenty workers. Under NEP, peasants were permitted to sell what remained of their crops on the free market after paying set taxes in money and kind, and they were eventually permitted a limited use of free labor and a restricted lease of land.

3. Andreev's footnote: "Molevoi splav" [free floating]. Logs floated separately, not bound into rafts.

4. Andreev is quoting a famous adage from nineteenth-century fabulist Ivan Krylov's "Shchuka i kot" [The Pike and the Cat].

Chapter 3

1. *Udarnichestvo* was the term given to Soviet economic shock tactics used to increase the tempo of production. The *udarnik,* or worker who broke production records, was celebrated as a hero and awarded special privileges, such as better living quarters and more food and consumer items.

2. Stakhanovism was an official campaign to increase productivity in all areas of industry. It was named after Alexis Stakhanov, a Donets basin coal miner who reportedly hewed 102 tons of coal in a single shift—fourteen times the normal production quota—in August 1935.

3. Andreev's footnote: At the time, a quarter-liter of vodka cost 3 rubles, 15 kopecks.

Chapter 4

1. Literally, "to combine," that is, to make unofficial business deals, not accounted for in the plan, through various complex barter agreements and often accompanied by the illegal exchange of money under the table.

2. Andreev's footnote: Under the law of August 7, 1932, regarding the "plundering of socialist property," sentences of ten years and even the death penalty were handed down for thefts in factories, on kolkhozes, and in other workplaces. Peasants were convicted under this law for taking ears of cereal grains from collective fields or for gathering up ears from already harvested fields, and workers, for stealing pieces of soap, leather, and the like from factories.

3. *Krokodil* [Crocodile], a leading Soviet humor magazine, well known for its satiric cartoons, which were frequently reprinted in the West.

4. Chichikov is a character in Nikolai Gogol's famous novel, *Dead Souls*, who makes a profit by buying up "dead souls" (serfs who have died since the previous census and for whom their former owners continue to pay the poll tax) for nothing and using them as collateral for loans.

5. Little Octobrists was the Soviet youth organization for the youngest age group. Most children belonged to the Little Octobrists from the time they began going to school until they were about nine, when they joined the Pioneers organization. These clubs provided a wide range of social activities as well as political indoctrination groups.

Chapter 5

1. Andreev's footnote: This happened before 1940, when the law on absenteeism and tardiness was introduced.

2. An agency established in 1921 to analyze resources and propose production targets, Gosplan (the State Planning Commission) was eventually responsible for drawing up the Five-Year Plans.

3. Andreev's phrase is an ironic gloss on Lenin's famous April 1918 treatise, "The Immediate Tasks of the Soviet Government": "The decisive issue is the organization of the strictest, nationwide accounting and control of the production and distribution of goods" (V. I. Lenin, *Sochineniia* [Collected Works], vol. 27, February–July, 1918 [Moscow: Gosudarstvennoe, 1952], p. 217).

4. A *maevka* was an outlawed prerevolutionary May Day gathering. Here, the term is used loosely to mean a party or outing.

5. The *barynia* and *trepak* are traditional Russian folk dances.

6. Andreev's footnote: ITP are "engineering–technical workers"; MOP are "junior service personnel."

7. Dachas are popular part-time residences, ranging from tiny, simply built summer cottages without utilities to more substantial houses, that are found in the greenbelts surrounding Russian cities. Many families own their dachas; others rent.

Chapter 6

1. GUM, the initials for *Gosudarstvennyi universalnyi magazin,* the large State Department Store on Red Square, across from the Lenin Mausoleum.

2. *Partizanshchina* refers to economic activity that is independent of the plan or in violation of official regulations.

Chapter 7

1. *Intelligent,* literally an intellectual. As used here "intellectual" means a member of the "intelligentsia," that is, a person who usually has some higher education or training and works in one of the middle-class professions, in the government bureaucracy, and the like.

2. The Lubyanka is a notorious prison in central Moscow and the headquarters of the KGB.

3. Political officers at all levels of the Soviet military services operated independently of the military command. Their functions included keeping tabs on the troops' morale and infusing them with Party spirit through various methods of education and indoctrination.

4. Marshal Mikhail M. Tukhachevsky, a former imperial officer and Chief of Staff of the Red Army, was one of eight prominent generals whose execution for "espionage and treason to the fatherland" was announced in *Pravda* on June 12, 1937.

5. The census was taken in 1937, not 1936.

6. Andreev referred here to large-scale border clashes between Red Army and Japanese troops near the Siberian–Mongolian border in 1939.

Biographical Sketch

1. Quoted by Leonid Rzhevskii in "Pamiati Gennadiia Andreeva (Khomiakova) [Recollections of Gennady Andreev-Khomiakov]," *Novoe Russkoe Slovo* [New Russian Word], February 18, 1984, p. 4.

2. Andreev, "Solovetskie ostrova," p. 229.

3. Ibid., pp. 265, 269–271.

4. Gennady Andreev, "Mertvaia petlia: pamiat' ottsa" [Tailspin: In Memory of My Father], *Mosty* (Bridges), 1961, 6:83, 94–98.

About the Book

One dusty summer day in 1935, a young writer named Gennady Andreev-Khomiakov was released from the Siberian labor camp where he had spent the last eight years of his life. His total assets amounted to 25 rubles, a loaf of bread, five dried herrings, and the papers identifying him as a convicted "enemy of the people." From this hard-pressed beginning, Andreev-Khomiakov would eventually work his way into a series of jobs that would allow him to travel and see more of ordinary life and work in the Soviet Union of the 1930s than most of his fellow Soviet citizens would ever have dreamed possible. Capitalizing on this rare opportunity, Bitter Waters is Andreev-Khomiakov's eyewitness account of those tumultuous years, a time when titanic forces were shaping the course of Russian history.

Later to become a successful writer and editor in the Russian émigré community in the 1950s and 1960s, Andreev-Khomiakov brilliantly uses this memoir to explore many aspects of Stalinist society. Forced collectivization, Five Year Plans, purges, and the questionable achievements of "shock worker brigades" are only part of this story. Andreev-Khomiakov exposes the Soviet economy as little more than a web of corruption, a system that largely functioned through bribery, barter, and brute force—and that fell into temporary chaos when the German army suddenly invaded in 1941.

Bitter Waters may be most valuable for what it reveals about Russian society during the tumultuous 1930s. From remote provincial centers and rural areas, to the best and worst of Moscow and Leningrad, Khomiakov's series of deftly drawn sketches of people, places, and events provides a unique window on the hard daily lives of the people who built Stalin's Soviet Union.

Gennady Andreev-Khomiakov was imprisoned as a teenager in Soviet Russia in 1926 and released in 1935. During World War II, he was a German prisoner of war and did not return to the Soviet Union at war's end. He later served as coeditor of the Novyi Zhurnal (New Journal) and chief editor of Mosty (Bridges).

Ann E. Healy is a lecturer at the University of Wisconsin at Milwaukee and the author of Russian Autocracy in Crisis: 1905–1907. She is currently writing a book about the Jewish issue in U.S.-Russian relations.